Social Development of Learning Disabled Persons

✲ ✲ ✲ ✲ ✲

Examining the Effects and Treatments of Inadequate Interpersonal Skills

Doreen Kronick

�֎ �֎ ✖ ✖ ✖

Social Development
of Learning
Disabled Persons

✼ ✼ ✼ ✼ ✼

Jossey-Bass Publishers
San Francisco • Washington • London • 1981

SOCIAL DEVELOPMENT OF LEARNING DISABLED PERSONS
Examining the Effects and Treatments of
Inadequate Interpersonal Skills
         by Doreen Kronick

Copyright © 1981 by: Jossey-Bass Inc., Publishers
                        433 California Street
                        San Francisco, California 94104
                                &
                        Jossey-Bass Limited
                        28 Banner Street
                        London EC1Y 8QE

Library of Congress Cataloging in Publication Data

Kronick, Doreen.
    Social development of learning disabled persons.

    Bibliography: p. 240
    Includes index.
    1. Mentally handicapped children. 2. Social
skills. 3. Learning disabilities. I. Title.
HQ773.7.K76 *1981*   305   81-81960
ISBN 0-87589-499-2   AACR2

            74853
Manufactured in the United States of America

JACKET DESIGN BY WILLI BAUM

FIRST EDITION

Code 8113

*The Jossey-Bass
Social and Behavioral Science Series*

❊ ❊ ❊ ❊ ❊

Preface

 When I entered the learning disability field in the mid 1960s, I accepted the prevailing belief about a learning disability: namely, that it primarily affects academic functioning and that the solution lies in academic remediation. However, as I watched a generation of learning disabled children grow to adulthood—and noticed that some, although remediated academically, remained friendless, lonely, and unproductive—I doubted that their problems could be attributed entirely to their feelings about having been poor students, or to secondary emotional problems, as the literature suggested. There was a quality of social ineptitude and imperviousness that had yet to be explained.

My doubts were reinforced and fresh perceptions provided by Ernest Siegel, Sol Gordon, and Betty Bader, who were among the first to stress the disabling effects of social inadequacy in the learning disabled. We all shared the feeling that, when one takes a lifetime into consideration, social disabilities tend to be far more handicapping than academic deficits. However, despite evidence of a more comprehensive disability, the prevailing belief persisted.

In my attempts to understand the quality and etiology of social deficits in the learning disabled, I familiarized myself with the fields of human development, social and rehabilitation psychology, sociology, family dynamics, and the literature on death and dying—the latter offering insight on human reactions to extreme stress and our ways of dealing with societally sanctioned issues. All these areas contributed profitable insights, as did Robert Jay Lifton's remarkable treatise on imagery, *The Broken Connection* (New York: Simon & Schuster, 1979).

Nonetheless, there were two critical gaps in the literature. The first was a virtual absence of information describing *healthy* development of exceptional children—how a family socializes an exceptional child in an optimal fashion from birth onward or, conversely, how an exceptional child alters his interactional environment. The second gap was an absence of literature describing typical peer interactions of North American children and adolescents at each juncture of their development—for instance, the ways that an eight year old or a fourteen year old initiates or terminates a telephone conversation with a peer, breaks into a closed group of children, or converses with a peer, a younger or older child, or an adult. Their developmental tasks and cognitive levels have been exhaustively documented but this does little to enlighten us on their social intercourse. No one has recorded the differences in interactional behavior between children of various ages and adults in our culture.

I wrote this book at this time because of my conviction that we have ignored and hence neglected both the social disabilities in the learning disabled and the appropriate education and counseling for them and their families. We have failed to deal with the feelings of parents and siblings or to explore the ways in which those families are similar to and different from other stressed families. In this book I have attempted to address these neglected areas. I hope that it will stimulate research in the many untapped spheres that are related to the etiology and remediation of social deficits in the learning disabled. In those instances where there are gaps in the literature, I have made assumptions. Perhaps they will tide us over until we have a more comprehensive understanding of the etiology of learning disabled persons' social imperceptions and the dynamics of their families, or alternatively, they might generate other hypotheses.

Since one cannot look at the manifestations of a disability and service provision without taking the sociopolitical environment into consideration, I hope also that this book will encourage the reader to examine our perceptions of learning disabilities and the focus and quality of service delivery in the light of North American beliefs and pressures. It is only then that we can distance ourselves sufficiently from practices to decide whether they have arisen in response to the client population's most critical needs or reflect, instead, our cultural values and the inertia of service provision.

The learning disability field is so young that a definition acceptable to all practitioners has yet to be articulated. Ironically, everyone who works with this population knows what a learning disability is; yet few can agree on descriptive terminology. I have no desire to create yet another unacceptable definition of learning disabilities. However, to enable the reader to appreciate the population to whom I refer throughout the book, here is my working definition. A learning disability is a deficit in the organization of one or more of the following areas: attention, memory (visual, spatial, auditory), spoken and written language, some forms of cognition, motor coordination, and social information processing in a person who demonstrates some aspects of normal to above normal intellectual functioning. Such a person typically will demonstrate disparities in performance, from competence in some areas to incompetence in others. These disabilities frequently respond, in some measure, to directed remediation.

This book should be of value to the spectrum of professionals involved in therapeutic intervention and education of learning disabled persons and their families. (I refer to "persons" rather than to "children" because the disability and its attendant problems rarely disappear at the termination of childhood.) I anticipate, with pleasure, my readers' added observations and suggestions for social deficit remediation.

Chapter One describes the North American perceptions of children within a historical and cultural framework. It suggests some of the difficulties that are encountered in meeting the needs of all children, particularly those with special needs, when a culture is in swift transition. The historical evolution of learning disabilities and dyslexia are traced and their differential manifestations outlined. I propose that there has been a shift in the North American perception of learning disabilities from that of developmental disabilities to that of written language deficits, so that learning disabilities now are perceived as dyslexias. I attribute this altered perception to legislation that has mandated that the state provide appropriate education to all children and to the shift in remedial emphases from the habilitation of psychological processes to the modification of learning tasks.

Chapter Two proposes that the acquisition of social adequacy depends upon the ability to develop imagery. For example, parental uncertainty about their child's prognosis and probable opportunities hinders their ability to imagine the child's adulthood and to fashion their childrearing to that image. It describes the development of schematic thought processes as the underpinnings of imagery, and hence, the prerequisites of bonding and attachment. The difficulties that learning disabled persons may experience in social competence if they lack stable perception or are deficient in temporal or experiential organization and imagery are explored.

Chapter Three describes the effects both of stressful information and of subtle developmental deviations in the child, upon parents, and the impact of such information upon childrearing practices. These alterations in childrearing are described as they, in turn, affect subsequent development. The interface of developmental deviations and parental reactions can result in intrusive childrearing practices and competition for control between the parents and the learning disabled member; I discuss passive means of control, such as hypoactivity, by which the child mobilizes the attention of his teachers and family members by his lack of productivity. I also explore the relationships between profound frustration and its attendant aggression and between the learning of behavioral and social boundaries and being allowed the freedom to be an individual.

Chapter Four examines the factors that affect the development of a realistic self-concept and some of the sequelae of a distorted concept of self. The ways whereby sheltered and mainstream education may contribute to or detract from an adequate concept of self are explored. I delineate the difficulties that the learning disabled experience in the processing of social information and in conceptualizing the quality of relationships as they affect self-perception. The development of an adequate concept of self is further explored in terms of the use of the learning disabled person's social skills to meet his ego needs and to reinforce the needs of others, the ability to organize his emotional self, effects of labeling, and parental embarrassment and intrusiveness, among other issues. The following consequences of inadequate self-concepts are explored: unrealistic levels of aspiration, a lack of opportunities to assert the self, the need to compromise, and the relationship between compromising the self and rigidity and constricted perception.

Chapter Five traces the manifestations of egocentrism as they appear in each developmental stage and describes the behavior of older learning disabled persons whose conceptual levels are at an earlier stage of development. The stages of moral development are traced in a similar fashion, with a concomitant discussion of the primary and secondary factors that might preclude a learning disabled person from attaining expected moral and conceptual maturation. I look at problems related to the victimization of learning disabled persons by erstwhile friends, unscrupulous organizations, and untrustworthy salespersons.

Specific categories of social inadequacy are related to subclusters of learning disabilities in Chapter Six. I support these observations with an extensive overview of current research. The difficulties that learning disabled persons experience when they lack peer-valued attributes are described. The acquisition of friends is the main focus of this chapter, which also considers the transformation of acquaintanceships into more intimate friendships and sexual adequacy.

Chapter Seven deals with the many considerations around the establishment of social remedial programs. It discusses possible program models, priorities, and the implementation of individual and group goals. The elements that should be incorporated into a carefully conceptualized program are described, and remedial premises and activities are suggested for each area of social deficit addressed in Chapter Six. The strengths and limitations of sheltered and integrated program models are compared in terms of their probable effectiveness for the remediation of social deficits. Guidelines are provided for choosing integrated programs, and for the planning, implementation, and evaluation of sheltered programs for building social skills.

Judith Wiener, the author of Chapter Eight, was invited to contribute to this book because she is among the first and one of the few professionals to have thoroughly studied a social and remedial program for the learning disabled. She is a member of the special education faculty of York University. In Chapter Eight, Wiener deals with the value and limitations of several traditional and untraditional therapies for the growth of social adequacy. Steps are outlined for implementing a variety of therapies addressed to specific social remedial needs; these therapies include the mutual story-telling technique, the lifespace interview, behavior modification, and training in social skill building and role taking. These techniques are augmented by charts for contract reinforcement, teasing, and self-help, as well as suggested training formats for adolescents and descriptions of commercial materials.

In Chapter Nine, I suggest indications for therapeutic intervention with families of the learning disabled and with the learning disabled person himself. This chapter delineates the maternal and paternal roles in rearing learning disabled offspring and the therapeutic needs of each parent, of siblings, and of the learning disabled adolescent and adult. The different therapeutic needs of healthy but stressed families and of pathological families, each with learning disabled members, are described. I offer alternative premises for traditional therapeutic assumptions. The educational needs of parents of the learning disabled are examined, and the evolutionary stages of volunteer organizations and their ability to help parents at each juncture of their development are discussed.

In the early days of my interest in this area, the social imperceptions about which I wrote and lectured were unsubstantiated observations. However, in the past six years, a body of research has emerged which has supported my hunches—always a pleasant feeling—and immeasurably augmented my perceptions and comprehension. Some impressive research has been and is being carried out by my colleagues in Toronto. These same professionals are noteworthy for the sophistication whereby they undertake task analyses of social deficits and design specific remediation. I am particularly grateful to Judith Wiener and Marc Wilchesky for their investigations, which have added immeasurably to this book. I am indebted also to James and Tanis Bryan and Melinda Parrill-Burnstein for the promising research that they and their colleagues are pursuing, which they so generously have shared with me.

Toronto, Ontario   DOREEN KRONICK
July 1981

Contents

✻ ✻ ✻ ✻ ✻

The Author

✣ ✣ ✣ ✣ ✣

✣ Doreen Kronick is on the special education faculty of York University, a consultant in teacher training for the Ontario Ministry of Education, and a consultant to the Institute for Research in Learning Disabilities, University of Kansas. She earned her B.A. degree in special education from Skidmore College in 1974 and her M.A. degree in interdisciplinary studies (psychology, sociology, and sociolinguistics) from York University in 1976.

She received the President's award for distinguished service from the U.S. Association for Children with Learning Disabilities in 1973 and the Founder's award from the Canadian Association for Children with Learning Disabilities in 1977.

Kronick is the author of *Three Families* (1976), *Involving Impaired, Disabled, and Handicapped Persons in Regular Camp* (1976), *What About Me? The Learning Disabled Adolescent* (1975), *A Word or Two About Learning Disabilities* (1973), *Learning Disabilities: Its Implications to a Responsible Society* (1969), and *They Too Can Succeed* (1969). Her articles have appeared in such journals as *Ontario Medical Review, Academic Therapy, Learning Disability Quarterly, Chatelaine, American Camping,* and *Canadian Vocational Journal.* She is contributing editor of *Academic Therapy* and on the professional advisory board of the *Journal of Learning Disabilities and Perceptions.*

Kronick is particularly interested in the psychosocial aspects of learning disabilities and in creative sheltered and integrated therapeutic recreation and camping. She cofounded the Ontario and Canadian Associations for Children with Learning Disabilities and the Integra Foundation, which is devoted to a comprehensive remedial approach that includes social remediation and family education and counseling.

To Tanis and James Bryan, Melinda Parrill-Burnstein, and Marc Wilchesky for their generous and invaluable assistance. To my husband Joseph and children Noah, Sarah, and Adam for being interested, supportive, and proud.

Social Development of Learning Disabled Persons

❋ ❋ ❋ ❋ ❋

*Examining the Effects and Treatments
of Inadequate Interpersonal Skills*

Chapter 1

Perceptions of Ordinary Children and Those with Special Needs

"The history of childhood is a nightmare from which we have only recently begun to awaken. The further back in history one goes, the lower the level of child care, and the more likely children are to be killed, abandoned, beaten, terrorized, and sexually abused." (De Mause, 1974, p. 8). DeMause and his colleagues, in their chronology of the history of childhood from prerecorded times to the twentieth century, describe a span of over two thousand years in which children were perceived as selfish and unpleasant, requiring stern punishment and deprivation if they were to grow into desirable adults. Up to the twentieth century, children in countries such as Britain and Germany were reared in a spartan fashion with cold baths, unappealing food, and a paucity of affection. Sutherland (1980) contends that upper-class British children still are reared in a similar manner.

Such attitudes are not easily discarded. We no longer kill female offspring at birth; yet many of us still feel that a male child is more desirable. The whip, paddle, and cat-o'-nine-tails may be out of fashion in this century; yet many children still are punished if they fail to conform to adult expectations, regardless of how unrealistic such expectations might be. Although we in North America do not deny children pleasures as extensively as our great grandparents did, our persistent belief is that many pleasures must be deferred until adulthood. Certainly we place far more limits on children—restricting their opportunities to choose pursuits, foods, times to eat, sleep, bathe, and play—than on adults, nor do we allow children the freedom to avoid activities that they dislike or do poorly. We still harbor the notion that children develop best if they engage in predetermined endeavors; that their conversation is secondary to adult discourse; and that their presence is unwelcome at adult social gatherings and in public places such as movie theaters and airplanes. We feel that they have the right to indulge in gourmet foods or expensive trips only after they have earned the money to pay for them.

Nonetheless, our approaches to the weak, the dependent, and the deviant have become increasingly humanistic. Perhaps the most compelling modifier of our negative perceptions of children was Freud, who transferred our concept of evil from something that resides in the child to something that results from a failure of maternal nurturing. This concept, in combination with the American egalitarian dream of education and opportunity for all children, seems to be largely responsible for our present concern for the quality of a child's experiences. Treatment of children and of children with special needs reflects this trend. Despite our failure to create a population of children who are universally educated, conforming, fulfilled, and stable, and who develop into mature and vocationally acceptable adults, we keep trying to reach those goals notwithstanding the attendant ambivalence, ineptitude, or inappropriateness of our efforts.

Our ambivalence reflects, in part, the reverence with which the individual in America is held. This reverence carries an assumption of success, intellectual competence, and affluence. The individual who cannot make it on his own or seems unlikely to achieve excellence in culturally valued areas of endeavor is devalued and deemed less worthy of our financial, human, and physical resources than his more competent peers. Thus, we locate special education programs in discarded space and are reluctant to teach plodders or to become involved in athletics with those who are clumsy. We also have confused "equal opportunity" with "equal attributes," assuming that all persons, afforded comparable occasions to grow, will emerge with equal achievements. If some have achieved less, we assume that somehow the quality of the opportunity is at fault. We are uncomfortable with the notion that achievement is related, in part, to differences in ability and environment. Similarly, many of us find it hard to believe that teaching styles need to be modified to individual children's learning styles and that expectations of production have to be related to the person's ability to express himself.*

Our evolving humanism is further tempered by the uncertain value that contemporary children represent. Traditionally, a society produces children so that the culture can reproduce itself. A culture in swift transition creates disequilibrium to the extent that adults become uncertain of the techniques, attributes, and values that are to be transmitted into the future. Indeed, parents lack the certainty that the future depends on the current population of children or that many of them will be needed to perpetuate the culture. Since we have created a style of living and a set of acquired needs for constantly changing goods and services that the family no longer produces, we have, in the process, relinquished the image of our children's adulthood; the world is changing so rapidly that we cannot image what life will be like when our children are adults. During the most profound periods of disequilibrium, adults must utilize so much mental and physical energy to ensure their own optimal place in the culture that there is less surplus energy for one's own children and for society's children in general.

Although we have become increasingly aware of the importance of the family as the child's nurturing agent and buffer between child and culture, we downgrade its authority and exclude

*The traditional use of the pronoun *he* has not yet been superseded by a convenient, generally accepted pronoun that means either *he* or *she*. Therefore, the author will continue to use *he* while acknowledging the inherent inequity of the traditional preference of the masculine pronoun.

and circumvent it in service provision. We devalue women's role as housekeeper and childrearer yet deny them the requisite supports, such as adequate child care, that would allow them to return to work. We make it difficult for parents to function as their children's advocates, since professionals resent the concept that lay persons have the right or ability to question their approaches. As Novak (1977) suggests, we have ignored the family as a mediating institution between the increasingly isolated individual and the increasingly powerful state: "We ignore it at our own peril because every advance in every scientific field from nutrition to pedagogy, from neurology to ethics, adds new significance to the role of the family in the welfare of the individual. The more we learn, the more clearly we see the many ways in which the family can fail. No generation in history has seen in such precise scientific detail how much children depend upon the habits, conduct, and spiritual life of parents" (Novak, 1977).

The days of extended family networks with an accessible supply of grandparents, aunts, and close neighbors to lighten the physical and emotional demands of childrearing, particularly with the child who creates extensive stress, have disappeared. The two-parent family has undergone amputation. Both parents frequently are employed yet try to find the time to remain faithful to themselves, their children, and all others to whom they feel indebted. These self-imposed and externally imposed demands are so extensive and the projected payoffs so uncertain that the inclination is a wish to reduce the debt—to narrow the group and the length of time for which one is expected to be responsible. In short, we are less committed to long-term relationships with spouses or with children. At the same time, such relationships, in fact, last longer than they did in former times in our nation and currently in developing nations. In previous centuries children assumed adult roles at an early age, and one's commitment to one's spouse was brief because life was short. We now struggle with an extended commitment while feeling cheated that our spouse and children do not provide us with the satisfactions that we expect of them. Whereas we had modest expectations of marital relationships in previous generations, we now expect them to provide love, romance, companionship, stimulation, support, empathy, sharing of tasks, and protection from want or stress. Although our forefathers did not become unduly upset at having a child who did not achieve as much as his brothers and sisters—and indeed seemed to expect that as being the probable order of events—we now expect our children to be competent athletically and academically, handsome, caring, and possessors of a host of other positive attributes. As a consequence, there is a conflict between our feelings of responsibility toward our marital and parental roles, which often extend throughout the entire span of our adulthood, and the lure of self-actualization, which we have been led to expect as a right. The inability to resolve this conflict has contributed to the dissolution of many marriages and the choice of many couples to remain childless.

Our children reflect this conflict by being self-centered, less positively reinforcing, and less willing to defer gratification than we remember previous generations of children to be. Since they may not be as enjoyable to rear, to teach, or to encounter publicly, the commitment to children individually and collectively is further questioned. In a society where "carrying on the culture" no longer entails the perpetuation of a marital, parental, or vocational tradition, it is exceedingly difficult for parents to visualize their offspring's adulthood. Lacking stable imagery, they are uncertain of direction. Similarly, children are no longer projected as direct sources of eventual physical and financial support for parents, so that the extended and extensive effort of childrearing may not always be recognized as worthwhile.

Confident childrearing practices have been further undermined by the widely held belief that adult caretaker behaviors are the precursors of the child's eventual emotional status. That this assumption is open to question is not widely known. As Kagan, Kearsley, and Zelato (1978) point out, the fact that psychologically unhealthy adults remember an unhappy childhood does not mean that imperfect childhoods (brought about by a specific set of parental treatments) universally create disturbed adults. In any event, the child encounters many critical influences other than parental in the process of maturing, so that few parental behaviors are likely to have long-term impact. Even these are attenuated by time and experience, so that they may become detached from the original stimulus and profoundly altered. Since this position is not generally known, parents in our culture are intimidated by the awesome prospect that their every behavior will have a lifetime of import. They and others perceive each imperfection in their children as a consequence of their failure as nurturers. Professionals and parents alike are incredulous that the most psychologically enabling adults are not always able to mold children into adults with culturally valued attributes. Compensatory efforts directed to equalizing biological, intellectual, temperamental, or environmental differences have led to frustration.

It is within these contexts that the anomalies become apparent: the belief that we are child centered versus the reality that our temporal, financial, and psychic priorities are adult centered. As a result, we vote against increases in school taxes, are loath to pay school taxes if we have no children or if our children are grown, build adult-only apartment buildings, and devote virtually no time to the community's children. Some adults fearfully avoid children and adolescents because they equate those stages of growth with malevolence. In contrast with other cultures—cultures where neighbors help with child care and assist children with homework, cultures where "baby sitters" are unknown commodities and children are included in adult social activities, cultures where there appears to be a well-defined concept of the desired current and eventual roles for children—our culture places a premium on the self. At this juncture in history, "doing one's own thing" has reached its zenith, with the attendant impatience with children's needs and particular impatience with children who present extensive or extended needs. Since we do not consider the future of our culture's children a priority, their presence represents a low valence in our value system: "We seriously must consider the notion of a child-centered society, that we use this term in an unexamined way. . . . [Possibly] we never had a child-centered society. We are for children to the degree that children are for us; but in this adult-centered society, each person is first and sometimes only for himself. One would be hard put to find sufficient evidence to reject this characterization of ourselves" (Blatt, Biklen, and Bogdan, 1977, p. 25).

Cultures perceive and focus on developmental attributes that are consonant with their value system. Since Americans regard vocational status as the most salient feature defining adults, they concentrate on those attributes in children that will determine vocational access. The vocations that we prize most highly require advanced levels of education and a degree of educational excellence. Those who falter along the way are streamed into educational routes that provide access to more limited and less valued vocational choices, whereas those who continue to progress receive passing grades that acknowledge their incremental competence. It is not surprising, then, that our focus on human development has been overwhelmingly oriented toward intelligence and academic adequacy. We examine pre, peri, and postnatal environments primarily in terms of their subsequent effects on scholastic competence and develop tests to determine intelligence from infancy onward. We promote educational toys and emphasize parental activities designed to maximize a child's intellectual ability. As Kagan, Kearsley, and Zelato (1978, p. 58) suggest, tests to determine infant empathy, strength, sociability, or irritability have not been devised. It is understandable, then, that parents and professionals should be disproportionately concerned with the presenting academic deficits in the learning disabled while minimizing, overlooking, or failing to perceive other areas of disability, or attributing them to the child's feelings around school failure.

Being ambivalent in our feelings toward children and uncertain about the attributes that they will require in their adult world, we are handicapped in designing institutions that will address their needs. Should our educational institutions focus on vocational readiness and access, an expansion of general knowledge, an increased ability to conceptualize and solve problems, or an infusion of values and, hence, attitudes? In the absence of a unitary goal, education tries to be all things to all people; consequently, no matter which goal each one of us considers primary, education fails and disappoints us.

I suspect that our most serious error in educational planning has been our failure to remember the sustaining aspects of our own school experience. As a result, our primary expectation of education tends to be the imparting of skills or information. We expect the student to be taught to read, spell, compute, and know the names of the states in the union. Regardless, when we recall our own educational experiences, our memories essentially are of attitudes and social encounters rather than information acquisition. Laudatory articles written about memorable teachers describe educators who led their students to the threshold of discovery and shared their own infectious enjoyment of art, music, and nature. Such teachers tend to model respect, afford students the dignity of having demands made of them and anticipate that the demands will be met, and find humor in pursuits that others take too seriously. No one ever memorialized a teacher who taught facts or mechanical abilities.

Our other services directed to children too frequently fall prey to the "too limited, too restrictive, too late, too few alternatives, and too unimaginative" syndrome. They, too, reflect our questionable commitment, our uncertain goals, and our confusion about methods. When we have no clear sense of direction in our childrearing and education and, indeed, see little purpose in producing children, how can we hope to conceptualize approaches to children with special needs? When we have omitted consideration of what life should mean to all people in our planning of services for children, we surely have failed to consider the requisite attributes for a rich process of living for exceptional persons. When we devalue individuals who do not meet our criteria of success and provide programs merely from humanistic dictates, how can such programs be effective? As a result, we attempt to create optimal therapeutic change within stressed and directionless systems. Our educational system is monolithic, stagnant, and elitist; our family system is undergoing transformation that creates conflicting priorities. Necessarily, then, our piecemeal efforts to adjust the learning disabled to these systems or the systems to them must net imperfect results. These systems no longer function adequately for the majority for whom they were designed. It stretches the imagination to suggest that in their present form they can meet the needs of the deviant.

Perhaps the limitation that most pervasively restricts us in planning and providing for children is the loss of our childhood perspective. We have forgotten and are unable to retrieve the essence of our own childhood; therefore, we create an imagery of childhood that is based on adult perceptions. Adults have traveled beyond the possibility of planning and providing for children as insiders. Since children lack the depth and variety of experience to place their perceptions and imagery of childhood within a continuum of possibilities and alternatives, and lack the linguistic facility to describe the uniqueness of their world, they have no choice but to accept our version of it, while recognizing the disparity between the two. They lack, as well, the power to alter cultural stereotypes and institutions; and, in any event, we have not deemed them capable of self-determination or of sharing in policy planning. Children's liberation is so heretic a concept that on the rare occasions when it is conceptualized, it is described in a "Lord of the Flies" manner, as democracy gone rampant.

Because of the increasing power and benevolence of the state and the increasing isolation of the family, parents and bureaucrats no longer know whether family or state should assume ultimate responsibility for children and for children with special needs. As a result, each system tends to create unrealistic expectations of the other and to distrust the competence of the other, so that it excludes the other from therapeutic information, planning, and execution—with predictably disappointing results.

Legislation such as the Education for All Handicapped Children Act (Public Law 94-142, 1975), which mandates school boards in the United States to provide appropriate education to all children, carries with it an unstated promise that school boards know how to reach all children, not only children who appear to resist learning but those whose attributes make some form of learning exceedingly difficult. Since education has been delineated as the possessor of answers, the entire onus of remediation has been placed at its doorstep. In order to believe that education is capable of effecting a cure, our perception of learning disabilities has been altered from that of a multifaceted disability affecting several areas of development to an academic disability. The consequent expectation is that, on receipt of appropriate academic remediation, the learning disabled person will no longer have nonacademic deficits.

Our current perception of learning disabilities can be more fully appreciated when viewed within a historical perspective. In 1947 Strauss and Lehtinen described the brain-injured child as essentially a mentally retarded child with exogenous etiology. Some years later Kephart (1971) described the unevenness of the retardation in such children and developed a remedial program that emphasized the development of basic processes as the underpinnings of higher cognitive functions. In 1963 Kirk coined the term *learning disability* as descriptive of a child similar to that described by Strauss and Lehtinen and Kephart but with near normal, normal, or above normal intellectual potential. The Kirk model, which was widely adopted, delineated a population of intelligent persons who typically were disabled in a number of primary areas of functioning in addition to academics. The deficit areas most frequently noted in the literature were linguistic/conceptual disorders, emotional/behavioral dysfunction and immaturity, social ineptitude, dyscoordination, perceptual immaturities, and disorders of attention, memory, and activity.

A parallel special-interest group evolved simultaneously. This group, adopting Orton's (1937) description of dyslexia, concerned itself with persons who essentially were developmentally intact but could not process and produce written symbols. Orton also noted the possibility of linguistic inadequacy and mixed dominance in this population. The Ortonians felt that presenting difficulties other than academic, such as lack of friends, were a result of the dyslexic's feelings about his academic failure. The assumption was that if the dyslexic experienced academic success, social adequacy would follow (Eisenberg, 1966, 1975). In contrast, proponents of the "learning disability school" believed that many of the learning disabled person's presenting difficulties resulted from primary deficits which were compounded by secondary factors.

However, in the 1970s the differences between learning disabilities and dyslexia lost their clarity. Regardless of the extent to which learning disabled persons are malfunctional in the nonacademic areas, their disability increasingly is being perceived solely as an academic deficit. This narrowing of concentration seems to have been initiated in 1979, when a political definition of learning disabilities was articulated for the U. S. Office of Education.

Children with special learning disabilities exhibit a disorder in one or more of the basic psychological processes involved in understanding or using spoken or written language. These may be manifested in disorders of thinking, listening, talking, reading, writing, spelling, or arithmetic. They include conditions which have been referred to as perceptual handicaps, brain injury, minimal brain dysfunction, dyslexia, developmental aphasia, and so on. They do not include learning problems which are due primarily to visual, hearing, or motor handicaps, to mental retardation, emotional disturbance, or to environmental disadvantage.

The overwhelmingly educational focus of this definition was designed to ensure the inclusion of learning disabilities in mandatory legislation for the handicapped. However, the definition served to focus our perception of the disability—a perception reinforced when the process approach to remediation (the emphasis on remediation of underlying processes) was found to be supported by questionable evidence (Lieberman, 1980). By the late 1970s, then, academic remediation was expected to eliminate the disabilities and to produce an intact, age-mature, socially adept, moral, and organized person. Such a belief proved to be a comfortable one for parents. It absolved the family of feelings of responsibility in having caused or perpetuated the disability and limited the manifestations of the disability to the school years. Thus, the focus of learning disabilities shifted from that of multiple primary manifestations to a unitary cluster of manifestations (reading, spelling, writing).

The alteration in focus from process to task has occasioned more than a modification in remedial approach. It appears to have obscured the importance of remediating the primary processes, such as language and coordination, for the sake of the processes themselves, irrespective of their relationship to academic functioning. We somehow have forgotten that people who are disabled linguistically, motorically, spatially, and socially—people whose attention, memory system, processing ability, and expressive ability are deficient—experience considerable difficulty with the life process irrespective of their ability to read, spell, and compute. Sadly, there is a current body of literature and research that examines primary processes in learning disabled children solely in terms of their predictability for subsequent literacy.

Once the shift in the perception of learning disabilities changed from a constellation of primary disabilities to dyslexia, the new focus proved to be so much more palatable for parents and so much simpler for educators that apparently no one has attempted to clarify the difference between the two exceptionalities. I am unaware of any articles delineating the difference between dyslexia and learning disabilities in terms of presenting behaviors, assessment features, remedial planning, and prognosis. We seem to have avoided the task of differentiation purposely, since to do so would be to illustrate that, in similar fashion to the blind man and the elephant, we are feeling the tail and describing it as representative of the animal.

This has resulted in a confused and confusing situation. Parents and professionals are exposed to literature and speakers who use the terms *learning disabilities* and *dyslexia* interchangeably, regardless of the population they are describing. Remedial rationale and outcomes are generalized in equally sloppy fashion. Because of the massive emphasis on the dyslexia aspects of learning disabilities and the propensity to perceive these as the entirety, a generation of parents have come to believe that the academic disability is the most salient feature of their offspring. They therefore suppose that all learning disabled persons are overwhelmingly similar in response and prognosis. If one learning disabled child reacts favorably to a remedial approach, in their comprehension, all should. If one becomes an esteemed professional or politician, it is expected that each one can. Conversely, if a child does not attain the hoped-for goal, education has failed. In short, when we attribute the child's misbehavior, regardless of how extreme, solely to his response to academic failure, the solutions we devise tend to be academic ones. However, alternative or more intensive academic remediation may not effect the desired personality change, and we may find that our expectations of education as the "great white hope" result in disappointment.

This reductionist phenomenon has locked the learning disability field into a constricted, linear concept of the disability that ignores the Gestalt of the exceptionality, ignores dynamic considerations, and denies the vast intrinsic and extrinsic differences that shape the learning disabled as they shape all persons. Thus, parents may be insufficiently cognizant of the role that personal attributes play in molding a person—attributes such as intelligence, temperament, talents, creativity, motivation, and courage.

Since we seem to believe that all learning disabilities are dyslexias, we have not evidenced any need to investigate social, emotional, and vocational prognoses. A generation of identified learning disabled persons have reached adulthood; yet no study has been undertaken to determine the intrinsic and extrinsic factors that are predictive of outcomes. We have yet to research adjustment in terms of disability clusters, temperament, measured intellectual functioning, family dynamics, rank order, and socioeconomic status. The few adult case studies that have been published typically describe rigid, controlling behavior which is simplistically attributed to illiteracy. The absence of data on which residual disabilities, if any, are the most handicapping in adulthood allows us to continue to put our faith in academic remediation without questioning whether there are more disabling aspects of the disability. We do not know the effects that poor spelling, slow and inaccurate reading, limited computation ability, clumsiness, or linguistic deficiences have on adult vocational and interpersonal competence. We have not determined which attributes lead to one learning disabled adult's ability to circumvent his academic disabilities in adulthood or comfortably ask others to assist him with difficult tasks and another learning disabled adult's devastation and immobilization by similar disabilities. Neither have we determined whether the areas on which we concentrate less—areas such as social inappropriateness, rigidity, disorganization, and poor judgment—are the most profoundly handicapping in adulthood.

This constricted perception of learning disabilities, which enables parents to envision a narrowly delineated and time-limited disability that the educational system will eliminate, spares parents the pain of facing a more global disability that may represent some degree of encumbrance for a lifetime. When humans find that facing a situation in its entirety is too threatening, they reduce it to simpler components and treat those components as if they were the whole. Consequently, a promised cure directed to some facets of the disability is perceived as a cure for the entire condition. Furthermore, a treatment that addresses itself to one possible etiology of learning disabilities, or which claims to eliminate one behavior, is embraced for all learning disabled persons, since some of them manifest that behavior. There appears to be insufficient understanding that humans possess a repertoire of behaviors that they are able to produce as a response to stress, regardless of the stress agents. Consequently, a behavior such as hyperactivity can represent many possible etiologies, so that a treatment for hyperactivity will not eliminate that behavior in all hyperactive persons, nor is it necessarily a treatment for learning disabilities.

Many parents become confused between issues of prevention and remediation. Much of the speculation in the chemometabolic sphere is addressed to future generations; eventually some learning disabilities might be prevented or minimized by genetic counseling or prenatal diet. Once a child has a learning disability, energy is most profitably focused toward remediation of existing deficits. Moreover, parents are unaware that, even if an immediate cure were discovered for their child, he still would be different from his peers. His years of altered perceptions, behaviors, and responses have created a different set of memories, concepts, feelings, and expectations than his peers have experienced.

In any event, we are unable to cure learning disabilities, just as we are unable to cure any organic condition such as diabetes or high blood pressure, although we are able to control, minimize and circumvent most dysfunctions to the point where they are of minimal inconvenience. Parents feel certain that educators possess the knowledge to cure learning disabilities because they have been legislated to provide appropriate education for all children. Legislation notwithstanding, educators are acutely aware of the limitations of their remedial knowledge. They find that they are able to create moderate improvement in the deficit areas of most children, while being unable to make anyone ultimately competent in his areas of disability. At the same time, there is the occasional child who fails to respond to the remedial efforts of skilled practitioners. And remediation, being legislated into the sphere of education, leads parents to expect that elimination of the child's academic problems will result in the disappearance of his social ineptitude, immaturity, and behavioral difficulties, since they are all attributed to the child's feelings about school failure.

The shortage of quality special education services further focuses parents on the academic aspects of the disability. Many parents find that they must remain vigilant activists throughout their child's school career to ensure that he receives competent and sufficient remediation with understanding teachers. This intense involvement in the child's education further narrows the focus toward the academic aspects of the disability; as a result, parents perceive the disability as the most important aspect of their child's being.

It is common for parents of the learning disabled to be overwhelmingly absorbed with the disability and to use it as an explanation for their offspring's behavior. Consequently, much of their investment in their child is around an aspect of him that is viewed as undesirable, bad, and frightening and for which he is not expected to be accountable. As long as parents view the disability as an acquired insult to an intact brain, their energies and anxieties will be directed toward its disappearance. If we directed some of our priorities to helping parents perceive the learning disability as an intrinsic aspect of their child, just as his physical appearance, intelligence, and humor are part of him, a speedier and healthier adjustment would ensue.

Susanne Langer (1951, p. 19) describes constricted perception in this way: "The limits of thought are not so much set from outside, by the fullness or poverty of experiences that meet the mind, as from within, by the power of conception, the wealth of formulative notions with which the mind meets the experiences. Most new discoveries are suddenly seen things that were always there." In the learning disability field, the issue is not our failure to acquire a comprehensive perception of learning disabilities but the apparent attenuation of an original perception.

Chapter 2

❋ ❋ ❋ ❋ ❋

How Thinking Difficulties Affect Social Development

❋ We live by way of images—images of our bodies and our minds, images of our birth and eventual death, images of others, shared imagery. Boulding (1956) suggests that our behavior depends on imagery, and Lifton (1979) relates personal development to our image of self and the world.

Imagery, in turn, is contingent on the acquisition of concepts, concepts of the size and shape of self, of the feeling and passage of immediate and extended time, of the temporal qualities of the life span, and of historical time. Imagery subsumes a knowledge of the life process, which is the pace and substance of human biological and intellectual maturation and humans' life tasks and stresses at each stage. The antecedent of imagery is an understanding of the ways whereby one is related to others, which dictates the ways that one will relate to others. The more extensive man's imagery is, the greater the number of interpretations he will be able to bring to a situation and the more varied his repertoire of possible behaviors will be. In turn, more extensive behaviors generate more responses from others. Conversely, limited imagery will result in

16

more impoverished behavioral possibilities that will evoke limited responses. These circumscribed responses from others restrict the number of behaviors to which one is exposed, which further limits imagery.

Since our very humanness is predicated on imagery, and since deficits in concept formation, abstract symbolic thought processes, and, hence, imagery have long been recognized in the learning disabled, it is a compelling model around which to build a discussion of development. Imagery molds behavior, which elicits response, which is incorporated into the imagery and modifies subsequent behavior. As a result, a discussion of imagery and human development must be transactional. It makes no sense to believe that the learning disabled person's current difficulties are directly traceable to a genetic difference or a perinatal insult without taking into account the years of mediation afforded by environment. Sameroff and Chandler (1975) found that infants whose perinatal environments increased their risk for developmental problems did not demonstrate a greater incidence of developmental deviations than in a control population if lower socioeconomic infants were excluded from the group. Thomas and Chess (1977), in their description of the temperamental attributes with which people are born and the effects of environmental response to such attributes, have been enormously influential in demonstrating the reciprocity of nature and nurture.

However, it is not sufficient to state that environment acts upon temperament, or that temperament alters environment, without recognizing that each changes over time and that each system attempts to compensate for deficits in its functioning. Therefore, rather than looking at the effects of a disability upon environment or of environment upon a disability, we must take the dynamic properties of both into account. This enables us to view behavior as the response of a particular person to a particular environment at a specific time rather than as a definitive expression of the essential nature of the child.

Notwithstanding the self-righting, dynamic properties of development and environment, there can be occurrences in either system that alter the quality of reciprocity and have implications for immediate and subsequent development. This can represent a difference in the child's presenting behavior from the expected, which can alter the family's perceptions of the child's intent. Parental interpretation of the behavior will depend on the conceptual level of parenting (Sameroff, 1979).*

Parenting is most comfortably handled when a child's behavior is consonant with parental expectations. As Erikson (1963, p. 67) described, the intact child achieves this consonance of balance or goodness of fit between parental expectation and development: "The healthy child, if halfway properly guided, merely obeys and on the whole can be trusted to obey inner laws of development; namely, those laws which in his prenatal period had formed one organ after another and which now create a succession of potentialities for significant interaction with those around him. While such interaction varies widely from culture to culture, . . . proper rate and proper sequence remain critical factors guiding and limiting all variability." When discontinuities of behavior create parental anxiety, disappointment, guilt, and rejection, then parental response may perpetuate or exacerbate the disability.

External information also can alter the quality of reciprocity. Parents, upon learning that their child might be or is disabled, may view behaviors as deviant which they previously considered normal.** Essentially, the quality of parental response to unexpected

---

*Sameroff formulated stages of parenting that correspond to Piaget's (1950) stages of cognition. He suggests that at the *symbiotic* level parents interpret their child's behavior as being directly related to parenting. At the *categorical* level parents see their children as separate entities and assign labels to them such as "my good" or "my bad" child. These labels tend to persist despite evidence to the contrary. Parents at the *compensating* level relate their child's behavior to age-expected norms. If the child produces a behavior that is not deemed age-expected, he will be perceived as deviant. Parents at the *perspectivistic* level see behavior as originating from individual experience with specific environments. Deviancies are perceived as representing the difficulty of a particular child is having with a particular environment, rather than as a static expression of the child's intrinsic nature.

**Klaus Minde (as cited in Sameroff, 1979), in a study of children from an intensive care unit, noted that the behaviors which parents viewed as normal became suspect after they were informed that there might be something wrong with their child.

behavior or threatening information has important implications for the child's acquisition of compensatory behaviors. In this book I will illustrate a few of the many possible interactional alterations that a learning disabled infant, child, adolescent, and adult might introduce into his environment, the responses such behavior might elicit, and implications for continued development. Intervention strategies may eventually reach the level of sophistication whereby supportive assistance is afforded to families at junctures of most profound discontinuity between the expectation of family members and the production of the learning disabled member. Such intervention would encourage parental responses geared to the reduction of the deviant behavior and would allow parents to consider the discontinuity in developmental terms, and as a response to the situation at hand rather than deviance.

Elements in Imagery Production

Schematization. Imagery is dependent on one's ability to conceive schemata of objects, space, and time. Schemata are formed from environmental feedback—the smile, the frown, the smell and feel, the fit and movement of animate and inanimate objects in the environment. The younger the child, the sparser his experiences and perceptions will be. As a result, the constancy of his schemata will be vulnerable to a loss of information, such as maternal absence. He lacks the store of previous experiences which would create an image of her in absentia and predict her return. Similarly, the accurate categorization of experience depends on a plentiful backlog of experiences, so that one is enabled to judge the precise quality of the current encounter. Marris (1974, p. 6) describes this phenomenon: "The ability to learn from experience relies on the stability of the interpretations by which we predict the pattern of events. We assimilate new experiences by placing them in the context of a familiar, reliable construction of reality. This structure in turn rests not only on the regularity of events themselves but on the continuity of their meaning."

Like the young child, the learning disabled person may lack stability and storage of schemata and imagery. Although he may frequently have encountered similar experiences, he may not have noticed, critically assessed, or remembered them. Since he may be insufficiently aware that all human experience falls into predictable patterns, he will be uncertain about which stimuli are relevant or irrelevant to the schemata at hand. He thus may process only part of an interaction or conversation or include extraneous information in his concept of what has transpired. This results in inaccurate storage, illogical thought processes, distortions of judgment and skewed responses. For example, Dan heard his mother discuss someone's poor health on the telephone and remark that he was "failing badly." Had he taken the entire conversation into account, he would have realized that it could not have referred to him. However, he focused on the one phrase and was devastated. Neil broke a window at the summer camp his father owned, and, fearful of punishment, ran away. He wanted to return to camp but was on some of the camp property that had "no trespassing" signs. As a result, he hid from the camp vehicles that were looking for him because he was trespassing on his own property.

Since the learning disabled person is unaware that all behavior falls into predictable patterns, he lacks the notion that his behavior and that of others are predictable (Parrill-Burnstein and Baker-Ward, 1979). Thus he will be unable to imagine a social situation in advance, rehearse his interactional strategies, and imagine his interactor's responses to his strategies. Neither will he comprehend the reasons that others react in specific ways to his interactions and adjust them accordingly nor appreciate the meaning and hence importance of noticing others' behaviors.

Church (1961, p. 42), in describing the evolution of schematic thought processes in the human infant, states: "Schematization occurs in the course of having his needs attended to, being played with and talked to, and, increasingly, of actively exploring the environment. We should note, too, that the taboos the baby encounters, for his own safety or for parental comfort, enter into his schematization."

Since nuclear and extended family members often manifest learning disabilities or some of the behaviors associated with learning disabilities (Hartcollis, 1968; Wender, 1971), some parents of the learning disabled are disorganized. A child in such a family may not have his needs attended to with sufficient structure that would enable him to note patterns and construct schemata. The child whose parents do not gear their ministrations to his needs and level of development may be too distressed or bewildered to conceptualize schemata.

We have become increasingly aware that the infant himself plays a crucial role in establishing the quality of the interactions he will receive. The care of the neonate is so time consuming and wearing that the parents may lose interest in him, or feel that the effort expended on his care is not worthwhile, if he does not adjust to routines and smile and babble and respond to parental overtures. The learning disabled infant who does not notice a positive overture or does not assess it as positive will fail to respond or be unpredictable in response. The learning disabled child who does not comply with parental efforts to socialize him, who is toilet trained with great difficulty, who is clumsy, easily frustrated, rigid or embarrassing; and who demonstrates less linguistic, conceptual, motor, and social growth than expected will, of necessity, create an environment in which the responses are diminished or less positive. The child who says little will be talked to less than the child who initiates enjoyable conversations or makes "cute" observations. The child who screams with frustration whenever he is clumsy will be played with less. The hyperactive child will exhaust family members, who have little energy remaining for enjoyable interaction, even if they were able to keep their child's attention long enough to sustain an interaction or catch him to cuddle.

When parents are confident that a child is achieving expected developmental milestones and behaving in an age-expected manner, they feel comfortable in exposing him to the peer group. "In this way," states Hartup (1979, p. 948), "the social system (family) ensures contact with a second social system (the peer group) that in turn can contribute on its own to the growth of various social competencies; that is, the two social systems are conjunctive." On the other hand, when the child is inadept, immature, easily frustrated, and uncooperative and/or the parents are ambivalent and insecure, peer contact will be anticipated as unpredictable and potentially embarrassing and hence avoided. The parents will fear other adults' assumptions that their child's behavior reflects their childrearing practices. Instead of parental encouragement of peer

engagement, there then is discouragement, which results in reduced exposure to peers and fewer opportunities to observe peer
social behavior and to practice interacting with peers.

  The Relationship of Imagery to Bonding and Social Adequacy. It is
likely that imagery has its egis in infancy. If the infant is to bond
adequately to the mother, presumably he must create some imagery that discriminates her from others. As he matures, he develops
the ability to retain her image through absences, so that her proximity can be symbolized as a mental bridge to reappearance. In her
overview of research on the infant's perception of the mother's
face, Izard (1977) relates such perception to visual and auditory
adequacy and to tracking ability. She stresses the relationship
between recognition of the mother's face, the development of
attachment behavior and social adequacy. The infant who has
difficulty in processing and retaining visual/spatial and auditory
stimuli and in predicting temporal events—who consequently is
inefficient in the analysis, synthesis, and memory of events—may
well experience deficits in the comprehension of the boundaries
and nuances of human form, sound, and smell. Thus, he may be
unable to retain the maternal image through time or to create the
temporal imagery to predict her return.

  Kaslow and Cooper (1978) suggest that the infant who is
deficient in holding a visual/spatial image or perceiving facial expressions accurately may fail to respond to the mother's smile and
may scream when she alters her clothing or hairstyle. In turn, she
may become confused, anxious, and disappointed in the discrepancy between the hoped-for baby and reality; she may become an
ambivalent and insecure parent. Brazelton and his associates (1975)
note that the intact infant, even at a few months of age, initiates and
modifies interaction with the mother. It is probable that the infant
who fails to notice a positive stimulus, such as a smile, as early as
intact peers or is not as attentive or predictable in response to social
stimuli will not take the initiative as early or as extensively. Lacking
the reinforcement of prosocial and reciprocal behavior, parental
interest will not be aroused. Parents who themselves do not notice
visual/spatial detail will not process the infant's wordless language,
a probable requisite of social development.

Attachment behavior appears to depend on perception, motor coordination, and cognition (Mahler, Pine, and Bergman, 1975; Sigman, 1980). When a child's development follows the expected course, his increasing mobility and demonstrations of ability alert parents to allow increasing amounts of freedom. The child who is delayed or deficient in the acquisition of such skills will be poorly equipped to produce the behavior that cements attachment and subsequently the behavior—such as crawling, walking, or talking—that promotes exploration, cognitive reorganization, and separation.

It is through mechanisms such as these that disturbances in processing and, hence, imagery may threaten the adequacy of bonding from child to parent and parent to child. It also may have implications for future social adequacy. Bryan and Sherman (1980) found that learning disabled children had shorter periods of time in which they maintained gaze or smiled. The brevity of gaze and smile caused mothers who watched videotapes of learning disabled children's interactions to rate those children as having negative attributes.

Research into the infant and maternal attributes that are predictive of adequate bonding is in its infancy. It seems probable that the presence or absence of specific behaviors in the infant is more critical to the bonding process than the extensiveness or possibly the type of handicap. Roskies (1972), in her research on thalidomide babies, found that parents who were able to engage the child in eye-to-eye contact or mutual smiling strongly believed that their child was normal, notwithstanding the absence of limbs. Similarly, specific handicapping conditions will be perceived as more or less serious and as greater or lesser tragedies to the extent that the handicap prevents the person from meeting personal, familial, or societal goals.

Bonding and Social Adequacy. There is a body of research which relates adequacy of bonding to the acquisition of independent, socially competent functioning. Ainsworth (1979) argues that a secure attachment facilitates the growth of healthy self-reliance. Matas, Arend, and Sroufe (1978) found that two-year-old children who had been assessed as "securely attached" at eighteen months of age were more enthusiastic, persistent, cooperative, and generally more effective in peer interaction than were insecurely attached infants. Independent observers also rated infants who had secure attachments as being better able to function effectively in the face of frustration, to utilize extended assistance appropriately, and to refrain from excessively self-defeating behavior. Lieberman (1977) reports that young children who had formed secure attachments as infants were more responsive to peers and engaged in more protracted social interaction than those who had bonded less well. Waters, Whippman, and Sroufe (1979) found that six-year-old children who had secure attachments were (1) socially active rather than withdrawn, (2) sought out by other children, (3) peer leaders, (4) active in making suggestions, (5) sympathetic to peer distress, (6) not hesitant in responding to initiations for interactions from other children. Ainsworth (1979, p. 936) comments on adequate bonding in relationship to social development: "The implication is that the way in which the infant organizes his or her behavior toward the mother affects the way in which [the infant] organizes behavior toward other aspects of the environment, both animate and inanimate. This organization provides a core of continuity in development despite changes that come with developmental acquisitions, both cognitive and socioemotional."

As Wilchesky (1980b, pp. 14–15) points out, positive correlations between secure attachment and social adequacy are not necessarily indicative of a cause-effect relationship. "Children," he suggests, "who enjoy successful peer relations may also establish secure attachments owing to some inherently positive attributes, such as brightness, even-temperedness, or attractiveness." Hartup (1979, p. 948) cautions: "It is risky to conclude from such evidence that secure attachment is a necessary precursor of success in peer relations." Nonetheless, whether one is the precursor of the other or both are dependent on a similar set of variables, once each is operant, they surely are reciprocal. In subsequent chapters I shall be describing the social ineptitude that a significant number of learning disabled children demonstrate. A fruitful area of potential research would be an exploration of the effects of social imperception on bonding and the effects of inadequate bonding on the acquisition of social skills in the learning disabled.

Temporal Imagery

A Schematization of Time. Church (1961, p. 40) tells us that the schematization of time begins at birth: "Our knowledge of time has its foundations in the biological rhythms of activity and repose, of feeding and digestion, and the external events with which these rhythms are coordinated. All animal organisms, and at least some plants, have daily and seasonal cycles, which are to some degree under the control of external stimulation (such as the alteration of daylight and darkness, the rise and fall of the tides, the phases of the moon, and so forth), but which also become stabilized under fairly constant conditions, as biological clocks which regulate the organism's activities from within." Church explains that the orientation of time is psychological as well as physiological and comes to include the abstraction of time from space and activity patterns, a vocabulary of words with a temporal index, an understanding of the scales used to measure time's passage and accumulation, a knowledge first of growing up and then of growing old, a sense of how time slips by at an ever faster rate as one ages, a sense of history and destiny, and the ability to coordinate activities and events in rational sequence and fit them into a larger time scheme.

Many learning disabled persons have a poor concept of the passage of time. They experience difficulty in learning and remembering the terminology that labels time, in sequencing information logically, and in learning to tell the time. They cannot readily learn the names of the parts of the day, such as midafternoon and evening; the days of the week; the months of the year; and the seasons. Even when they do learn these words by rote, they often are unable to generalize the information—what comes before Monday or after February, when Christmas falls, or in what month spring arrives. Some will transpose "yesterday" and "tomorrow" or shortly after breakfast inquire when supper will be ready. Some are unaware of the rules whereby we denote the passage of years (1979, 1980, 1981), nor will they state a year if asked when they were born. Some lack a sense of time, be it five minutes, a month, or a lifetime. If expected to complete a homework assignment within two weeks, they may not comply because of their deficient imagery of that length of time and their lack of temporal organization and sequential planning skills. They make poor use of their time because they cannot judge the number of tasks they can accomplish in a period of time, or relate the amount of time one should spend on a task to the importance of a task, or determine when one should begin a task or set out for a destination. Some have not differentiated between repetitious conversation that is reinforcing and repetition that is perseverative and irritating. Some do not know when to terminate clowning behavior; and some cannot tell a joke so that the punch line is discontinuous and hence funny. Some are unaware of the timing of spoken language and do not regulate timing with affect, nor do they give other people an opportunity to pause without filling in the gaps (Bryan, Sherman, and Fisher, 1980). They seem unaware of which interactions should be cursory and which should require an in-depth investment. Being deficient in temporal imagery, they generate excessive anxiety around upcoming events and insufficient anxiety around long-term goals.

Some, being insufficiently aware of the organization of experience, do not draw on past experiences to predict subsequent outcomes. Since some learning disabled persons perceive events unitarily rather than in a temporal context, the events have reduced impact on them. Humor is not amusing unless we can relate it to analogous past situations and imagine an atypical result. Similarly, a situation such as death is not sad unless we have an imagery of the importance of our past relationship with the deceased and project a future without him. This deficit in temporal imagery—combined with egocentricity, misperception of affect, and deficient knowledge of the words and language that express feeling—produces a blunting of expressed affect or an apparent shallowness of affect. However, although Strag (1972) found that parents rated learning disabled children as less affectionate than their siblings, there is no indication that the learning disabled care for others less than their peers do; they merely may be ill equipped to express their caring.

Some lack the imagery of the temporal life span. They are unaware of man's body size in each temporal period of development, his cognitive and linguistic ability at each juncture (Bryan and

Pflaum, 1978), and his life tasks. They do not know when humans stop growing or the changes that the body undergoes in each developmental phase. They are uncertain about one's vocational role over time and the stresses that accompany each of life's passages. This reduces their ability to empathize with others, to imagine themselves over a life span, and to regulate their activities in accordance with anticipated future events. They will be ill equipped to place the life span of others in a perspective as it relates to theirs.

Most certainly they will lack an image of themselves in relationship to historical time. They may be unable to imagine their life span, their childhood, adolescence, and stages of adulthood in relationship to a historical continuum that includes the past and future history of their family, their subculture and the human race. Thus, they will be hampered in adopting a role in life that is consonant with their historical tradition while being addressed to current and future concerns. Those of us who possess adequate temporal imagery tend to be fascinated by the history of the human race, by our roots and our relationship to them. We select roles that are compatible with our roots yet contribute to the present and future of mankind; the imagery of this projected contribution makes our efforts seem worthwhile. It is almost beyond our ability to comprehend the static quality of life of those learning disabled persons who lack temporal imagery; they are locked into the current moment in a meaningless and directionless existence.

Imagery of One's Life Span. Neugarten (1979) suggests that individuals develop a concept of the "normal expectable life cycle," a set of anticipations that certain life events will occur at certain times and a mental clock telling them where they are and whether they are on or off time. She has found that people have a concept of their own best age to marry, to have a child, to become a grandparent, to be settled in a career, to reach the top, to retire, and the salient personality characteristics for each life stage. "People," Neugarten states, "readily report whether they themselves are on time and if not, why not." She elaborates: "Being on time or off time is a compelling basis for self-assessment. Men and women compare themselves with their friends, siblings, work colleagues, or parents in deciding whether they have made good, but it is always with a time line in mind. It is not the fact that one reaches forty, fifty, or sixty which is itself important, but rather, 'How am I doing for my age?'" (p. 888).

Learning disabled persons tend to be saddened when they have not achieved milestones at the same ages as their siblings and peers. Some, however, lack the ability for self-appraisal in relationship to peers and culture. They are thus hampered in molding assumptions of the appropriateness of their behavior and achievements; these assumptions take into account not only the achievement of others of their age and cultural expectations but also their own rate of development, abilities, and disabilities. We mainstream them with intact students. Their siblings and neighbors are intact, so that their reference group is the nondisabled. If they fail to achieve an amount of growth commensurate with that of their peers within the same time span, their disappointment may well supersede an appraisal of their personal time clock.

Some learning disabled persons lack the ability to take the perspective of others (Parrill-Burnstein and Hazan-Ginsburg, 1980). So much concern has centered around them and typically few demands made of them to be other-centered that some remain egocentric throughout adulthood and cannot interact appropriately with other people. Since they may not realize the importance of being attuned to their interactor's role projections and may, in fact, not notice interactional detail (Winner and Gardner, 1977), they will be limited in the acquisition of information about other humans and their life processes, and deficient in gearing their interactions to effect optimal responses.

Ignorance of the components of the life cycle and deficits in temporal imagery render the learning disabled ill equipped to visualize a personal life plan. They experience difficulty in imagining themselves as an intimate, a wage earner, and a contributor to the culture. Intact children begin this task in preadolescence, and it is well defined during adolescence (Ausubel and Sullivan, [1957] 1970). Adolescents also evolve an image of the quality and extensiveness of their moral and ethical roles throughout life. However, the person who lacks an imagery of his own and others' personal and geographical space, of his own and others' life space and the temporal components thereof, will be ill equipped to map his life plan and conceptualize his life's meaning.

Parents of the learning disabled are handicapped in developing an imagery of their child throughout life and imparting this to him. Our emphasis on creating services solely in the academic sphere has relegated parent education and counseling to the volunteer organizations. They, in turn, consisting primarily of parents, have largely concentrated information services around the newest treatment rather than the information requisite for parenting a learning disabled child. Similarly, most volunteer organizations have not developed formal counseling programs. As a result, parents may be aware of a plethora of treatments but may not comprehend what a learning disability is. They realize that their child has difficulty in some aspects of functioning but are unaware of the differences between his processing style and that of intact children, and implications for coping and development. Many parents are only marginally aware of the different learning disability clusters. They are unable, then, to appreciate the difference between their child's learning disability and those of other learning disabled persons. Neither are they able to take his particular disability and other attributes into account in developing a current parenting and educational plan and a concept of his adult life. Since many parents are unaware of the variations of learning disabilities and the possible nuances of learning style, they may not realize the importance of a prescriptive remedial approach. They thus are ill equipped to judge the applicability of a remedial method for their child, nor do they have the knowledge to assess the adequacy of his current program or one under consideration. Not only are such parents vulnerable to each remedial fad they encounter; they also are impeded in conceptualizing their child's probable future.

We are able to supply our intact children with imagery of their probable adult social and vocational roles in early childhood. We frequently comment to them about what they are likely and not likely to do as adults. The messages that parents of the learning disabled convey to children about their eventual adulthood are related to the extent to which each parent has come to terms with the disability and the pervasiveness of their current acceptance or denial. This level of acceptance is, in turn, colored by the quality of their other life events. If highly stressed, they are likely to convey a gloomy outcome and, if comfortable, an optimistic future. When they are exposed to a life history of a learning disabled adult who has succeeded vocationally, they tell their child that he, too, will turn out in this fashion. Conversely, when someone implies that learning disabilities render one at risk for delinquency, the child is expected to become delinquent momentarily. The end result is parents who convey a host of contradictory messages to the child and others—suggesting, at different times, that the child is incompetent and competent, retarded and intelligent, worthless and worthy, troublesome and a blessing; likely to become a professor and sure to become a criminal or dependent for life.

Since the learning disability field is in its infancy, no honest practitioner can predict with certainty or guarantee the extent of an individual's response to remediation. Practitioners have a sense of which approaches appear more promising but cannot assure improvement for every person or suggest the amount of projected improvement. Not only are professionals puzzled by the occasional person who responds to remediation in a limited fashion but they are also surprised by those who respond more comprehensively than expected. Because of this unpredictability, even the most sophisticated parents cannot conceptualize their child's life span with clarity; the child, in turn, is hampered in conceptualizing his own emerging and eventual self.

Even more unpredictable is the quality of the remediation a particular child will receive. Parents cannot predict, from year to year, the amount of remediation he will be offered each week, the number of children with whom he will share remedial time, the quality of the special educator's training, or the competence of the educator; nor do they know whether the teacher's orientation and interests coincide with the child's deficits. Parents have no crystal ball to tell them how flexible mainstream teachers will be throughout their child's school career. They also do not know which academic track he will be put in, and each track limits access to vocational choices. Similarly, they have no way of predicting the degree of flexibility of eventual employers or postsecondary institutions, all of which impinge on choice of eventual career. Most important, they do not know how their child will mature, which current behaviors will disappear or be expressed in modified fashions, or how disabling some behaviors—such as disorganization, rigidity, proneness to frustration, or perseveration—will be to him in adulthood. When one's intact offspring reach mid to late adolescence, the form of their probable adulthood comes into focus. However, immature learning disabled youth take much longer to "jell" and may progress well into adulthood with their eventual vocational, social, and parental status still unclear. We are in the process of "becoming" through much of our lives. However, when we do not know what it is that we are becoming, then substance and direction are lacking.

When parents are unclear about what their child's future holds or are frightened by their image of his probable future, they discard the processes whereby parents typically visualize their child's adulthood. Instead of imagining an adult life based on an amalgam of attributes and likely opportunities, they relate future probability to present satisfactions (Wright, 1968). Therefore, if they receive some positive information about the child or note an increment of growth, they generalize this to a bright future. However, in these instances, prognosis is vulnerable to the moment-to-moment vicissitudes of the learning disabled child's performance and ranges from optimism to despair.

Moreover, until children reach adolescence and begin to take charge of their future, they do not necessarily separate realistic goals from merely wishful ones. When decision making and personal responsibility for the future are delayed for whatever reason—for instance, because the child is disabled or has been overprotected—the young adult will be further delayed in relating future aspirations to personal competence and likely opportunities (Wright, 1968).

Childrearing in our culture is directed toward eventual adulthood: "Children in American society are molded for their futures. We ask of them, demand of them, train them, so that they will 'turn out all right.' They are creatures to be socialized, to be readied" (Bluebond-Langner, 1978, p. 210). Inkeles (1968, p. 75), in describing parental direction, states: "In their efforts to social-

ize the child, parents are guided, however fallibly, by their awareness of such social expectations and their image of what the child
must become if he is to live successfully in the world as the parents envision it will be at the time the child becomes an adult."
Bluebond-Langner (1978, p. 212) depicts the process whereby parents rear the future adult: "When children succeed they are rewarded; when they fail they are punished or ignored. All of these
actions are done 'for their own good.' This justification for discipline is also the rationale for withholding certain things from children, and not indulging them materially or nonmaterially. Many
goods, rights, and privileges are for a later time, when they are
older, when they have earned them. Complete gratification is for
the future, after one has 'made it.' Children, in American society,
are in process, not yet full formed, as childhood is a period of
formation, of becoming. Socialization is by definition forward
looking."

When the imagery of our offspring's ultimate adulthood is
amorphous, the parental role is partially aborted. Parents are hampered in creating an adult image toward which they and their child
can work. The shaping of that image through childrearing practice, the teaching, the modeling, the expectations, the denials, and
the rewards, lack purpose and direction. Parental behavior becomes inconsistent, compensatory, and momentary instead of being
consistent, assured, and future directed.

Parents assess their child's attributes and relate them to
probable adulthood on a covert as well as an overt level. Aberle and
Naegele (1968) suggest that parents evaluate their child's behavior
not only by direct extrapolation but also by vaguer and less conscious processes in which the connection between present and
future behavior is more indirectly and symbolically reckoned.
Therefore, future directing will be based not only on the child's
presenting attributes but also on the parents' feelings around having parented their learning disabled child and the effect that they
imagine he will have on the attainment of their own goals.

Time, Culture, and Self-Worth. Time is biological, ecological,
and cognitive but it also is cultural. Each culture has a shared imagery and hence value system concerning use of time. Cultural activities can be differentiated as "Being" and "Doing" (Murray and

Kluckhohn, 1953). "Being" is represented as beneficial, effortless, pleasurable, and almost spontaneous activity—for instance, watching or giving a concert or dance, telling a joke and laughing at it, or attending a party. "Doing" is a demand for action in the sense of accomplishment and in accord with standards external to the acting individual. In this type of activity, satisfaction is linked to the ultimate goal. Our American culture is overwhelmingly oriented to "Doing" as exemplified by our phrases of "don't waste time," "getting things accomplished," and "bettering oneself."

The value of achievement, rather than personal pleasure, is internalized by the learning disabled, their families, and most others in the culture. Consequently, the learning disabled child and his parents are pressured to attain developmental, academic, and athletic milestones at expected ages, and the biological time of the learning disabled person is ignored. The child and parents feel pressured into directing disproportionate time, energy, and concern into the remediation of deficit areas so that the child will catch up, keep up, and eventually succeed vocationally. The time spent on remediation and the concern generated around it magnifies the importance of the learning disabled person's inadequacies in his and others' assessment of his worth and interferes with his time to devote to the "Being" facets of self or belief in its importance. The learning disabled person's deficits in organization, judgment, and future imagery impede his ability to plan and execute his activities so as to actualize his "Doing" self. Anticipating failure, he also tends to generate anxiety that is disproportionate to the difficulty of the upcoming task and thereby cripples his success as a "Doing" person. Similarly, the temporal demands of being a parent or a sibling to a learning disabled person may conflict with the time that they wish to spend on the "Doing" and "Being" facets of their lives.

An Image of Energy

Each family and every member of a family imagines the ways in which energy is to be expended and the amounts of energy that are to be directed toward each immediate and long-term goal. Although individual family members demonstrate varying levels of available energy and different goals as to its use, they also share a concept of the use of energy in mutually approved ways and directed toward family goals. Some families value the completion of tasks, hence the proportioning of energy throughout the task; others are less concerned with completion, so that considerable energy is expended on initiation of multiple tasks and little on termination. Some families tolerate or enjoy high levels of overt demonstrations of energy, such as movement, loud laughing, sneezing, and crying; other families are more restrictive and subdued. Although beliefs about energy use are sociocultural to a large extent, there is also considerable intracultural variation.

Our beliefs about the expenditure of energy within interactions relate, as well, to the type of interaction. Formal interactions or those with persons of higher status than ourselves, interactions that might alter the course of our lives or those involving extensive intimacy are interpersonal encounters in which we invest considerable energy. On the other hand, we expect to expend minimal amounts of energy on casual encounters in such places as elevators, at parties, or on park benches. When we encounter someone such as a learning disabled person who does know or respect our shared understanding of the use of energy, and produces behavior that demands more energy of us than we are prepared to exert, we react with annoyance, fear, and avoidance.

Learning disabled children who are hyperactive or hypoactive frequently are out of step with their family members' beliefs about the use or expenditure of energy. Those who plan their time or tasks so poorly that their energy is dissipated with minimal return may clash with their family's value system. Those whose needs for assistance exceed family members' beliefs about the amount of assistance an offspring or sibling should require, or find that it conflicts with energies that they had hoped to direct to other activities, will be resented. Those who become loudly frustrated or move a great deal may irritate families who believe in self-control and restrained expression of self. Those learning disabled persons who perseverate or who do not perceive others' periodic need for solitude, will exceed their family members' willingness to expend energy at that time.

Similarly, those learning disabled persons who lack knowledge of the expected use of energy in a variety of social situations may overdo them by prolonging a cursory conversation, providing information that is anxiety producing, too intimate or embarrassing, monopolizing the conversation, introducing irrelevant or tangential information or violating the physical constraints by standing on the furniture or touching treasured belongings.

An Imagery of Meaning

Each family develops elaborate concepts of its beliefs about desirable behavior and about the religious, moral, and ethical beliefs that they practice and espouse. Their belief system encompasses the ways that family members use time and money, the way they dress, and the relationships that they have with persons outside the family. These beliefs are conveyed through their choice and arrangement of clothing and accessories, their use of language, body movement and facial expressions, and their behavior. Typically, members of a family learn to convey an image that represents a family's beliefs and maintains family secrets (Kantor and Lehr, 1975). However, a learning disabled member might not further the image that a family wishes to promote or conceal those aspects about which it is ashamed. He may be sloppy and not notice current fashions in dress yet have a family that values neatness and style. He may be prone to loud expressions of frustration and impulsivity whereas his family values controlled, quiet language and careful approaches to tasks. His parents may place importance on persistence and hard work whereas he may have a short interest span and become easily discouraged. They may feel that people should organize their use of energy whereas he may use energy randomly and show little propensity to set goals. They may value constricted, careful movement and he may be hyperactive; they may be productive, high achievers and he may be hypoactive. Moreover, the learning disabled person who has not learned the expected behavior in each social situation will freely expose family secrets so that the family is unable to present a face to the world that implies somewhat different circumstances than actually occur. In other words, a family whose child tells everyone everything will be unable to present themselves as having a healthy marriage or happy family life if such is actually not the case. Although many of our children do not necessarily promote all the behaviors that we value as a family, their deviations stem from choice. They are aware of family values and decide which values are consistent with the beliefs that they and their generation hold and which ones they must modify to conform to their plans. The learning disabled, on the other hand, fail to conform because they do not realize what the family's values are or have a disability which makes conformity difficult.

The learning disabled lack the imagery that enables us to visualize our own lives as they relate to the history of mankind, our family, and those around us. They may not recognize the beliefs that their culture values and subsequently do not share an understanding of the predictability of social experiences that would enable them to plan, judge, project, monitor, and defer behavior, to establish short- and long-term goals and to direct their efforts accordingly.

Chapter 3

✻ ✻ ✻ ✻ ✻

Relation of Developmental Problems, Parents' Reactions, and the Child's Progress

✻ At an early age, the infant begins to imagine himself as an entity with a specific size and shape that is separate from his mother and others. That is, tactile and kinesthetic sensations acquaint him with objects outside his body, and he develops a concept of his body's movement through space. As a result, by the time he has reached preschool age, a child ordinarily has developed a stable perception of his size, looks, and color. Some learning disabled children, however, develop these perceptions much more slowly.

These children have poor body awareness and therefore lack a stable concept of their physical selves.

This poorly defined concept of one's biological body and its capabilities hinders the development of shared cultural concepts of use of one's body socially and instrumentally (see Goffman, 1974), of predicting the body messages of others, and of being in control of one's body most of the time. The learning disabled person who has not generalized his own and others' physical activity is similar to the toddler learning to walk. The toddler must direct all his energy to placing one foot in front of the other without falling and has little excess energy to divert to other processes. The learning disabled person who must concentrate on finding his classroom, his desk, or his locker and not bumping into people or objects in the process has directed all his energy to the task and to the anxiety generated around the possibility of becoming lost or having others think of him as clumsy or foolish. The student who must use all his energy to write neatly between the lines has little left to direct to content. When disproportionate energy is diverted to the functioning of one's own body in space, there is less remaining energy for social processing and a more meager acquisition of information about the meaning of others' bodies in space.

One learns about objects—their identity, size, shape, color, and brightness—by organizing environmental feedback: the chair rung under which one cannot crawl, the table that is too heavy to move, the ball that rolls away. The child who fails to notice or integrate critical stimuli to hold a perception in his mind or organize it into a framework of experience may spend years bumping his head on door frames or lifting his foot for a phantom step. He uses too much or too little energy for the task, since he has effected a faulty relationship between his body strength and the physical world. As a result, some learning disabled children clump loudly up and down stairs, slam doors with vigor, pound drums with such force that they break, and hug friends so tightly that their ribs seem in danger of fracturing. Such learning disabled persons also find it difficult to modulate their walk and voice tones. Rarely do they succeed, as adolescents, in sneaking into the house undetected after a late date.

Early Ego Development and Childrearing Practices

The child from approximately six months to two and a half years of age feels that he must indeed be powerful, since—despite his helplessness—all his needs are met. Since few demands are made of him to this point of development, he probably believes that he can compel adults to gratify his desires and that they, in turn (particularly his mother), are infinitely capable of gratifying him. However, by the time he is two years old, the socialization process shifts into gear, and the child is expected to feed himself neatly, become toilet trained, and conform to a variety of expectations in the areas of routines, cleanliness, manners, and safety. The child who is emerging from the omnipotent stage begins to perceive his mother's limitations and fallibility. As Lasch (1978, p. 71) describes:

> He relinquishes the image of maternal perfection and begins to take over many of her functions—to provide for his own care and comfort. An idealized image of the mother lives on in the child's unconscious thoughts. Diminished, however, by the daily experience of maternal fallibility, it comes to be associated not with fantasies of infantile omnipotence but with the ego's modest, growing mastery of its environment. Disappointment with the mother, brought about not only by her unavoidable lapses of attention but by the child's perception that he does not occupy the exclusive place in her affections, makes it possible for the child to relinquish her undivided love (through a psychic process analogous to mourning) and incorporating her life-giving functions.

When a child is learning disabled, the developmental process may proceed less perfectly. It is possible that some learning disabled infants are not as enjoyable as intact babies are. Wiener (1978) hypothesizes that many of them may fall into the temperamental constellation that Thomas and Chess (1977) describe as "Difficult Child." Such children dislike changes—in routines, people, or food—and are noisy about their disapproval. The chances of there being a "goodness of fit" between the child's temperament and the parents' value system is poorer than it is with children whose temperaments represent more valued behaviors. Some were premature babies (Rabinovitch, Caplan, and Bibace, 1976) separated from their parents at birth, with the concomitant risk to the development of maternal/infant bonding. Those who are premature or neurologically immature can tolerate only a minimum of stimulation, so that the greater the parental investment in them, the sparser or more aversive their response. Similarly, neurologically immature or damaged infants may demonstrate difficulties sucking, gag readily and have difficulty establishing a biological rhythm.

By age two many learning disabled children have evidenced problems in development, sleep disturbances, sluggishness or excessive activity, clumsiness and frustration, stubbornness, resistance to change and the acquisition of self-care skills, and immaturities of language development. As a result, parental disappointment may well have occurred early in the child's life, with the compensating parental behaviors of inconsistent childrearing, maternal overprotection, and underinvolvement of the disappointed and excluded father.

A mother may compensate for her disappointment in her offspring by lavishing attention on him and by providing him with an excess of seemingly solicitous care, which may at times lack genuine warmth and possibly mask considerable ambivalence. As Lasch (1978, p. 171) states, "By treating the child as an 'exclusive possession,' she encourages an exaggerated sense of his own importance; at the same time, she makes it difficult for him to acknowledge his disappointment in her shortcomings." She intrusively continues to do too much for him, and he, being not too competent or flexible about acquiring new skills, allows the continuation of a dependent relationship that may well persist for many years. Some parents of elementary-age learning disabled children devote their lives to their child and to the remediation of the disability. Some present as martyrs and others as saviors. Such demonstrations of excessive devotion perpetuate infantile omnipotent thought processes and disallow any seeming disloyalty on the child's part. How can one think badly of a parent who demonstrates such apparent devotion? It certainly is too painful and contradictory to acknowledge maternal ambivalence, the hostile feelings that are masked by such devotion. The defenses that children adopt to handle these prohibitions include controlling behavior, loss of boundaries of self, magical thought processes, and persistence of impulsivity, since the child has not been expected to regulate his own behavior. The loss of boundaries of body and ego, the omniscience, and the magical thought processes further hinder the development of concepts of time and of cause and effect. Egocentricity is prolonged; and the learning disabled child, who could not perceive his mother as imperfect, is hampered in conceptualizing others as possessing a spectrum of attributes from undesirable to desirable. Consequently, some tend to judge people in absolutist terms, "good guys" and "bad guys."

Fathers, even more than mothers, tend to perceive their children as being extensions of themselves, so that the discovery that they have a learning disabled child is particularly disappointing. They generally do not verbalize their feelings to friends and relatives as readily as their wives do, so they may not reconcile their disappointment in their child as speedily or effectively as their spouses. Their broken dreams may be masked by their denial that there is anything wrong with their youngster. This fantasy of what their child is capable of doing can only be maintained if they have little contact with them, thus ensuring minimal exposure to their child's ineptitude. This reduced contact may be furthered by mothers who feel that the father will make harmful comments to his child such as "you clumsy fool," or "why don't you watch what you're doing?" Or mothers may fear that their husbands will expose the child to physical danger or embarrassment such as allowing him to climb a tree or participate in group sports even though he is awkward. Consequently, the role that parents most typically assume—mothers protect children and fathers expose them to novelty—may develop, for families of the learning disabled, into maternal overprotection and paternal alienation. The father's withdrawal and emotional absence may strengthen the mother-child alignment; the mother may try to meet her emotional needs, no longer satisfactorily met by her husband, from her child.

actions toward a specific member, may serve to extend or reinforce a son's slow learning ability and thus prohibit the growth and development of an entire family system."

Intrusive patterns of childbearing may well persist into adulthood. When parents of a learning disabled child do not want their youngster or themselves to be embarrassed by the child's ineptness, clumsiness, or inaccurate or tangential responses to adult queries, they will respond for him and perform his tasks. They may do the child's homework for him, so that he will not be penalized for faulty production. In their concern about whether he has a date, a friend, a job, or is using his time well and staying out of trouble, they may question his activities far more extensively than one should of an adolescent or adult. He, being cognizant of his immaturity, ineptitude, and occasionally faulty judgment and his dependence on his parents, may well allow parental intrusiveness to persist.

McDermott (1977) found that fathers of children with reading problems tended to behave toward these children in a directive, domineering, and intrusive manner—manipulating play materials and providing partial and complete task solutions. These same fathers were much less domineering toward their other children. McDermott also found that mothers spoke less frequently to their children with reading problems than they did to their other children. Doyleys, Cartelli, and Doster (1976) found that mothers of preschool learning disabled children dispensed more rewards and asked more questions than mothers of controls. However, these interactions often were proffered at inappropriate junctures, such as when the child complained that the task was difficult or left it uncompleted. Some of them questioned their children so extensively that they verbalized constantly. The researchers noted low levels of maternal criticism and child compliance. The authors conclude: "The mothers in the l.d. group judged their children to have a larger number of problems and more difficulty adjusting than the nonclinic mothers judged for their children. This implies that children with learning disabilities demonstrate problem behavior in nonacademic as well as academic areas. It is plausible, however, that these nonacademic behavioral and adjustment problems evolved from the reactions of the parents and other persons in the environment to the child's disability and to his behavior in general. That is, complete attention may be given to the child's learning disability while discipline is neglected because the parents perceive noncompliant or disruptive behavior to be a result of the l.d." (p. 375).

Warner and associates (1980) found that learning disabled adolescents perceived their mothers as more supportive than did low-achieving adolescents. Greenberg (1970) found learning disabled adolescents and young adults to be preadolescent emotionally. They were extremely dependent on their parents for assistance and direction. It would be interesting to determine whether the maternal support perceived by Warner's experimental group was age-appropriate or excessive. Humphries and Bauman (1980) found that mothers of learning disabled children exercise more authority than mothers of control subjects.

Fathers, in the quality of support in childrearing that they afford their wives, may be a critical ingredient in the rearing of learning disabled children and those with other problems. Cohen (1981) found that, in adoptions of older problem children, the success or failure of the adoption depended on the adoptive father's response to his wife's frustration and stress with the adopted child. If the father was able to tolerate his wife's anger, discouragement, and demonstration of weakness, be supportive of her, and relieve her of childrearing until she regained her composure, the adoption succeeded. Conversely, the adoption failed in families where the adoptive father needed a wife who was strong at all times. The dynamics in families of the learning disabled appear to be similar. The father who is unable to tolerate his wife's upset will ally himself with the child and ridicule the mother or with his wife and lash out at their child. The wife's response, in the latter instance, will be to turn on her husband, since she has assumed the role of being her child's protector. As this pattern runs its course, one finds a polarized family with an alliance of mother and child against the father, or father and child against the mother, or both parents against the scapegoated child.

Issues of Control. The child, in his second year of life, tests his emerging independence through resistance. "No" becomes a favorite word, and the youngster fights sleep and other forms of control. Typically, this stage passes with little difficulty as the child increasingly realizes that he can control greater aspects of his environment yet needs to depend on his parents for safety and nurturance. The onus, essentially, is on the child to determine a cognitive balance between assertion and dependence. As Erikson (1963, p. 69) points out, babies control and bring up their families as much as they are controlled by them. "The family," he states, "brings up a baby by being brought up by him."

In families of the learning disabled, the child's cognitive deficits and the parents' feelings about the child interfere with the child's transition from a need for ultimate control to a compromise position. Ambivalent parents may overcontrol until their guilt and the child's resistance cause them to undercontrol. Eventually the child's behavior becomes so untenable that the parents overcontrol once again. The parents' guilt is particularly pervasive when they attribute the child's behavior to the learning disability—something that he cannot help. Most of the information services in the learning disability field contribute to that parental assumption, since virtually every undesirable human behavior is described as being a manifestation of the disability. As a result, whenever learning disabled children are forgetful, irritable, fidgety, lively, disorganized, disobedient, clumsy, long winded, and so on, their behavior is assigned to the disability, with the assumption that it is not under their control. When parents or their intact children produce similar behaviors, they are attributed to more typical causes and result in typical sanctions.

Thus, learning disabled children may manipulate parental ambivalence by gaining tyrannical control of their childrearing, and frequently of the entire family. They may be allowed to watch television endlessly and indiscriminately, retire at midnight, climb into their parents' bed at three in the morning, maintain an unusual diet, interrupt family members' conversations, break their siblings' toys, and join their siblings' social groups. Their rigid resistance to compliance (Wender, 1971), as well as their limited ability to elect alternatives whereby they could comply yet save face, creates a polarization of parental demand, child refusal, and the consequent parental withdrawal when confronted with the child's noncompliance. All this, in addition to the parents' ambivalence and desire to compensate the child for having been cheated of his birthright, results in inconsistent and lenient childrearing practices when the child's need is for consistency.

The learning disabled child's assumption of absolute control is similar to that elected by ill, handicapped, or dying persons. Control of family members may be the only power he possesses and is an outlet and compensation for his unhappiness. Nonetheless, when his efforts to control are successful, he is frightened because family members' acquiescence signifies to him that his disability must be serious.

Battles for control within the family and rigid, polarized thought processes (I'm boss/you're boss, I'm right/he's wrong, he's good/he's bad) may persist into adulthood (Lenkowsky and Saposnek, 1978). As a result, the individual may lack ability to compromise and the linguistic skill and environment to encourage negotiation (Peck and Stackhouse, 1973) or the ability to convert the dissenter to his point of view (Bryan and Sherman, 1980). One notes, as well, passive behaviors whereby learning disabled persons control those around them. Their failure to conform and comply, their disorganization, hypoactivity, lack of productivity, and sparse production of goal-directed behaviors create frustration and impotence in parents, educators, and employers. The adolescent who sits at home even though he has been ordered by the court to attend school has parents, attendance officers, and educators completely mobilized around his passive/hostile behavior. The learning disabled person whose language is perseverative or rambling controls his interactions by preventing the person he's speaking with from interjecting; a mutually reinforcing, shared conversation is impossible. The learning disability itself can be an agent of control, since it focuses the adult world onto the disabled member. The controlling learning disabled person fails to learn that power is earned incrementally through meritorious behavior; he therefore maintains a concept of himself as someone who is powerful but, at the same time, experiences the powerlessness of the low-status student, the clumsy athlete, the ineffective interactor, and the person who is at the mercy of the moment rather than able to plan and execute desired change.

The learning disabled child attains the chronological age at which parents expect increased frustration tolerance and responsible behavior but may lack the imagery to project the satisfactions and rewards of a more advanced developmental stage. He may be loath to risk the period of disequilibrium that occurs between stages, wherein old meanings are reinterpreted and new behaviors tested. Consequently, he clings rigidly to old premises and satisfactions. Since he may have missed, or failed to perceive, the satisfactions of the omnipotent stage, such as nonambivalent maternal care and love, he may cling to the controlling behavior that earmarks that stage, in the hopes that his needs may yet be met. As a result, the rigid learning disabled person may rarely experience novelty and growth as being enjoyable and successful.

Most parents of the preschool learning disabled are unaware that their child is disabled and therefore attribute his nonconformity to willfulness or other behavior under his control. He is expected to be as accomplished as his peers—to dress, manipulate toys, eat neatly, ride a tricycle, demonstrate sphincter and bladder control, express himself understandably, and respond to language. The learning disabled child may become frustrated at his failure, which conflicts with parental expectation of increased frustration tolerance.

Frustration Tolerance. If children are to develop independence and frustration tolerance, learn how to set realistic goals for themselves, make reasonable demands on others, and acquire self-critical ability and capacity for resisting hedonistic urges, they must have firsthand experience in coping with frustration. (Ausubel and Sullivan, [1957] 1970). The learning disabled child who responds to demands with frequent and excessive frustration will not develop coping abilities or acquire patience and persistence en route to preferred goals. He may be so overwhelmed by the disparity between what he would like to do or say and his limitations that his anxiety precludes judgment about his level of accomplishment in relationship to peer ability and external demands. So much of his energy is diverted to frustration that he has little left to expend on an assessment of the task and the development of coping strategies. As a result, he approaches tasks in his deficit area with anxiety instead of utilizing a problem-solving approach. Being hindered in the process of determining his own capabilities (Bruinincks, 1978), he lacks knowledge of his own strengths and limitations as a baseline for measuring the capacity of others. Thus, we note learning disabled persons who approach others for friendships and dates without a prior assessment of mutual attributes, and are rejected. When one seeks friendships without a determination of similarity of interests and attributes and mutual compatibility, the possibility of failure is high.

Aggression. Traditionally, demonstrations of severe frustration in children have been attributed to excessive inhibition of the child's behavior by parents and other authority figures. This inevitably occurs in instances where the learning disabled member is extremely active, distractible, or impulsive; embarrasses others with his statements; or has a short interest span. However, the effects can be equally debilitating if the frustration is generated by the learning disabled person's own overwhelming anxiety in response to complexity and anticipation of failure; severe frustration produces aggression. The aggression frightens parents, who fear that their child's outbursts will cause educators or employers to reject or exclude the child or to assume that the child is mentally disturbed. Thus, the aggression that is generated by frustration, by anger at a world in which one cannot succeed, and by overinvested parents may not be allowed expression. Similarly, parents of the learning disabled may feel frustrated, misunderstood, cheated, and hence angry. Their aggression also may be disallowed even justified expression because it labels them as "angry parents" and the cause of their child's disability. Since we rarely afford them opportunities to work through their feelings about having parented a learning disabled child, much of the aggression around that issue can remain unresolved. Thus, they may be poor models for their children around socially productive ways of channeling anger, and their children may respond to their own anger with hyperactivity, withdrawal, or misplacement of behavior.

Some learning disabled persons internalize their anger and become dreamers or persons who are uncomfortable with any expression of conflict or disagreement, however minimal. Others become hostile to an entire class of persons, such as teachers. Yet others may become disproportionately angry at the most innocuous of precipitants, and their anger is exacerbated by their misperception of expressions of affect (Wiig and Harris, 1974; Wilchesky, 1980a). Some, being morally/conceptually immature, become angry at a situation because they have interpreted it in a primitive, egocentric, or literal manner rather than in a manner that is consistent with intent. The literature in the learning disability field suggests that parents of learning disabled children should teach them to channel their aggression into hitting punching bags. However, Argyle (1967) points out that one does not discharge anger by attacking physical objects or watching aggressive scenes on television. Instead, the child might be encouraged to practice directing aggression to the anger-evoking person; or he might be taught to verbalize his concerns in a fashion designed to effect optimal response. Similarly, families might be counseled to model and allow appropriate demonstrations of anger.

Behavioral Boundaries. Parents who are permissive or inconsistent in limiting their children fail to provide sufficient prohibitions through which the child can experience a copable dose of frustration. Such children are not taught the boundaries of acceptable behavior. Even when parental ambivalence is not an issue and parents sincerely attempt to teach their learning disabled children the boundaries of desired behavior, their task tends to be considerably more difficult than it is in socializing their intact child.

Parents of young children consistently define boundaries and limitations. As the child demonstrates increasing motor, linguistic, and conceptual skills, his freedom to explore is expanded and behavioral boundaries are redefined. Through continued exposure to prohibitions and freedom, intact children soon learn to generalize the behaviors that are permissible in the home, neighborhood, in other homes, in the religious and subcultural groups, with peers, with each teacher, and so on. They develop schemata of the typical organization of each social event—be it a visit to the physician, classroom behavior, a trip to the supermarket, or a visit to relatives—and the behavior that is expected of them in each situation. Young children are quick to perceive the signals that convey leeway or conformity—which parent will be lenient and in which context, which parent is "tough," which teacher is permissive and which one is strict, which one should be taken at his word—and the signals that indicate an adult or peer's momentary mood. Children soon realize that what is permissible in their own home—

dropping clothing on the floor or standing on the furniture—is not permissible in other homes.

However, when parents attempt to socialize their learning disabled child through the usual processes of limitations and exploratory freedom, they may well find that he fails to generalize the differential expectations. He may lack judgment about behavioral acceptability; if he is not dashing about and touching objects inappropriately, he may be conveying information that is too personal to share with a casual acquaintance. When I moved in with three families of learning disabled children (Kronick, 1976), I found that the learning disabled children used the same behavior with their peers that they saw their parents use (such as scapegoating), regardless of its appropriateness with the peer group, whereas their siblings chose more age-appropriate behaviors.

The learning disabled child may do a poor job of determining the behavioral boundaries acceptable to each teacher, or the contexts in which boisterous behaviors are permitted; he may be unable to perceive the cues that signify a switch from exuberant behavior with one teacher to studious behavior with another. The hyperactive or impulsive child will not take the time to assess the type of experience in which he finds himself and hence behave in a fashion that is acceptable and safe. He produces little behavior that would assure his parents that he can handle increasing freedom without harm, gross error, or embarrassment to himself and family. As a consequence, such freedom may be disallowed. Even reasonable error, whereby all children learn independence, eventually becomes too threatening for parents to allow their learning disabled children to experience, particularly since error is attributed to the disability. Their intact children will be allowed to travel on public transportation, and the thought of their becoming lost once or twice can be tolerated. In contrast, the parents will drive their learning disabled child everywhere because the thought of his becoming lost results in profound anxiety. This is consistent with Strag's (1972) finding that parents of learning disabled children rated them as more clinging than their other children.

Some parents, wearied and defeated by their efforts to reduce the hyperactivity or impose their will on a hyperactive, perseverative child, no longer see themselves as agents of change (Kronick, 1976). As Barsch (1976, p. 243) points out, it is difficult to convince an egocentrically directed child to relinquish his immediate desires, demands, and behaviors in order to conform. Barsch found that mothers of "organic" children felt that disciplining their children was more of a problem than it was with their other children and that fathers also were insufficiently strict. Doyleys, Cartelli, and Doster (1976) found a low level of conformity in learning disabled children. Wender (1971) conjectured that learning disabled children have reduced feelings of pain and pleasure and hence are unresponsive to the socialization process. As the child matures, he is expected to become more independent and self-assertive to combat his own and parental ambivalence about his capabilities and dependency needs—a difficult task, indeed, when a child has not adequately learned behavioral boundaries and acceptable parameters of freedom.

The learning disabled child, by failing to produce the behavior which signals parents that he is ready for increased independence, is protected and overassisted. Realistically, these children do require more assistance and intervention than their capable peers do. However, we have not taught parents how to elicit behavior from the child that is appropriate to his level of development, they are poorly equipped to promote the child's conformity other than by performing activities for him that others expect him to do, such as getting dressed. When the child is thus protected from forays into the world, child and parental anxiety is minimized; at the same time parents and child fail to achieve the increased freedom that denotes a child's expanding assumption of responsibility.

Parents who persist in mourning the fact that their child is learning disabled, or who feel that no one understands the disability, may reduce their contact with the extended family, neighbors, and friends, so that they become too tightly bounded. When I moved into the homes of three families, each with a learning disabled child, the outstanding feature that I noted was their loneliness and aloneness. They did not share feelings about their disabled children with anyone, and their social contacts were limited or nonexistent. Since one of the roles of friends, relatives, and neighbors is to be sympathetic to stresses and to allow one to express concerns and disappointments, this aspect of interpersonal interaction was not modeled for the learning disabled children. Moreover, since these children's parents had little contact with intimates, the children had few opportunities to observe other families' models of establishing boundaries. Their siblings, however, spent considerable time in their own friends' homes and therefore were able to observe alternative models. Being too tightly bounded, these families conveyed to their learning disabled children that interaction with outsiders is unrewarding and possibly unsafe.

The child, then, may have his learning disabilities responded to by overprotective and intrusive parental behavior, which reduces opportunities for problem solving, decision making, individuation, and social skill learning. Parental ambivalence may have denied the child the requisite support, protection, freedom, and acceptance to transverse the developmental stages with assurance. Admittedly, since the learning disabled child evokes negative responses in peers, teachers, and strangers (Bryan, 1979), parental intervention and protection are to some extent required. When such intervention persists beyond the point of being developmentally functional, the family presents as an enmeshed system. Therapeutic considerations are similar to those utilized with any enmeshed family except that the learning disabled member's idiosyncratic needs for assistance, clarification, structure, and support must be taken into account. Family members must continue to be helpful and to be buffers, on occasion, while allowing their offspring and siblings room to mature and individuate. Marris (1974, p. 20) aptly describes the processes of attachment and separation:

> As he grows up, in John Bowlby's (1970) words, "first the child, then the adolescent, and finally the young adult moves out in a series of ever lengthening excursions." . . . Each step follows the previous one in a series of easy stages. Though home ties may attenuate, they are never broken. Thus, the self-confidence of maturity is not a rejection of support but an ability to turn for reassurance when need arises, trusting that it will be met. The confirmation that more primitive wants are securely satisfied renews confidence to confront the uncertainties of growth. Conversely, if

these wants have never been fully met, growing up does indeed become a succession of bereavements; the grown person is a banished child with forged papers of maturity.

In order for a child to progress from one developmental stage into the next, he must be prepared to relinquish the satisfactions of that stage, to undertake increased autonomy and greater risks. He discards the well known for the uncertainty of the less familiar and the particular discomforts of the transition period. The learning disabled child of age two or three may well have realized his difficulties with coordination, language, activity level, and compliance. He may have attained the behaviors requisite for his present developmental stage with difficulty. Any new situation to be adjusted to requires a new set of concepts and behaviors which threatens his image of his probable ability to comply. As a result, he rigidly attempts to maintain the known, in this instance, the omnipotent stage of development.

For most children, entry into the educational system provides a source of status other than the family. School makes them feel important for their own achievements and through their identity with schoolmates and teachers. These new identities and feelings of importance cause them to question their parents' omnipotence. However, the school experience is less likely to make learning disabled students feel important. They are less likely to produce the academic, athletic, and social behaviors that merit educator and peer approval and so are less likely to identify with them and their values. Thus, it is less probable that they will question parental values or develop the concept of the validity of a range of values.

Derived-Status Stage of Development

The developmental stage which succeeds omnipotence and persists until adolescence has been described by Ausubel and Sullivan as "the derived-status stage." In this stage of development, the child realizes his relative powerlessness but acquires status from being valued by people who are powerful, by being accepted and made to feel important in his own right. During this period the child is motivated to undergo changes in personality development in order to obtain and retain parental approval. Only in this way can he be assured that the status he derives from being a member of his family will continue. His sense of security and adequacy becomes increasingly dependent on conformity to parental expectations for more mature behavior. That is, if he acquires the skills, concepts, and attributes that the family, subculture, and culture value, he is likely to be accepted and, in turn, will exert more conscientious effort to retain adult approval—so that a circular process is established.

The child who is intrinsically valued at home is likely to be independent, task oriented, and able to postpone gratification; such a child demonstrates emotional control and makes few demands of adults. One of the critical functions of the derived-status stage is the child's identification with his parents and the consequent learning of increasingly sophisticated social behavior through teaching and modeling.

However, the learning disabled child, deficient in skills and concepts, is a poor candidate to acquire the behaviors valued by parents, subculture, and culture. He is not necessarily neat, obedient, agile, competent, or verbally adept. He may have difficulty in learning the family's language of origin, such as Chinese or Yiddish, or in standing quietly and still at church. He may not excel athletically or scholastically or produce achievements that his parents can be proud of. One cannot expect parents to enjoy the child for his intrinsic worth when so much of the day is spent dealing with his failures or misadventures.

In some instances, the learning disabled child and family find that identification with one another is difficult because there is a dissonance of "fit" between child and family. One notes clumsy children in athletic families; language-handicapped children in fluent families; children with extensive academic difficulties in high-achieving families; lethargic children in energetic families; hyperactive children in phlegmatic families; disorganized, unproductive children in organized, productive families; socially inadept children in polished families; and erratic, impulsive children in controlled families. When the child and other nuclear family members do not share similar values or behaviors, and when parents do not value the child's characteristics, they will provide less social modeling. If the learning disabled child is friendless, he will spend much of his time in the home and be limited to whatever social learning is available there, however inadequate it might be.

When a child fails to acquire the attributes that parents value, they may magnify the attributes he has acquired and generalize them to the whole, which supports mutual pretense. Mutual pretense allows parents to aspire to the same heights of attainment that we establish for our intact children. This pretense is nurtured by literature and lectures which refer to the supposed learning disabilities of Einstein, Edison, and Michaelangelo, and implies that the child need but be remediated to achieve equally well. Each time the child produces academic or social behavior that is similar to that of intact children, the mutual pretense is sustained.

Mutual pretense can coexist with disproportionate emphasis on the disability. When parents have produced a learning disabled child, they have what Goffman (1964) calls "a spoiled identity." They are afraid that the child's imperfections will be blamed on them—on their failure to provide adequate genetic inheritance and competent childrearing. Some parents, in their efforts to defend their childrearing competence, will go out of their way to inform everyone about their child's learning disability and relate the tale of their struggle to each passing acquaintance. They presume that the imparting of such information will create an understanding that the child's behavior does not reflect on their parenting ability. Similarly, they may remark that the listener should see their other children, which ostensibly would repair their damaged image.

Parents who feel successful are able to be in control, to be powerful, and to protect. Children who feel competent are able to become increasingly independent. When the learning disabled child has gained control over the household and professionals exclude parents from treatment processes, parents no longer feel powerful. They cannot convey to their child that they have protected him from failure, from sadness in childhood, and from cruel treatment. They feel that they have failed to provide their child with a competent mind, an athletic body, and access to the American dream of ultimate success. Some even harbor a fear that, as a result of their ineffectual childrearing, their child is emotionally disturbed rather than learning disabled. Such parents feel that if they are honest with professionals about the child's behavior or their home life, their secret will be revealed.

In exchange for parental protection of children from physical and emotional want, pain, and fear, society promises parents fun and happiness (Wolfenstein, 1955). Indeed, the absence of fun and happiness in the tension-filled existence of families of the learning disabled confirms the parents' perception of themselves as failures; they feel that they must have done something wrong and hence do not deserve to enjoy their children and their lives.

Chapter 4

�֎ �֎ ✷ ✷ ✷

Factors Contributing to Adequate and Inadequate Self-Concepts

✷ Man's concept and feelings of self have been described in many ways. Gergen's (1971, p. 293) model seems particularly apt: "The way in which a man conceives of himself will influence both what he chooses to do and what he expects from life. For one to know his identity is to grasp the meaning of his past and his potential for the future. Equally important to the problem of self-definition is man's concern with self-evaluation. What feelings should a man have about himself, how should he value himself? A major issue can be traced to the long-standing feeling of basic conflict between self and society. . . . The self is treated as a set of core feelings or perceptions the person has about himself, which demand reverence because they uniquely distinguish the individual from others."

A child in the derived-status stage—when he receives his status from his family, peers, and school—acquires a concept of what he is all about and what he can expect of himself. This accrues from feedback from adults and peers; from attempting tasks and learning what he is and is not able to do; and from assessing his capabilities, looks, humor, talents, and temperamental attributes in relationship to peer and adult accomplishment in his subculture and culture at large. Our concept of self and aspiration level are fluid throughout our lifetime. They are adjusted to instrumental and interpersonal success and feedback.

Learning disabled children are lower in self-esteem than their achieving counterparts (Rosenthal, 1973; Larsen, Parker, and Jorjorian, 1973; Guthery, 1971). There are many factors which can interfere with the learning disabled person's acquisition of a realistic and positive concept of self. Certainly the meaning of his subcluster of learning disabilities to his family, subculture, and culture will relate strongly to his self-perception. For instance, some families and some subcultures value verbal ability or academic attainment so that a language disability or academic disability will be more devastating to them than to those less oriented toward verbal or academic achievement. Similarily, his feelings about his worth will relate to the discrepancy that he feels exists between his present level of attainment and where he feels he currently should be, as well as where he feels he should be going. He will be confused by the less-than-truthful feedback he receives from some persons who attempt to conceal their impression that he is unintelligent, clumsy, and strange by being overly kind; the stronger their aversion is, the more they will compensate with solicitous behavior and the more distorted his self-image will be. If his disability is treated with discomfort, shame, and secrecy, he probably will feel guilty for being learning disabled or will assume that he really is mentally retarded and psychotic. There are additional, less obvious factors which may impinge on self-concept yet do not receive the serious attention they deserve.

Factors Affecting Self-Concept

Dissonant Environments. Rosenberg (1979), in discussing the adjustment of school children in dissonant contexts (blacks in predominantly white schools, Jews in predominantly Protestant schools, Orientals in Caucasian schools), found that such children were teased more than were children in consonant settings. If the children in dissonant contexts accepted and internalized the general standards and values of the dissonant context, they were at risk for self-devaluation: "We may come to despise ourselves—to believe that we are strange and different, that we are inept at the skills and talents valued in the new environment, that we are ignorant of the things that count. This kind of attack is particularly devastating for it is an attack from within" (Rosenberg, 1979, p. 113).

The learning disabled person is in a dissonant context much of his life, since he is surrounded by intact family members, neighbors, and friends from whom he differs. Since they do not share his disability, they cannot comprehend his experience as insiders, nor can they teach him to maximize his position in the culture, a lesson that minority parents pass on to their offspring. Until or unless he encounters other learning disabled children, he may feel that he is alone in the world. Having been socialized to value the traits of the majority, he is bound to feel inadequate and inferior much of the time.

Nonetheless, if he is placed in a sheltered educational setting, his academic world will, in large measure, consist of a value system modified to his production. Whereas in the mainstream he may be the one who is considered "strange," "out of it," "low man on the totem pole," in sheltered education he may be a conformist in relationship to his classmates, be well integrated into the group, and able to excel in some areas. Siperstein, Bop, and Bak (1977) found that classmates acknowledged a learning disabled child's looks and athletic ability, when present. Since we are exposed in depth only to segments of the culture, and derive self-esteem from our ability to conform to those segments, it is important to consider the effect of sheltered education and mainstreaming on the learning disableds' concept of self.

Rosenberg (1979) reports that although black students obtain slightly higher marks in white schools than they do in predominantly black schools, their self-esteem is lower because they compare themselves with whites. Blacks in black schools, however, compare themselves with other blacks. "Self-assessment," Rosenberg points out (p. 118), "is as much dependent on the performance of the comparison reference group as on one's own performance; and the evidence is consistent in indicating that, at least among children, those in the immediate context constitute the comparison reference group."

When a child moves from a sheltered context to the mainstream, it is important to consider the shift in emphasis in terms of the qualities that are reinforced. In the special education classroom, the teacher may have been effusive in his praise of the child's ability to sit still for five minutes, to write neatly, and refrain from loud comments in the classroom. In the mainstream such behavior is likely to be taken for granted or even belittled as not sufficiently acceptable, regardless of the improvement such behavior might signify in terms of the individual child's growth. Essentially, in a special education setting, a child's work is assessed in relationship to his level of development, whereas in the mainstream it is compared to that of his peers, particularly when his teacher has been told that his intelligence is normal. Intact children can reconcile disparities in expectation and produce the behaviors that will evoke an optimal response. Some learning disabled children, on the other hand, neither perceive the subtleties of expectation nor possess the behavioral alternatives to match their production precisely to expectations.

A person checks the accuracy of his concept of self through environmental feedback. Rosenberg (p. 121) suggests, "An individual requires confirmation of his self-hypothesis from the behavior of others toward him. For example, if a person considers himself likable, others must act as if they like him. If he perceives of himself as intelligent, others must show some respect for his intelligence." So others must afford the learning disabled individual feedback that is consistent with his image of himself if he is to maintain a stable self-concept. However, a learning disabled student in the mainstream may find that his teachers do not confirm any positive impressions he may have of himself if he is unable to function in the same academic and behavioral fashion as his fellow students. The disparate feedback he receives, in combination with the unevenness of his own competencies, contributes to an inconsistent and unstable image of self.

Consequently, when we return children from self-contained classrooms to the mainstream or offer them a combination of mainstream teaching and remediation, we need to teach them the cues that signify teacher expectation and provide them with a store of behaviors that usually evoke positive educator response. The mainstreamed student should be able to explain his disabilities simply and request the necessary alterations. Most important, if we cannot ensure him opportunities to excel in activities that are highly valued by his peer group, the benefits of mainstreaming should be seriously questioned.

Processing of Social Information. One must consider, as well, the learning disabled person's ability to notice and process social information accurately and its effects on his ability to evaluate himself. A number of studies have dealt with this problem, and the following findings have been reported: Learning disabled children respond more inconsistently to success and failure than controls do (Robbins and Harway, 1977). Children with heterogeneous learning disabilities have problems responding appropriately to feedback on hypotheses, whereas children with language learning disabilities respond in the same fashion as controls (Parrill-Burnstein and Baker-Ward, 1979). Learning disabled children and adolescents are inaccurate in judging the affective states of others (Bachara, 1976; Bryan, 1977; Wiig and Harris, 1974; Wilchesky, 1980a). Learning disabled children are less accurate in judging their social status than controls are (Bruinincks, 1978). Learning disabled persons exhibit marked deficiencies in social perception. Adults with acquired right brain damage do not notice visual detail (Winner and Gardner, 1977). Learning disabled children, being unable to process feedback accurately, may experience difficulty in evaluating their abilities (Robbins and Harway, 1977). Parrill-Burnstein and Baker-Ward (1979, p. 24) conclude their research by commenting: "Children with learning disabilities have difficulty processing information at the levels of attention, memory, and social perception. Problems attending selectively to the most relevant information interfered with both memory and social perceptual skills. Problems recalling social cues reflected deficits in attention and hindered the development of appropriate social behaviors. In addition, in view of the proposed analysis of social cognitive processing, children with learning disabilities were less successful than children without learning problems at the level

of stimulus differentiation, selective attention, response generation, response execution, and, particularly, appropriate responses
to feedback."

Since the learning disabled person's interactions are not always based on an assessment of all the critical cues in a situation
and the implications of that situation to past and future, others are
unable to predict his responses and assume his reliability. They are
uncertain whether he will protect the secrets of the group, and
their lack of confidence in this regard often proves to be justified.
When role projection is dissonant with culturally accepted social
behavior, people become uncomfortable and alter their interactions to the dissonant person. Even minimal differences such as
briefness of gaze or smile, excessive or atypical use of the hands, or
ignorance of some of the rules of conversational language will, as
the research by James and Tanis Bryan and their colleagues has
shown, affect the ways that people view the learning disabled and
interact with them.

Similarily, we create behavioral expectations of persons we
encounter from the setting in which we find them, the knowledge
we have about their family and subculture and the way they look.
Therefore, we make one set of assumptions about persons we meet
at a presidential reception and another about students at an inner
city school. When one encounters a learning disabled person, one
initially may assume that he is competent and socially adept since
he may be handsome, alert, well-dressed, a member of an accomplished family, and a student at a prestigious school. However,
when he destroys our assumptions about him by being clumsy,
illiterate, gauche, or verbose, we find ourselves uncertain as to the
reasons for his unexpected ineptitude, and hence feel uncomfortable. Such discomfort tends to evoke anger and a feeling of having
been misled. Since we are uncertain about whether he is intelligent or sane, we are unwilling to share information or feelings with
him. Lemert (1962) suggests that such uncertainty results in a reduction and distortion of feedback to the person as to what he is all
about, an affect, on the interactor's part, that is unrelated to the
ideas being conveyed. He also suggests that our uncertainty about
what such a person will do with the information we provide and
our lack of assurance that he will protect the secrets of the group

result in an ambiguous message being conveyed concerning the situation at hand or the group image.

Consequently, the learning disabled person, who already has an unclear self-image, receives less truthful, sparser, and less confirming feedback. His difficulties in perceiving the organization of social situations, of social roles, and of groups are compounded by the ambiguous information that is transmitted to him concerning the situation at hand, the social roles of his interactor, and the group image. His literal interpretation of events and his absolutist stance that events and people can have only one meaning make it particularly difficult for him to reconcile the ambiguity between message and reality. Since the learning disabled person is unable to perceive these messages as pseudocommunication, he models his own communication from them. This, in turn, contributes to his lack of clarity and to shallowness and inappropriateness of affect (Bryan and Perlmutter, 1979; Bryan, Donahue, and Pearl, 1980). However, learning disabled children are less likely than controls to request information that will clarify ambiguity (Pearl, Bryan, and Donahue, in press; Pearl, Donahue, and Bryan, 1980).

Bryan (1979) suggests that the learning disabled, in a similar manner to emotionally disturbed adolescents, may be more likely than their nondisabled peers to interpret friendly initiations from others as hostile—which would explain their initiation of more hostile interactions (Bryan, 1975, 1976, 1977). Therefore, if learning disabled children and adolescents are inaccurate in processing affect and other forms of feedback to the self, this must result in inaccuracies in their comprehension of messages that confirm or disconfirm the self. Since many of them are egocentric, they also may not recognize the importance of interactional feedback. If one is unable to process external feedback accurately or recognize that the interactor's behavior is, in large measure, a response to one's own, then one is handicapped in the ability to predict social responses to one's interactions and to conceptualize the expected and typical organization of social situations. Therefore, the safest course is to remain at home, where responses are predictable.

Whatever affect the learning disabled are able to process accurately may be negative and rejecting, both from peers (Bryan, 1974a, 1976; Siperstein, Bop, and Bak, 1977; Bruinincks, 1978) and from adults (Bryan and Perlmutter, 1979; Bryan and Sherman, 1980; Keogh, Tchir, and Windeguth-Behn, 1974). Learning disabled students were found to be the recipients of more teacher criticism, but also more praise and feedback (Chapman, Larsen, and Parker, 1976; Forness and Estveldt, 1975).

Wiener (1978) found that the severity of the social ineptitude and the degree to which the self-concept was negative were directly proportionate to the severity of the learning disability. Weitman (1974) found that the level of academic achievement in the learning disabled was related to their ability to take the perspective of others. These studies suggest that social cognition may be dependent on general cognitive adequacy. It appears, as well, that the more learning disabled one is, the greater the negative feedback is likely to be, with the resultant decrement in self-esteem.

Interaction as Confirmation of Self. Interaction is used to forward a definition of the self and the situation that we want others to entertain. Goffman (1959, p. 142) describes the process:

> When an individual appears before others, he knowingly and unwittingly projects a definition of the situation of which a conception of himself is an important part. When an event occurs which is expressively incompatible with this fostered impression, significant consequences are simultaneously felt in three levels of social reality.
>
> The social interaction may come to an embarrassed and confused halt; the situation may cease to be defined, previous positions may become no longer tenable, and participants may find themselves without a chartered course of action. The minute social system created and sustained by orderly social interaction becomes disorganized. In addition to these disorganizing consequences for action at the moment, performance disruptions may have consequences of a more far-reaching kind. Audiences accept the individual's particular performance as evidence of his capacity to perform the routine and even as evidence of his capacity to perform any routine. We often find that the individual may deeply involve his ego in his identification with a particular part. When a disruption occurs, we may find that the self-conceptions around which his personality has been built may become discredited.

When the learning disabled person misinterprets the organization of a social event, is clumsy, expresses himself poorly, or provides information that discredits the self, such as being in a special education program, he has created disequilibrium in the interaction. As a result, it loses both direction and the investment that the interactor had in continuing the interaction. This disorganization of interaction further reduces the learning disabled individual's exposure to social schemata and his ability to organize his social world. Others readily generalize his presenting deficiency to an assumption of total imcompetence. Their feedback then will disconfirm whatever positive assumptions he has of self. Goffman (1959, p. 123) points out that an individual who implicitly or explicitly signifies that he has certain social characteristics is expected to be what he claims to be. He also forgoes all claims to be things he does not appear to be. As a result, regardless of how discrepant his role projection may be from the actuality of his essential self, he is presumed to be that which his social behavior and context implies that he is.

The generalizing of one behavior or cluster of behaviors to the Gestalt is done not only by strangers encountered but also by the learning disabled person's relatives, teachers, and others, who imagine the disability in every behavior. This stereotyping of the individual as being comprehensively inadept has enormous implications for the concept of self. Shur (1971, p. 38) suggests: "Because stereotyping involves a tendency to jump from a single cue or a small nucleus of cues of "kind of person" being referred to, stereotyping can have an overwhelming impact on the individual, so that the person may find himself unable to sustain any alternative definition of himself."

Watzlawick, Beavin, and Jackson (1967, p. 84) contend that, on the relationship level, people do not communicate about facts outside their relationship but offer each other definitions of that relationship and, by implication, of themselves. As a result, whatever content is being communicated, the metacommunication will consist of the interactors' perceptions of themselves. Martin Buber (1957) describes this process as a confirmation of self.

The learning disabled person who does not notice others' role projections, lacks perspectivism, or has difficulty with the recognition and labeling of affect will not use language or nonverbal communication to confirm his own and his interactor's perceptions of their present and hoped-for selves nor judge the type of self that the interactor wants confirmed at that juncture. His language is likely to be shallow and self-concerned, with little sharing of his inner self. He is unlikely to attract the friendship of persons who are conceptually ready to seek relationships that involve mutual sharing and appropriate levels of independence and interdependence. His friendships may be limited to immature peers or younger persons if the latter are not deterred by the age difference. Thus, role models that confirm the self are lacking.

Since the learning disabled person's communication may reflect only his superficial self, communication, in his instance, is not a confirmation of self. Because he presents himself as being subtly different from others' expectations of him, others' responses may represent a rejection and disconfirmation of self. Disconfirmation occurs when peers, teachers, and other adults ignore him. It also occurs when others deny his reality because they are unwilling to face his experience; parents and other significant adults, who cannot cope with the pain of his unpopularity or mishandling by educators, deny its existence. He is disconfirmed when his responses are discredited as inappropriate or where feedback to his production is false. Eisenberg (1975, p. 12) describes it well: "We expect reassurance to offset psychic distress that can *only* be overcome by acquiring competence and not by being given credit for 'trying hard' or praise for washing blackboards when you can't read."

Disconfirmation of self is most evident in the parents' desire to have the youth conform academically, socially, and vocationally, even if such conformity is achieved by the parents' doing his homework, dressing him for social outings, and providing answers for him in public. It must appear to him that they prefer their fantasy image of him to the reality.

The ways in which parents present their learning disabled offspring varies with the response that they wish to elicit. They will present him as handicapped if they are seeking understanding from educators or sympathy from friends or relatives, or they will present him as intact if they want him hired by an employer.

Whereas intact persons are able to conceptualize the intent of mixed messages and absorb them into an integrated concept of self, the learning disabled may be unable to resolve the disparity. Thus, the everyday mixed messages which commonly are conveyed to everyone by everyone, in which we say one thing but mean something else, and are resolved with ease, even by young children, may be interpreted literally by the learning disabled.

When generational boundaries have not been adequately conceptualized or parental overprotection and intrusiveness have confused the expression of generational roles, the ability to judge interactional intent is not well defined. We typically learn the boundaries whereby specific interactions, however demeaning they might be in other contexts, are handled casually. In other words, "You idiot" can range from being the ultimate insult to an expression of endearment, depending on our relationship to the person, the situation in which the utterance occurs, and the accompanying affect. Similarly, slights from significant persons are far more threatening to the ego than slights from casual acquaintances or strangers. One, then, must be able to conceptualize the extent of commitment in a relationship and the importance and quality of a specific interaction, in order to weigh intent. The learning disabled person who processes interaction from nonmeaningful persons as assaults to the ego, because he does not comprehend his relationship to them or their expected role or affect, will demonstrate the same fragility in interactional boundary setting as the neurotic. However, his deficit may well be conceptual rather than neurotic.

Being Labeled as Learning Disabled. Just as parents, on discovering that their child is learning disabled, begin to perceive him and his behaviors differently, the child himself undergoes a status change. In the preschool years, his behavior is usually not so alarmingly deviant that he is labeled as handicapped. Behaviors such as high activity level and sloppiness may be valued in the young child as indications of his being "all boy," whereas they subsequently are devalued and relabeled "hyperactivity" and "lack of coordination." Once he encounters academia, deviations in development are not as liberally tolerated by educators as they are by the family. He thereby experiences a status shift from "normal" to disabled, with the accompanying devaluation of status, depression, and mourning for the intact child who has been lost, and the forfeiture of the promises that accompany intactness.

In part, some of the social problems that the learning disabled evidence may be the result of their voluntary distancing from peer interaction because they now have "a spoiled identity" (Goffman, 1964). They cannot hide the disability by denying it, because it is felt that they cannot be remediated until they acknowledge their areas of incompetent functioning. They cannot conceal the disability because the volunteer associations have largely eliminated the element of shame, so that the fact that one is learning disabled tends to be common knowledge, and considerable information about oneself is readily available. Thus, they now must relate to others as learning disabled and find few opportunities to present their public selves as competent. We judge ourselves and others judge us by our friends, so that other children are not eager to befriend a low-status person. Neither is the learning disabled person eager to remind others of his low status by befriending other learning disabled. As long as he avoids friendship with those having similar problems, he can cling to the illusion that he still is like everyone else. The issue to be determined is whether his differences are more apparent, and hence stigmatizing, in sheltered education or in the mainstream.

The Many Roles of the Individual

We project a multiplicity of selves that are based on the type of relationship in which we momentarily are involved and the particular circumstances of that relationship. During the course of a day, we well may be a parent, spouse, child, sibling, niece or nephew, aunt or uncle, grandchild, neighbor, intimate friend, casual friend, boss, fellow professional, employee, customer, and stranger encountered in a cursory interaction. Within each of these roles we assume subroles. As children, we sometimes assume the role of our parents' peer or parent, particularly as we reach middle adulthood and our parents become old. As teachers, we sometimes behave toward students as a teacher and sometimes as a peer. As spouses, we are, on occasion, a child or parent; however, we never are a child for long if our spouse does not want to be a parent, nor are we a parent if the spouse does not need to be a child at that moment. Thus, all role taking is based on a schematization of our typical behavior to the particular type of person with whom we currently are interacting in a particular environment. It takes into account the relationship we have with our interactor and the momentary needs he conveys, both verbally and nonverbally. The learning disabled person who does not realize that people project roles and subroles will fail to treat his interactor in a culturally expected manner; neither will he be other-centered. Similarly, the learning disabled person who fails to notice or misinterprets body language will not project a role that is consonant with others' image of what he should be. His discordant role projection will cause interactor confusion, fear, and anger, so that his feedback will consist of rejection or avoidance, which hinders more adequate role learning. The conceptually immature person may not appreciate the importance of projecting a self that is consonant with the interaction at hand; therefore, he produces the first behavior that comes to mind.

We have, as well, an intimate self, a family self, a public self, and an ideal self. The learning disabled person who has difficulty understanding abstract concepts will experience equal difficulty conceptualizing a self that presents different faces to his interactors depending on who the interactor is and the expectations of the interaction. He may feel, for instance, that a presentation of one's public self is duplicity since it does not reflect one's basic beliefs. Therefore, he may find it impossible to resolve the ambiguity of a multiplicity of selves without feeling that he has compromised his essential self. He may try to achieve resolution through splitting himself into discrete entities. Some learning disabled persons and their families split the failing and nonconforming student (the "bad" self) from the family member (the "good" self).

Factors Affecting Self-Concept

Language as Self-Expression. The acquisition of language enables the child to progress from concrete pictorial thought processes to more representational, linguistically mediated thoughts. This higher-level thought process enables him to develop a unified concept of self—himself as a totality, the essence of his body and roles in life. Since language shapes thought and thought shapes language, children who experience linguistic delay must also demonstrate a corresponding delay in a developed concept of self.

Furthermore, the child who says little or nothing evokes no response, so that there is reduced feedback to the self. One cannot minimize the importance of response in promoting conceptual growth in preschool children. This is the stage of life where children comment on the world with their freshness of perception, and adults respond to their observations with delight, while correcting their precepts and concepts. A parent can be impressively nurturing yet cannot respond with wonder, warmth, and clarification to a child's comments if the child has said nothing. Nor is the parent as likely to return messages of love if the child never says "I love you, Mummy and Daddy." Preschool children use language to structure the world around them. The child with deficient verbal skills is thus less able to make sense of his incredibly complex environment.

The Ability to Organize the Emotional Self. According to Becker (1962, p. 15), the ego allows the organism to hold several conceptual processes and stimuli simultaneously. This permits the organism to imagine diverse outcomes without immediately acting; it makes reasoned choice possible; it allows the organism a freedom unknown in nature. The ego, through its store of schemata and hence ability to interpret and predict others' behavior, can replace action with imagery. As the child's cognitive and behavioral scope increases, there are more persons, activities, and concepts with which he is able to become empathically involved and more things that have meaning for him. With increasing age he is increasingly likely to assume the role of observer without plunging into action each time he is stimulated. As he acquires the ability for efficient mobilization, he becomes able to perform two or more actions efficiently in rapid alteration. Since some of those actions will be automatic, he will be able to devote attention to issues requiring an empathic response.

The learning disabled child does not compensate for his deficient areas of processing until his schemata have been organized or until he realizes that his processing is inefficient and is taught compensatory mechanisms. Before compensation can be effected, he must acquire sensory and ego integration. Since one needs to perceive in order to determine patterns of experience and needs to have concepts or schemata to realize what it is that one is perceiving, deficits in attending, processing, and memory influence the circular process of perceptual and conceptual maturation, and hence the organization of the ego. Lesser and Easser (1972) postulate that this, in turn, creates developmental delays both in areas close to the deficit and those seemingly distant, such as emotional expression, conscience formation, motor control, imitation, and identification.

Lesser and Easser suggest that impulsivity is closely connected with the child's deficient ability to express his needs and feelings and to the paucity or noncomprehension of corrective feedback. "Impulsivity," they suggest, "is directly related to the organization of emotions for the self and the understanding, the naming, if one likes, of the emotions by the self. Once an affect can be named, it can come under the sway of ego control and ego use" (pp. 462, 463).

Lesser and Easser further suggest that the delay in organizing the emotional self is clearly related to the child's difficulty with empathic responses. "Emotions are used to feel out the other person and to adjust oneself quickly to the feelings noted in the other. This difficulty with the use of emotions creates a seeming bluntness in social relationships. It delays and stunts the feelings of sorrow and shame" (p. 463).

When the ability to attend to, process, judge, and retain a multiplicity of simultaneous stimuli and concepts is deficient, exposure to novelty is limited and feedback is reduced or inaccurately processed, then the proficiency to weigh, plan, act, and assess one's actions is hampered. As a result, the child is unable to assess situations in a thoughtful manner, presenting instead the immature responses of impulsivity, hyperactivity, and delays in ego and moral development. Since adults do not trust children and adolescents who behave so precipitously to handle new experiences safely, new opportunities for experiential learning are withheld. Impulsive, hyperactive, and aggressive children evoke feelings of failure in teachers and parents, who may react to their lack of control with rigid disciplinary measures. Considering that the immaturity perpetuates feelings of omniscience, the learning disabled child may see no reason to be accountable to his parents and culture and hence to restrict his impulsivity and hedonistic urges. Such a child, feeling little allegiance to his parents, will identify with and imitate them less, which hinders the learning of most social skills. Since he is not empathic, he infrequently will demonstrate sensitivity to others' situations, so that family members and peers will lose interest in him as an interactor. The resultant shallowness of affect represents, in part, the distance that has been created by the delayed acquisition of self, and perhaps a stereotyped concept of roles, such as "Men are not supposed to show feelings."

The learning disabled person, then, is uncertain that his precepts and concepts are consensual with those of others. He is unsure of his own feelings, others' feelings, and others' feelings about him. He may well begin to doubt his own capacity to perceive, generalize, abstract, and react accurately; and this contributes to dependency and a less than confident self.

One must wonder about the extensiveness of self-prostitution and self-denial that we have perpetrated on the learning disabled person when we insist that he conform regardless of cost or attendant loss. What, indeed, has he forfeited when we attribute his successes to our efforts? When one feels worthless and, in fact, is unpolished and hence unsuccessful socially, one expects rejection from others and produces behavior that ensures such rejection. The projected rejection is coped with by withdrawal or attention-seeking behavior, both of which are self-defeating.

Thus, we have an anomaly: the learning disabled person who feels that he has little worth and yet may expect to achieve goals as lofty as those that other presumed-to-be learning disabled persons and intact persons have achieved. Rigid adherence to unrealistic goals results in devaluation of self and a life in which one rarely experiences true feelings of accomplishment.

Our feelings about ourselves are directly related to our explanations for failure or success. The person who believes or has been led to believe that he is irrevocably inept, clumsy, unintelligent, or lacking in judgment may attribute failure to himself and success to luck or the manipulation of others. If he is convinced of his inability to perform, he plans to fail, so that failure comes to

represent a predictable commodity that is less frightening than
success. Once he perceives failure as being his dominant experience, it is difficult to reverse the trend (Kagan, Kearsley, and
Zelato, 1978). His failure reinforces his image of himself as incompetent, which results in further failure.

The explanations that educators and parents have for a
child's success or failure contribute, as well, to his belief concerning the egis of responsibility for his performance. Generally, we
tend to believe that our own behavior is affected by external factors
but that the behavior of others is a function of their personality.
Beckman (1970) found that teachers believed that they were responsible when children's performance improved but not when it
deteriorated. Observers, on the other hand, reported that the
teachers had been more responsible for performance deterioration than for improvement. Similarly, some parents attribute
their child's unacceptable performance to the learning disability,
whereas they attribute his acceptable production to their or others'
remedial efforts. The use of a chemotherapeutic approach to controlling behavior, or external imposition of structure and reduction
of stimuli, as essential as they assuredly are, may leave the child and
significant adults with the impression that the child is unable to
control his own behavior.

Pearl, Donahue, and Bryan (1980), Chapman and Boersma
(1980), and Hallahan and Reeve (1980) found that learning disabled children and adolescents attributed failure to their lack of
ability or effort and success to luck or teacher's benevolence. Tanis
Bryan (1980) reported that learning disabled adolescents perceived
themselves as performing more poorly than classmates on all academic subjects and on nonacademic activities such as following directions and relating to peers. Chapman and Boersma (1980)
observed that teachers and parents had low expectations for learning disabled children's future academic achievement and generalized the child's current failure in specific academic subjects to
future failure in other academic areas. As reported by Dweck and
Repucci (1973), children who believed that their failures were due
to lack of ability rather than lack of effort were likely to exhibit
learned helplessness after experiencing failure. Pearl, Donahue,
and Bryan (1980) found that children's belief in internal locus of

control correlated with their understanding of implicit feedback. Since the learning of most social behaviors occurs through the integration of implicit information, the child who does not believe that he controls his fate appears, as well, to be the child who is handicapped in social perception.

Parents of the learning disabled may also exhibit learned helplessness in response to their failure to rear a functional, well-behaved child, to mold professional attitudes, and to arrange effective services for their offspring. When I lived with the three families of learning disabled children (1976), I found that the parents did not perceive themselves as agents of change with their learning disabled offspring, although they did with their intact children, and consequently arranged problem-solving experiences for the latter but not the former. Peck and Stackhouse (1973) found that parents of reading disabled children used closed system communication. When parents do not believe that their behavior can create alterations, they no longer teach or model interactional negotiation or conceptual skills or convey to their child that he, too, is in control of his destiny. Bryan (1980, p. 14) sums up the research on the factors to which the learning disabled attribute their successes and failures:

> Learning disabled children are more likely than non-disabled children to make causal attributions likely to lead to "learned helplessness" when they experience failure. In addition, teachers and mothers hold little expectation that these children will improve academically across time. Not only do learning disabled children have to cope with their own negative feelings about failure, the persons upon whom they depend for evaluation are also likely to judge them as doing badly. This pattern of not taking credit for success, plus feeling responsible for failure, and a dependence on others for feedback and evaluation has been found by about age nine, and there are data that suggest this pattern remains unaltered when the children are in high school. However, there is some evidence that by junior high ages the child no longer depends on adults for evaluation; by this age they have decided that any failure is the result of their ability.

Generalization of Failure

Our culture's overwhelming emphasis on productivity, success, and the need to excel generates feelings of little worth in the minimally productive learning disabled, who may be inadept athletically, academically, and socially. Overwhelming feelings of worthlessness can be aroused by perceived failure in one or two aspects of a complex personality. A child might be affable, intelligent, creative, humorous, and cooperative yet become discouraged and depressed over his academic or athletic limitations. If he is unable to limit his feelings of failure to the situation in which he has failed, relate the failure to a component of the situation, and find compensatory ways of handling or avoiding the difficult component, then his depression and anxiety will result in disorganization and hence successive failure in other areas of functioning. Eventually he will feel that he has lost so much ground that he becomes overwhelmed and immobilized by his lack of success. Some learning disabled persons seem able to salvage feelings of value by contemplating future successes. However, this requires the ability to evoke temporal imagery and some indication that future success is possible. When learning disabled children and adolescents have few feelings of esteem in areas they value, they may express totally unrealistic aspirations. After all, if one can salvage nothing about which to be proud, one might as well fantasize about the impossible.

Consequences of Self-Devaluation

Unrealistic Aspirations. Ausubel and Sullivan ([1957] 1970, pp. 261–268) point out that the child who does not feel sufficiently loved and wanted cannot acquire the necessary status in the derived-status stage. Not only is it impossible for him to enjoy current self-esteem but his aspirations for power or prestige must either be projected outside the home (for instance, at school or in the peer group) or into the more distant future. The issues that militate against the learning disabled child's feeling loved and wanted have been discussed. One must add, in addition, the probability that children with perceptual and/or memory deficits may not perceive all the loving behavior directed toward them. Unlike intact children, the learning disabled child cannot augment or substitute the feelings of power and prestige that he may lack within the family through the peer group because he may have few friends and be a low-status member of the group. Certainly, the school is not an arena wherein he can achieve prestige, and rarely is he afforded positions of power. Children who perceive themselves as intrinsically valued tend to conceive of their capacities in less omnipotent terms and are less tenacious about maintaining unrealistically high levels of aspiration despite realistic considerations to the contrary. Conversely, many learning disabled children, adolescents, or adults verbalize unrealistic goals in terms of their capabilities and likely opportunities. This would be consistent with the findings of White and his associates (1980) that learning disabled young adults were less satisfied with some aspects of their lives than controls.

Insofar as the learning disabled child is exposed to typical expectations, he is subject to chronic failure. Once his disabilities are recognized, however, he may be reared and educated in a controlled environment, where he is protected from failure. He may be told that he is a failure now but that an impressive future awaits him. Both excessive exposure to failure and excessive protection from it, or noncontingent reinforcement for behavior not ordinarily considered praiseworthy, result in unrealistic self-estimates, a tendency to underperform, and a concept that both success and failure are extraneous to one's efforts (Cobb, 1966). The child who has been afforded opportunities to experience realistic doses of success and failure and to organize and direct his production toward a successful outcome is likely to be realistic about his capabilities. Similarly, the child who has been afforded opportunities to achieve esteem in activities that are highly valued by his peers is likely to discard aspirations that are unrealistic, taking into account one's attributes and prospects. Finally, the expression *unrealistic aspirations* may signify denial of the disability (Wiener, 1978), or magical thought processes. The learning disabled adolescent may state lofty goals in the same manner that he overestimates his status, both representing ignorance of the process or degree of difficulty whereby such goals are reached. After all, he has achieved other goals, such as passing a grade in school, without having produced the expected level of work.

Opportunities to Assert Oneself. Self-esteem is inseparable from one's acts and one's power to act. If we are afforded limited executive possibilities, we are, necessarily, low in self-esteem. The learning disabled often lack opportunities to exert power in a positive manner and to find genuine areas of self-expression. In the school system, no one in the educational hierarchy is allowed much assertion of self without the risk of penalty. Educators who have been disallowed opportunities to strive for their significant selves would be unlikely to foster their students' expressions of self, particularly those students who are noncompliant or unproductive. In any event, educators may be so overwhelmed by the task of teaching reading, writing, spelling, and computing to their learning disabled students that little, if any, time or energy survives for ideas, creativity, and questioning. Rarely do we ask such students the relevance of current learning to their life experience and aspirations, or determine the aspects of self of which they are most proud. Children in our culture are disallowed the power to effect significant change. The learning disabled, being devalued, are particularly powerless.

Since the learning disabled child is unsuccessful, he is vulnerable—vulnerable to exclusion from educational opportunities and peer social arrangements, vulnerable to imagined and real banishment from the family and into a world with which he feels ill equipped to cope. Vulnerability itself renders one dependent on teachers and parents, who, in turn, contribute to it. Henry ([1957] 1973, pp. 89–90) describes the dynamics:

> The child's vulnerability is sustained and intensified by the elementary school, where he is at the teacher's mercy. The teacher, clearly through no fault of her own, is the agent of vulnerability; and she transmits the sense of it to the child through two weapons thrust into her hands, sometimes against her will—discipline and the power to fail the child. Before these absolute weapons the child is even more vulnerable than with his parents; for with his parents the agony of vulnerability is allayed in part by love, and he can, within limits, fight back. In school, however, this usually is not the case, for in the first place, in the contemporary overcrowded

classroom, fighting back is a negation of order and routine, and fear of failure is the pulse of school life. Remove the fear of failure and education in America would stop. Yet we cannot blame the feeling of vulnerability on fear of failure, for, after all, without fear of failure nobody would try for success, and without striving for success there could be no contemporary culture. Thus, another characteristic of vulnerability—its roots in the idea of success.

The Need to Compromise Oneself. In a culture that worships success to the extent that man must excel in something in order to feel worth (Becker, 1973), and is terrified of failure, we all are placed in the position of selecting goals we are likely to attain and behaving in ways directed toward that attainment. That means that, regardless of the inclinations of the self, we will conform, in large part, to expectations of parents, teachers, bosses, and valued peers, because the penalty for not doing so is failure. Each acquiescence is a prostitution of self until we reach the point where the self is so repressed that we no longer recognize our compromises.

We compromise, as well, on the goals we set for ourselves, be they selection of spouse or job. Rather than strive for a job that would represent the ultimate in personal satisfaction, we select a job in which we are reasonably certain that our attributes will be acceptable resources. We establish a value and weight on our intelligence, appearance, wit, affluence, energy level, popularity, and so on, and seek persons who are likely to date or marry someone with those attributes.

Although all of us compromise our inner selves and must eliminate many life possibilities and curb expressions of self, the learning disabled child or adolescent is expected to repress himself far more extensively. His impulsivity, hyperactivity, loudness, inappropriate social behavior, and short interest span are restrained for the sake of conformity. He is not allowed the playfulness and pranks that highlight his peers' social life because his parents are afraid that he lacks the judgment to "get away with it" and because they are apprehensive that his misbehavior will be used by educators to effect reprisals. Some parents, having heard that learning disabilities are equated with delinquency, perceive normal noncompliance as precursors of future unlawful behavior. The learning disabled person may be excluded from possible vocations because he cannot cope with the steps en route, notwithstanding the extent to which those steps are utilized by the practitioner. By the time he reaches adolescence, giving up, giving in, and repressing a variety of impulses that are socially unacceptable may have become so thoroughly integrated that he has erected a wall of resistance. This resistance may present itself as balkiness, rigidity, and absence of compromises or as a barrier between his and others' access to his inner self. Consequently, he becomes someone who talks about himself extensively but shares few of his feelings.

Henry ([1957] 1973) comments that the penalty for invulnerability to our compromises of self is isolation and illusion. Illusion can take the form of unrealistic aspirations or "if only" fantasies, both for the learning disabled person and his parents— if only he had received more effective remediation, he would have been able to . . . Alternatively, when there are no compromises of self or a deficient ability to assess one's attributes and relate them realistically to opportunities, the learning disabled adolescent attempts to date the valedictorian or beauty queen or to become a mathematics professor when he lacks basic mathematics concepts. Such a youth is exceedingly vulnerable to assaults on his concept of self. One must seriously explore his failure to effect a concept of self that is comfortable and compatible with opportunities.

When the self is excessively compromised and the inner self commensurately defended, this defense presents itself as constricted, unspontaneous functioning and thought processes. Such a person become rigid and limited in his willingness to allow other persons the validity of their points of view. Becker (1962, pp. 83, 85) describes the process well: "Character armor, as we know, refers literally to the arming of the personality so that it can maneuver in a threatening world. It refers to the shoring-up or damming-up of the individual's fragile sense of self-value, in order to keep that self-value safe from undermining from events and persons. In other words, character armor really refers to the whole life style that a person assumes, in order to live and act with a certain security. We all have some because we all need to organize our personality. . . . Some people, of course, have more than others—more self-protecting constraint. This makes them remarkably stiff, as though they actually wore armor. It makes them remarkably unsympathetic to points of view they have decided are not worth entertaining, or are too threatening to entertain. It shuts them very tightly toward others who risk invading their world, and perhaps upsetting it, even if they upset it with kindness and love.

Chapter 5

✻ ✻ ✻ ✻ ✻

Understanding the Problems and Behavior of Older Learning Disabled Persons

✻ The egocentricity evidenced by some of the learning disabled appears to result from their conceptual immaturity and the environmental response to their disability. In turn, it has implications for maturation, social adequacy, moral development, and abstract thought processes. So it both creates and is created by deficits in concept formation. It appears helpful to determine the conceptual level of the presenting egocentricity, since that will provide clues for growth needs and remedial direction.

Stages of Egocentrism

Sensorimotor Egocentrism (0–2 Years of Age). Toward the end of the first year, the infant demonstrates his ability to represent absent objects internally. We have no research as yet to determine whether infants who subsequently present as learning disabled are delayed

at this level of symbolic conceptualization. Nonetheless, the difficulty that learning disabled children and adolescents demonstrate
in conversing with someone on the telephone or in describing an
object that is not in sight seems to indicate some breakdown in early
representational imagery.

Preoperational Egocentrism (2–6 Years of Age). Symbolic functioning becomes fully active at this age—as is evidenced by rapid
growth in the acquisition and utilization of language, the appearance of symbolic play, and the first report of dreams. Early in this
period, a child fails to differentiate between words and their refer-
ents and between his play, dream symbols, and reality. He believes
that the name inheres in the object.

The preoperational child demonstrates his egocentrism by
the use of many indefinite terms and the omission of important
information (Elkind, 1974). This can be attributed to the child's
failure to consider the other person's point of view or to his assumption that words convey the property of the objects they represent—so that, in fact, words seem to carry more information
than they actually do. Research suggests that preoperational behavior occurs in school-aged learning disabled children. Bryan and
Pflaum (1978) found a higher percentage of incompetent communications in learning disabled children than in controls, particularly by white males to peers and white females to younger
children. They found that white learning disabled children in
elementary school did not gear the complexity of their language to
the age of their interactors, whereas intact four-year-old children
were able to do so. Bryan (1978) also found that learning disabled
children, in instructing other children in how to play a game, in-
structed so continuously and overhelpfully that their behavior
appeared intrusive and meddlesome rather than helpful. Parrill-
Burnstein and Hazan-Ginsburg (1980) found that children with
heterogeneous learning disabilities had more trouble with visual
perspective taking than children with language-learning disabilities
and controls. They suggest that the inability to reorganize a visual
image so that one can imagine how others see it would affect the
understanding of others' social roles. Weitman (1974) noted that
high-achieving learning disabled subjects achieved perspectivism
whereas low-achieving ones did not. A learning disabled person

who functions at the preoperational cognitive level may walk between two persons who are involved in a serious conversation and interrupt them with a statement that can be understood only if one knows what this person has been thinking. Such a person seems to assume that surely everyone knows what he is thinking.

Toward the end of the preoperational period, a child achieves concrete operational thought processes, the ability to hold two dimensions in mind simultaneously. This enables him to conceptualize symbol and referent at the same time, thereby distinguishing the two. The learning disabled child with poor auditory, visual, or spatial memory, or deficient ability to synthesize and stabilize his impressions, or the child who responds catastrophically to complexity, may break down at this juncture and be limited by his unidimensional understanding of information, be it in the interpersonal, linguistic, or academic/symbolic spheres.

Egocentrism in Middle Childhood. The major cognitive task of the school-aged child is that of mastering classes, relations, and quantities. If the cognitive breakdown occurs at this juncture, in addition to its effect on mathematics, science, reasoning, and judgment, the learning disabled child's social cognition will be impaired. He may experience difficulty in understanding the relationships of grandparent, aunt/uncle, niece/nephew, in-law, step-relative, or cousin. He may not comprehend that a person usually is a member of many classes, being a daughter, sister, sister-in-law, wife, mother, aunt, librarian, and so on, simultaneously. He may not appreciate the stability of relationships through time or may perceive relationships egocentrically; as a result, he may say that a grandparent cannot possibly be a parent's parent because he or she is too old to have children. Or a child may claim that her uncle cannot be her uncle because he died before his niece was born or that relatives cannot be related if they do not spend time together. Another such child may assume that passing a grade indicates an automatic increment in cognitive ability; so he states that now that he is in grade 6 he will be able to handle multiplication.

Similarly, the child may be confused about the relationship one assumes with the multitude of people one encounters and the level of intimacy or formality one should elect. Should one pat one's teacher affectionately on the backside, or address one's adult neighbor as "Mary"? To whom is it appropriate to convey personal or intimate family information, and with whom is one free to criticize behavior or appearance? When is it appropriate to use "Ms.," "Miss," "Mrs.," "Dr.," "Sir," "Madam," "Your Honor," "Hey you," or other appellations? He also is likely to have difficulty determining the age and status of persons he encounters by their size and other physical characteristics. A learning disabled person at this level of cognition may classify people and objects according to extraneous rather than salient features, which further distorts the thought process. For example, because size usually signifies age in children, he may assume that the larger an adult is, the older he must be. He may be equally unclear about the complexity of language that people of different ages can comprehend or the topics of conversation that interest them.

The egocentrism that the child demonstrates at this stage of development is an inability to differentiate clearly between what he thinks and what he perceives (Elkind, 1974). As a result, he will rationalize information to conform to his premise and will blame others for the failure of his premise to work, instead of attributing the failure to a faulty assumption. Learning disabled persons who persist in this form of egocentricity will continue to produce illogical or tangential premises, fail to develop a problem-solving approach to situations, and continue to believe in external locus of control. Because such persons tend to reject or reinterpret facts to fit their hypothesis, they make assumptions about reality on the basis of limited information, which they will not alter in the face of new and contradictory evidence. This method of reasoning results in rigidity and will affect academic performance, since the child will apply a rule or conviction to all situations, regardless of applicability. The child also may create faulty social assumptions; he might conclude that his parents' current argument is attributable to a behavior he produced earlier, and so he will feel guilty for behavior external to the boundaries of the parental disagreement.

With the achievement of concrete operational thought, the child discovers that his parents are not omniscient after all (Elkind, 1974). Indeed, in the young adolescent's eyes, they are not even too bright. If he is able to demonstrate that he is brighter than they are in one instance, then he assumes that he must be more intelligent than they in all instances. Similarly, if he can catch his parents erring in one situation, they must, then, be wrong in everything. However, when parents become overinvolved in or martyred to their learning disabled child, the child is not allowed to acknowledge their imperfections. In fact, he may feel so much less competent than they that he may not recognize their fallability. He may lack the linguistic skill to demonstrate his superiority by tripping his parents up on their ambiguous or imprecise commands (Donahue, Bryan, and Pearl, 1980; Donahue, Pearl, and Bryan, 1980). As a result, it is difficult for the learning disabled adolescent to develop the cognitive conceit wherein he finds himself all-knowing and his parents useless, an assumption widely observed in intact adolescents in our culture.

Conversely, when parents have made the learning disabled child see himself as special, he is unlikely to make a realistic assessment of his and his parents' attributes and is likely, as a result, to have unrealistic aspirations and difficulty in assessing himself in relationship to others. Cognitive conceit in early adolescence is a normal manifestation of the developmental process. Adults indulge in it occasionally as a momentary fantasy ("I am more knowledgeable than my boss on one point, so I know more than he does altogether"), but they do not truly believe their assumption. However, when cognitive conceit persists as a belief that is carried into late adolescence and adulthood, the delusion of grandeur becomes a substitute for realistic self-assessment and planning. However, since the learning disabled person's life experience does not support his cognitive conceit, he is at risk for paranoid swings of overesteem and underesteem. The learning disabled child or adolescent who regards himself as superior to adults will see no reason other than fear of punishment to obey rules that adults have imposed. He may, in fact, break the rules as proof of his cleverness in evading detection. The child who makes judgments on the basis of assumptive realities rather than the facts may create assumptions about his wrongdoing that, in his mind, excuse or exonerate his acts.

Adolescent Egocentrism. The adolescent who has attained formal operational thought is able to conceptualize and critique his own thought processes and imagine what others are thinking.

However, he, too, is egocentric in his failure to differentiate between his own preoccupation with his appearance and behavior and others' impressions of him. When he is able to examine himself from the perspective of others, he becomes conscious of the discrepancy between his real self and his ideal self. Thus, the learning disabled adolescent who has attained formal operational cognition may experience his first real depression. His deficient time sense, his immaturity, and the delays in the need for reality planning may have cushioned him from conceptualizing the discrepancy between his attainment and wished-for goals until mid to late adolescence. Since all stress respresents loss or threatened loss, he is depressed until a conciliation between ideal and real self can be effected. Adolescents generally lack compassion for human failing; thus, the learning disabled adolescent may berate himself too extensively for his social, academic, and athletic inadequacies. Learning disabled adolescents who do not yet perceive the discrepancy between their real and ideal selves will persist in aspiring to the impossible.

Adolescent concept formation allows for duplicity, wherein the adolescent can make assertions yet believe differently and produce interpersonal behavior that is at variance with his concept of self. He then is able to conceal thoughts and wishes and to produce a social role that he feels will be most comfortably received, both to further his own social gain, relax others, and reinforce their social roles. The learning disabled adolescent, on the other hand, who feels that any presentation of self that is not totally honest is deceitful, creates his own social havoc with his ultimate candor. He is the antithesis of the delinquent, since each rule or law is literally obeyed.

An adolescent typically believes that his feelings, his pain, his frustrations, and his love are special and unique. He imagines that this personal uniqueness will ensure protection from misfortune and mortality. The learning disabled adolescent whose differentness, specialness, and preoccupation with his needs have been reinforced by significant adults may consider himself above harm and persist in perceiving magical rather than causal outcomes. His conviction of personal invincibility may result in reckless behavior because he is convinced of his immunity to discovery, just as his female counterpart is convinced of her immunity to pregnancy.

The intact adolescent, unlike the child, is able to utilize a second symbol system, which enables him to comprehend metaphor, double entendre, and cartoons. The concrete learning disabled adolescent, however, continues to respond to information literally, regardless of the senselessness of his interpretation in terms of the probable meaning of the interaction at hand. He responds to partials instead of deriving meaning from the Gestalt of the interaction. This, in turn, contributes to dyslogic thought processes.

Because adolescents typically are able to perceive a host of alternatives to parental directives, they are reluctant to comply without questioning. The learning disabled adolescent, being dependent on his parents, particularly his mother (Greenberg, 1970), may be reluctant to threaten that dependency with breaking-away behavior, particularly if he imagines that misbehavior will evoke parental hostility and result in expulsion. Having few friends, he is unable to test his decisions on peers or to gain peer support for rebellious behavior. Then, too, parents may be fearful that breaking-away behavior will cause educators to penalize him; therefore, they urge conformity when they should be encouraging individuation.

All of us are egocentric on occasion. Although we may demonstrate momentary egocentricity at one level of functioning, this does not necessarily preclude the presence of higher levels of cognitive and emotional development. The therapeutic issue is the frequency and extensiveness of the egocentric manifestations, the prevalence or absence of higher-level functions, and the degree to which the egocentricity and cognitive deficits are limiting socially and academically. Remediation entails the stimulation of abstract thought processes and correction of egocentric distortion.

Stages of Moral Development

As Ausubel and Sullivan ([1957] 1970, p. 467) note: "Moral obligation is one of the most important psychological mechanisms through which an individual becomes socialized in the ways of his culture. It is also an important instrument for cultural survival, since it constitutes a most efficient watchdog within each individual, serving to keep his behavior compatible with his own moral values and the values of the society in which he lives."

Although many learning disabled persons do not become delinquent, some present as morally immature. Adequate moral development is dependent on psychological environment; conceptual competence; and the ability to notice, assess, and initiate selected behaviors and to integrate a set of personal values that constantly are reassessed as new information is assimilated (Hemming, 1957). As Ausubel and Sullivan (p. 474) note, the development of conscience is predicated on alterations in dependency relationships and ego status needs; an increased capacity for perceiving social expectations and the attributes of social roles; and expanded ability to generalize, formulate abstractions, take multiple perspectives, and become more self-critical, less egocentric, and more objective in one's approach to values. The smooth acquisition of moral behavior is predicated on a complementarity between the child's cognitive development and childrearing practices. Dissonance can occur at any level of moral/conceptual growth. Thus, the consonance between the child's increasing ability to conceptualize moral expectations and parental ability to create an environment conducive to the assumption of moral behavior can break down at any level of the child's development.

Egocentric Stage of Moral Development. A child at this stage of development complies with parental injunctions from a fear of punishment rather than from conformation to a self-determined principle of behavior. The egocentric child learns to anticipate and avoid punishment, since conformity reduces insecurity. The child at this stage cannot separate the rightness of his act from his rationalization. The impulsive or controlling learning disabled child, the one who is deficient in anticipation and generalization, or the one who does not relate punishment to misbehavior may be particularly difficult to socialize to conformity. Some learning disabled children continue to confuse the assumptive reality with reality, failing to distinguish between their actual behavior and the fable they have constructed about their behavior.

Derived-Status Stage of Moral Development. The child in this stage of development, aware that he is not omnipotent, derives status from being a member of the family. He must identify with the family, and they, in turn, must accept and value him if he is to accept their standards of rightness and wrongness. At this stage of development, guilt reactions become possible. The child's motivation for conformity to parental standards is avoidance of guilt. The learning disabled child who is unable to meet family standards and does not feel intrinsically valued will not necessarily identify sufficiently to conform. Kohlberg (1964) noted that parents of delinquents were typically less accepting, affectionate, and solicitous than parents of nondelinquents. If the child lacks temporal imagery, he will be unable to project the consequences of his misbehavior or evaluate behavior that has occurred within a schemata, so that the development of guilt may be retarded. Wender (1971) attributes the difficulties that parents experience in socializing their learning disabled offspring to a blunting of the feelings of pleasure and pain, the latter relating to a blunting of guilt.

Since children in the derived-status stage are absolutist and heavily dependent on parents and other authorities in the community for rule setting, the learning disabled person who persists at this level of moral development, as a result of his social inexperience and dependency on the family, may go through life as a rigid moralist—one who feels that all issues are polarized as right or wrong, with no negotiation or compromise possible. He will experience difficulty as an employee, a spouse, and a parent, particularly when his own children reach adolescence. Such a person may continue to look to authorities for rule setting, rather than establishing his own set of ethical principles that are redefined through time.

Spivack (1957, p. 5) found that disturbed adolescents appear to feel a strong need to conform to what they perceive as parental values and standards of right and wrong, and they experience more than normal guilt when they disobey the authority of parental mores. They feel that a child who disobeys his parents is ultimately punished in some way, whereas normal adolescents disagree. This immature need for external standards and sanctions may also typify the learning disabled person in the derived-status stage of conceptualization.

A preadolescent child typically has completed his assimilation of parental values. As he becomes progressively more self-critical, he is able to perceive his wrongdoing exclusive of external authority. He becomes increasingly concerned with the spirit of moral duty and less with threats of punishment. His anticipation of praise or blame in response to his conformity to moral roles begins to control his behavior. He gradually becomes concerned with the rights and expectations of both rule enforcers and rule obeyers (Kohlberg, 1964). Some learning disabled children reach this stage of moral development and try exceedingly hard to conform but discover that their efforts to effect conformity are not always well received by others because they still do not meet age-expected norms. Other learning disabled children, because of aberrations in childrearing, meet difficulty at this juncture. Parents who have been intimidated by the child's behavior or his disability and respond with permissiveness, or those who orient their lives to their child and his specialness, will have a child who is not under pressure to conform. He will not see the need to curb impulses or aggression, nor has he been expected to be critical of self and responsible to others. Freund and Elardo (1978) found that learning disabled children from large families were more socially appropriate than those from small families—possibly because the children from large families were expected to assume increased responsibilities. According to Hunt and Hardt (1965), capricious and inconsistent parental discipline is associated with a lack of self-discipline in children and is more characteristic of delinquents than nondelinquents. It frequently has been suggested that learning disabled children perform delinquent acts in response to their need for peer approval. However, children who are susceptible to peer suggestion also lack self-sufficiency and self-assertiveness (Ausubel and Sullivan, [1957] 1970), and this deficiency relates to the extent to which they have been allowed to individuate.

Adolescent Moral Development. As the adolescent comes into contact with the multiplicity of beliefs that are ascribed to in our pluralistic culture, the rightness of a singular approach, that of his parents, is challenged. Parental values are then perceived in less absolutist terms. An adolescent increasingly turns to the peer group as a source of status and moral authority, so that peers come to replace parents as moral interpreters and enforcers. It is not necessary for an adolescent to reject parental and sibling authority in order to attain moral maturity. He merely requires a change in status and dependency needs and sufficient social experience to appreciate the functional basis of existing authority relationships (Ausubel and Sullivan, [1957] 1970). An adolescent can imagine and resolve conflicting norms. He becomes increasingly able to take multiple perspectives. His perception of social roles becomes more accurate. This expanded understanding of the behavior that is associated with specific social roles increasingly governs his own behavior and his judgment of the behavior of others. An adolescent demonstrates an increasing ability to detach himself from values, examine them hypothetically, and think in terms that transcend his immediate experience (Ausubel, 1968). He becomes correspondingly less egocentric and more altruistic, so that he is able to make judgments that are universal; this means that a behavior is acceptable whether one produces the behavior or is the recipient of it.

If parents continue to treat the adolescent as preadolescent and he lacks sufficient peer contact to experience and experiment with values, he may continue to conform to parental rules. Unfortunately, parents and educators may be so grateful for his compliance that they encourage its perpetuation instead of promoting a questioning or self-assertive stance. Fearing that peer friendships will result in antisocial behavior, parents may discourage these friendships or be overcritical of their teenager's friends. Although one has parented a learning disabled child, one still may devalue other learning disabled persons and dissuade one's offspring from associating with peers who might be prepared to extend their friendship. The egocentric adolescent will be unable to recognize that a behavior must benefit the recipient of the behavior as well as the producer of the behavior in order to justify it. For example, stealing benefits the thief but not the person who was robbed. The adolescent who is literal will be unable to imagine a value in general terms, to abstract it from specific situations, and incorporate it into his value system.

Social Adequacy and Moral Development

Zimmerman and colleagues (1978) found that, popular belief to the contrary, learning disabled adolescents are not more likely to commit delinquent acts than are those who are not learning disabled. However, they are likelier to be adjudicated—possibly because they fail to take the perspective of those persons in the judicial system upon whom they should make an impression, which would result in the most benevolent outcome. Perhaps they also are less able than their peers to mobilize parents and teachers to argue in their defense, since both may be "fed up" with them. These failures of social adequacy are penalized with adjudication.

In that we achieve the approval of others through imitation of their values, imitation and identification are powerful forces in value assimilation. The child who is delayed or deficient in establishing identification and in attending to, noticing, and emulating others' values, or who does not gain approval even when values are imitated, will be handicapped in developing a value system of his own. The rigid, concrete learning disabled person will persist in seeing values in absolutist terms rather than assuming a fluid schemata that alters as he, his relatives, and friends change life stages, as knowledge is extended, and ethics shift. He will see people as being good or bad rather than perceiving all behavior as falling within a continuum of possibilities. Neither will he see people as being many faceted and variable through time and circumstances. Similarly, he may not be able to resolve or tolerate moral ambiguity, to conceive of an act as being morally acceptable in one context and unacceptable in another. The person who lacks the linguistic versatility to project into the future and create alterations through verbal mediation or lacks the ability to express feelings verbally may act out his frustrations and fantasies delinquently.

Considerable attention has been paid to the learning disabled person as offender, but no one has considered his vulnerability to becoming a victim. The lonely learning disabled adult who is desirous of friendships or the one who takes all information at face value is ready prey for dating clubs that provide no dates, salespersons who sell worthless products, and friends who borrow money and disappear. The learning disabled person may be equally ill equipped to deal with the judicial process in order to obtain a fair hearing and retribution. His rambling language and generally poor social skills may result in cursory dismissal by judges and other authorities.

Moral obligation is contractual between the person and society. One complies with the culture's injunctions and expectations in return for the rewards conferred for conformity. Similarly, one acts out the role that society has assigned to him. Therefore, it is not sufficient to examine the cognitive and parental parameters of moral development in the learning disabled. We must consider, as well, our need to withhold from them some of our valued awards for conformity, unlimited educational and vocational opportunity, peer and adult acceptance and esteem. Furthermore, when society assigns some of its members deviant or nonconformist status, and when they respond with delinquency, we must consider the extent to which the prophecy is self-fulfilling. When learning disabled persons find that their efforts do not result in conformity, that regardless of their investment they do not succeed academically or socially, being denied the payoff for conformity, they may well elect nonconformity, be it in social behavior or delinquency. The nonconformity becomes, in turn, their rationalization for their failure, which strengthens their investment in it. Goffman (1972, p. 9) describes the reciprocal process of compliance to moral obligation: "Rules are effective (insofar as they are) because those to whom they apply believe them to be right and come to conceive of themselves both in terms of who and what it is that compliance allows them to be and in terms of what deviation implies that they have become."

Chapter 6

❀ ❀ ❀ ❀ ❀

Relating Specific Disabilities to Problems in Making and Keeping Friends

❀ Just as there are many definitions of self-esteem, there are equally many of social competence. The purpose of this book is not to join in the argument but to choose a comprehensive working definition. Wilchesky's (1980b) model appears suitable for this purpose: "Social competence is defined as a set of basic components which collectively permit the individual to successfully engage in interpersonal relationships, in the event that he desires to do so. The core group of components involved in this process is composed of (1) an ability to encode and decode both verbal and nonverbal communications, (2) a sensitivity to the needs and feelings of others, (3) an ability to independently utilize interpersonal cognitive problem-solving skills, and (4) an awareness of peer group norms and an ability and inclination to behave socially in a manner consistent with those norms. The socially competent individual will be able to affect the feelings and behavior of others in the way that he intends and within the recognized boundaries of his particular sociocultural context" (p. 11).

Although there is an extensive body of literature which describes the social-emotional development of children and a growing body of literature which describes adult social behavior, there virtually is nothing delineating typical social behavior of children in our culture at each age. Consequently, when we note that a seven-year-old child appears lacking in peer social skills, we have no description of seven-year-old American children with which to compare his behavior. Neither do we of four year olds, ten year olds, or any other age. This creates difficulty in the categorizing of children as socially atypical when a baseline of typical behavior is lacking. Similarly, we cannot readily devise prescriptive social remedial programs because we lack formulated descriptions of representative peer social behavior of children. How, indeed, does a nine-year-old female in our culture answer the telephone, call for another child at her home, break into a closed social situation, react to a child who has been accepted on her team, and so on? Opie and Opie ([1959] 1976, 1969) point out that children enjoy complex social and linguistic rituals which we have forgotten and of which we are unaware. They comment ([1959] 1976, p. 1): "The scraps of lore which children learn from each other are at once more real, more immediately serviceable, and more vastly entertaining to them than anything which they learn from grownups. The schoolchild's verses are not intended for adult ears. In fact, part of their fun is the thought, usually correct, that adults know nothing about them. Grownups have outgrown the schoolchild's lore."

The obvious danger in programming for children's social deficits while lacking descriptions of children's peer interactional behavior is that we will base our remediation on the body of social psychology that describes adult metacommunication. This could create miniature adults, which is the antithesis of our desired remedial direction; learning disabled children already seek adults with whom to interact rather than their peers. Regardless, we cannot wait until we have a body of knowledge descriptive of children's interactions. For the present, we will have to utilize observations of same-age children in peer interaction to provide remedial direction.

Not all learning disabled persons are socially inadept. Some, whose presenting problems primarily are in areas such as the memory, retrieval (Parrill-Burnstein and Hazan-Ginsburg, 1980), and sequencing of language (Wiener, 1978), are impressively socially adept. Their occasional periods of social isolation may represent depression about their academic inadequacies rather than a deficient ability to initiate or maintain friendships. However, they, too, may be immature, insecure, and embarrassed about expressing themselves. Recent empirical research has confirmed the observations of clinicians (Giffen, 1968; Johnson and Myklebust, 1967; Lerner, 1976; Minskoff, 1980) that learning disabled persons, particularly those with heterogeneous learning disabilities, are socially awkward. As I have discussed, this social ineptitude appears to be multifactorial, an amalgam of primary and secondary factors which are reciprocal and inseparable. Optimally, a therapeutic approach would deal both with primary processing deficits and with the environment. Nonetheless, since remediation entails the "teasing out" of singular factors, this chapter will describe, in part, the social expectations in our culture and some of the primary processing deficits in the learning disabled that make it difficult for them to meet those expectations, while recognizing the artificiality of assigning a biological weighting to specific behaviors. It is probable that social experience enhances social perception and that social perception leads to increased social experience, so that the person who is deficient in social processing or sheltered may well be lacking in social skill acquisition.

Research indicates that the presenting social inadequacies will be related to the areas of disability (Bryan, 1979; Wiig and Harris, 1974; Wiener, 1978; Parrill-Burnstein and Hazan-Ginsburg, 1980). As Bryan (1979) observes, the data suggest that children with short attention spans for visual presentation of the alphabet may also have limited attention spans for people's facial expressions.

Social Organization

Every social situation encountered in the course of a day has a predictable organization, whether we are traveling to work, shopping, or involved in a job interview. Everyone in the culture shares knowledge of the expected behaviors for each social activity. This allows one to process information as being central, peripheral, or extraneous to the interaction at hand. It means, as well, that people are able to anticipate interactions before they occur, imagine their structure, and practice strategies. While in an interaction, they can be several steps ahead in their anticipation and planning. When one learns of an upcoming job interview, one practices it in one's mind for days. While in the interview, one imagines what each party will say. When one knows of an upcoming date, one practices one's behavior cognitively before the date has occurred. Our prior understanding of typical and expected behavior for each social situation affords us the opportunity to organize our behavior in advance and in process, so that it will be the most efficient and effective. It also minimizes anxiety, because we can anticipate the sequence of events, our behavior within them, and others' reactions to us.

We are able to assess social situations in terms of the schemata into which they appear to fit, judge whether our perceptions of the situation are congruent with actuality (Bruner, 1951), and, if not, relate the information to other schemata. As we mature, our store of schemata increases, so that we are able to relate information to an increasingly sophisticated and larger number of possibilities. As we become more organized, we are able to organize increasingly complex social encounters.

We attend primarily to the stimuli that are relevant to the momentary social situation and relegate other stimuli to the background. As the social situation shifts, we transfer the information that was in the foreground a moment before into the background and reorganize the current stimuli into new schemata, order, or understanding of the current and expected behaviors in a situation. Thus, a person at a party or a child in a playground may need to conceptualize a host of schemata within a short period of time as he moves from interaction to interaction. Unlike reading or mathematics, in which the presenting stimuli are static and can be re-processed endlessly, social situations are transient. They must be processed and responded to with accuracy within the short time that they are perceived, or one has lost the opportunity to be socially appropriate, although one might be more proficient in subsequent interactions.

Learning disabilities are, in effect, disorganization at the levels of decoding, memory, and encoding. As a result, disorganization, at some level of functioning, may underlie much of the social inadequacy in the learning disabled. Those learning disabled persons who do not realize that all social situations fall into predictable schemata will attend to and process extraneous stimuli and relate them to the interaction at hand, with the consequent distortions in concept formation. Being imperfectly aware of the organization of social encounters, they will not organize their behavior efficiently and optimally. Those who take too long to conceptualize the schemata at hand, and hence process several steps behind the current social input, lose the essence of ongoing social information, and those who perseverate in attending to social stimuli will be unable to switch from stimulus to stimulus with sufficient competence to effect adequate comprehension. Much of the behavior that we associate with clumsiness, impulsivity, or social imperception is, instead, attributable to deficits on the level of imagery of social schemata and, hence, planning. Since the learning disabled may be inefficient in imagining the organization of an upcoming social situation and their own and their interactor's behavior within it, or even imagining successive steps once they are in a situation, they produce the first behavior that comes to mind, anticipate change with anxiety, and create an expectation of personal failure.

A child establishes new schemata through the process of creating inferences around events. He generates hypotheses about events in order to understand them more completely. These inferences are treated as valid beliefs until disconfirmed. The young child or the learning disabled child—who, by virtue of poor memory systems, disorganization, and circumscribed experiences, possesses a limited or less certain store of schemata—will generate inferences that are less predictable than those of children with a more substantial base of knowledge. The inferences of a learning disabled child may reflect his isolation, egocentricity, or magical belief system. The more fragile the knowledge base, the less predictable the inferences. Although the learning disabled person may be impressively knowledgeable in some areas of functioning, he still may make astoundingly immature or atypical inferences in other areas. This inconsistency makes it particularly difficult for others to believe that the erroneous inference was unintentional.

The disorganized child or adolescent may become overwhelmed by the prospect of arranging an ordinary social encounter, and so he spends his free time watching television. Even the seemingly simple task of inviting a friend to join him at a movie would require considerable organizational ability. He would have to (1) determine which movies are playing and decide which ones he would like to see; (2) determine who is likely to want to see that type of movie and who would consider spending time with him; (3) find out where the movie is playing, how to travel there and back, and how long the journey would take; (4) decide whether to meet the friend at the movie or travel together and where the initial meeting will take place; (5) determine the cost of movie, transportation, and perhaps a snack and where the money will come from; (6) decide whether to invite the friend to his house or to a restaurant before or after the film and, if so, whether it should be for a meal or a snack or other activity and the timing.

Role Organization

Shantz's (1975) model of role-taking ability in intact children suggests that, by about the age of six, children recognize that others have different perspectives but cannot yet produce interactions that are addressed to those perspectives. By age seven, children attend to highly salient surface cues of people and situations. Between the ages of seven and eight, attention is directed to temporal and spatial cues that were not previously within the child's frame of reference. Children between the ages of eight and nine are able to sequence or coordinate different perspectives. By age ten, children can assume and evaluate others' perspectives as well as their own.

Flavell (1974) suggests that the sequence of skills requisite for social behavior are *existence,* which is the recognition that social cues such as attention, motives, and beliefs are relevant; *need,* which is an attempt to act on cognitive cues; and *inference,* which is the implementation of social thinking. By ages eight to eleven, he suggests, children are able to view simple social episodes from the perspective of others.

Implicit in role organization is the projecting of a social role that is concordant with the knowledge that others have or assume of us. This role projection protects our vulnerable self and cues others to reinforce the aspects of ourselves that we value. We effect different roles with each person with whom we interact—our boss, neighbor, child, and spouse. The role projections are related to the degree of intimacy, the information one wishes to conceal (perhaps ethnicity, nationality, job, school placement, relatives, blemishes, disability or social class), and the image one wishes to project. As a result, we underplay or exaggerate, hide or expose past history and aspects of the self, depending on the person to whom we are acting our social roles. In social encounters we convey information that leads to others' judgment about our age, sex, race, social class, rank, occupation, education, nationality, regional origins, religious group, and family connections (Argyle, 1975). These assignations are conveyed by physical appearance, style and content of language, body stance, and the behavioral response that we adopt to people of the same and different categories.

In other words, we adopt one behavior for neighbors, another for same-sex friends, yet another for opposite-sex friends, bosses, servants, people of different ages, and so on. Children use one kind of language with peers, another with their parents, and another with educators. As Bluebond-Langner (1978, p. 212) points out, adult acquaintances who encounter one another inquire about activities, "What are you doing these days?" However, when they meet a child, they typically ask him what grade he is in. Not only is this descriptive of the different behavioral responses, adult-adult and adult-child, but it indicates our definition of children's social role as being school attenders. Children in our culture do not attend school solely to learn, but to actualize their social role, to be where their peers are.

Since others judge us by our appearance, language, gesture, and surroundings and by their preconceptions of persons in our category, a learning disabled person frequently is judged as competent on initial encounter. He then says the wrong thing and is clumsy, forgetful, inadept, illiterate, frustrated, or stubborn, so that peers and adults feel anxious and resentful that he has defaulted the role image they had of him. His uneven presentation of self and his confusing repertoire of competencies and incompetencies make it difficult for them to construct an altered image. The atypical information about his social role, that of a special education student, further contributes to a role organization that is discordant, or, as Goffman (1967) describes it, "out of face."

He may well lack the linguistic facility and ability to anticipate others' behavior so as to enable him to "save face" and hurt feelings by withholding some information about the self on certain occasions and presenting other information that will result in positive messages to the self. He may not recognize which person will praise modesty, from whom he can seek compliments, or who will respond to apologies. He may fail to avoid topics and activities that are inconsistent with the self he currently is portraying, as well as with the value system and current mood of his interactors, or fail to change subject or activity if it threatens the self or others. He may produce statements that result in affirmation of his bad or useless self, rather than protecting himself from such assaults, particularly when he is feeling vulnerable. He may not have separated his beliefs into those that represent his existential self and those of lesser consequence. As a result, he may feel that alteration of a minor belief, in order to conform to another's point of view, is a betrayal of self; hence, he adopts a rigid stance.

Parrill-Burnstein and Hazan-Ginsburg (1980) found that learning disabled children were unable to take the perspective of others, and Weitman (1974) found that high-achieving disabled subjects could do so but that low-achieving learning disabled could not. As a result, in conversational interchanges a learning disabled person may not necessarily define his social role, because he may fail to adjust his conversation to the age and status of his interactor; therefore, if he does not converse as a student does to a principal, an employee to his boss, or a husband to his wife, how, indeed, are others to conceptualize his role in specific contexts?

Similarly, being egocentric, he may not have considered it important to glean sufficient information about family members or other interactors in order to learn the areas of sensitivity idiosyncratic to that category of person (for instance, women's not wanting their age revealed) and specific to a particular person. As a result, he is unlikely to devise interactions that will save his interactor's face and feelings. There are numerous anecdotal descriptions of the tactless exchanges that learning disabled persons have had with others and of the personal, embarrassing, or taboo quality of the information they share or observations they make.

When we lack perspectivism, our interpersonal behavior is imperceptive, or, as Watzlawick, Beavin, and Jackson (1967) describe it, "impervious." They suggest: "For smooth, adequate interaction to occur, each party must register the other's point of view. Since interpersonal perception goes on on many levels, so, too, can imperviousness go on on many levels. For there exists for each level of perception a comparable and analogous level of possible imperception or imperviousness. Where a lack of accurate awareness, or imperviousness, exists, the parties in a dyad relate about pseudoissues" (pp. 76–77). As a result, the egocentric learning disabled person will demonstrate a shallowness of interactional content that will reflect neither his own essence nor that of his interactor.

One infers the state or characteristics of another person because the circumstances, behavior, or reactions of the individual are similar to those which the perceiver has personally experienced at some time in the past. The learning disabled person who has had fewer experiences, has not organized his experiences into schemata, or who fails to notice the behavior of others as having critical import will not demonstrate other-centered behavior or make logical inferences about the mood or behavior of others.

Visual/Spatial Processing

Argyle (1975, p. 157) notes that the visual-gestural channel plays a more fundamental role in communication than the linguistic. When a message is discordant, in that the body language and words convey different meanings, the nonverbal message will be the one believed. Nonverbal gestures normally are learned at the same time as language. Body movement, facial expression, and gesture can be utilized to augment, complement, clarify, or negate the words being expressed. For example, studies by Exline and Winters (1965) and by Mehrabian (1969) indicate that a speaker who is not telling the truth looks at a listener less, uses less gestural and body movements, talks less, and smiles more.

Interactions proceed only when they are reinforced by the interactor—such reinforcement being primarily nonverbal. Listeners provide commentary and reinforcement by facial expressions, mouth movements, nodding, smiling, shaking their heads, and mirroring their interactor's body movements (Kendon, 1972). Argyle (1975) points out that the signals which signify listener attention and interest are proximity; attentive posture; head nods at the end of clauses, intermittent gaze, smiles, and other responsive facial expressions; and body movements which are coordinated with those of the speaker.

The visual channel provides feedback on the style, color, quality, neatness, and type of dress of others, the sophistication and color of their hairdo, and the objects they wear and are carrying. A person's physical appearance suggests age, social class, wisdom, degree of conformity, extent of sophistication, conservatism, degree of extroversion, interests, intellectual pursuits, sexual persuasion, and so on. Through visual processing we assume a great deal about people from the state and contents of their homes. In a similar fashion, we surmise the quality and relative expensiveness of stores and restaurants and can guess the content of a book from its cover.

The visual/spatial channel assists us in creating assumptions concerning the relative importance of someone by the use of space in relationship to him—the oversize desk, the large office, the dais. We learn through visual/spatial observation how much space to keep between us and the person beside us, depending on whether he is an intimate, a casual acquaintance, or a stranger. We learn how to signal that we want to pass someone on the street and the spatial rules for lining up at the theater or standing in a bus. We come to know the distance to maintain when conversing with someone, depending on our relationship to him or her; when and how frequently to touch; and when hand shaking, hand holding, and light or prolonged kissing are permissible and expected. We learn to distinguish body contact as being aggressive, affiliative, sexual, or nurturant.

Argyle (1967) suggests that we learn to distinguish the expressions of happiness, surprise, fear, sadness, anger, disgust, contempt, and interest and that such information is collected through gazing. He suggests that the emotional states that can be perceived through body gesture are aggression, anxiety, self-blame, tiredness, relaxation, and interest. In the absence of speech, interactional forms such as silence, ignoring, or turning away must convey the entire message.

Youth who are poor visual/spatial processors or those with short interest spans may not notice the body language that clarifies the verbal and may not process the body signals that suggest lying, sarcasm, humor, doubt, distrust, disgust, pain, and so on. As Bryan (1977), Bachara (1976), Wiig and Harris (1974), and Wilchesky (1980a) found, such individuals may process expressions of emotion as the opposite of the emotion being expressed, whereas, as Wiig and Harris noted, intact adolescents make substitutions that are similar. The dichotomous perceptions of the learning disabled are not typical in that intact persons may confuse anger with fear or disgust but not with happiness or surprise (Argyle, 1967). Wiig and Harris found that the number of correct interpretations of emotions correlated positively with scaled scores on Block Design and Object Assembly on the Wechsler Intelligence Scale for Children. In my clinical practice, I found eight-year-old learning disabled children who were unable to differentiate smiles from frowns and twelve-year-old children who were unable to differentiate more subtle expressions of emotion. Bachara (1976) suggests that inability to interpret emotional expressions of affect hinders one's ability to empathize with others. Parrill-Burnstein and Baker-Ward (1979) found that children with heterogeneous learning disabilities were not as adept as children with language learning disabilities or controls in recognizing faces or retaining nonverbal social cues until they were taught memory strategies such as noticing unusual facial features. Pearl, Donahue, and Bryan (1980) found that learning disabled girls in grades 1 and 2 were less likely to revise their message in response to puzzled facial expressions than were control females, although learning disabled boys in the same grades were more responsive to facial feedback than controls.

The disturbances that some learning disabled persons experience in the processing of affect and of the body in space may create distortions in comprehension, so that benevolent intent is interpreted as malevolent. Such a child may cringe at an arm coming toward him, though the intent was a hug. He may not recognize silence and its accompanying body language or body messages that convey irritation, impatience, or a wish to be left alone. Once the child recognizes his inefficiency in judging intent, he may become withdrawn. This will compound his isolation, since the child with poor visual/spatial orientation has difficulty finding his way around the city in any event and therefore is reluctant to travel to friends' homes or to activities.

The learning disabled person who has not noticed others' facial and body expressions will lack models on which to mold his own body language. As a result, his movements may appear clumsy, constricted, or overemphasized. He may use his hands too extensively or intrusively. Bryan, Sherman, and Fisher (1980) noted a greater number of hand movements in an unstructured task. The learning disabled person's entire body may respond to stimuli with arms and legs moving, the plasticity of movement resembling the response of an infant. He may stand too close to people, with their resultant discomfort, or distance himself too extensively, thereby implying that he is less friendly than he means to suggest. He will not be able to rely on his gestures to convey the role he wishes to assume or the deceptions he wishes to further.

The person who does not notice a great deal of his visual/ spatial world may not be aware of or process the cues—from clothing and other accouterments, grooming, furnishing, and use of space—that signify age, social class, financial status, emotional state, vocation, avocation, and rank. Neither will he be able to determine the level of sophistication of an invitation to a party from the lettering, or of a store or restaurant from the window decorations. He may fail to reinforce others' conversation through positive body language and mimicry. When recognition of the facial and body attributes that suggest personal characteristics is deficient, the learning disabled person will be hampered in selecting compatible friendships. Similarly, persons who have not noticed the use of space through which successive degrees of proximity are achieved as increasing increments of intimacy are attained will find it difficult to deepen relationships.

The poor visual/spatial processor often does not notice the current clothing style adopted by his peer group, whether it be dress for school, summer camp, a party, or a proposal of marriage. As a result, his attire might resemble the style of his parents' generation. He typically presents himself as further differing from his peers by his sloppiness, his bulging pockets, unlaced shoes, partially untucked shirt, sweater on which holes and buttons are not synchronized, and his propensity to carry a briefcase whereas his fellow students have their books under their arms. He may be clumsy in sports and confuse the spatial organization of the playing field so that he scores points for the opposing team.

As he matures, he may miss the cues that denote others' interest in his friendship, including sexual interest. He may be equally inadept in conveying his sexual interest to others and in perceiving and executing the sequence of steps that signify the willingness for increasing physical and sexual intimacy. Wiener (1978) found that children ages eight to twelve with visual/spatial deficits were relatively well behaved in the classroom. They demonstrated good comprehension, creative initiative, and attention to tasks. They did not seem to demonstrate the significant problems of attention and impulse control that characterized the children in the sample who had language or sequential disabilities. Nonetheless, they experienced significant problems in developing positive peer relationships. Bryan (1977) found that learning disabled children were less accurate than controls in the comprehension of nonverbal communication. Bryan and Perlmutter (1979) found that learning disabled children's nonverbal behaviors resulted in the least favorable impression by observers. Goffman (1963, p. 35) comments on body messages: "Although an individual can stop talking, he cannot stop communicating through body idiom; he must say either the right thing or the wrong thing. He cannot say nothing. Paradoxically, the way in which he can give the least amount of information about himself—although this is still appreciable—is to fit in and act as persons of his kind are expected to act." Body messages, then, are powerful conveyors of social information. Deficits in visual/spatial encoding or decoding can consequentially reduce or distort the social information that is imparted or perceived.

Gaze

Patterns of gaze play an important role in establishing relations between people. Gaze provides the match between encoding and decoding. Exline and Winters (1965) found that people look more at those they like. Rubin (1973) noted that the extent of mutual gaze was proportionate to the amount that couples were in love, gaze being used as a courtship signal. Mehrabian (1969) found that if a subject was looked at more, he, in turn, liked the person who was gazing at him better. As Goffman (1963) points out, the eyes are used to convey considerable information: a willingness to interact, avoidance of interaction, unity emotionally or for a cause, alienation, withholding of information, catching one's eye, ignoring someone or signifying that one does not know someone or does not understand the content of the information being conveyed, and the staking of a claim on the sidewalk or parking space. The ways in which gazing is utilized and the extensiveness of gaze vary with the number of people in an interaction and the interactional setting.

Bryan, Sherman, and Fisher (1980) found that learning disabled children used less face-to-face behavior when talking. This caused peers and a group of mothers to view the learning disabled children as less adaptable and more socially hostile than controls. The poor use of gaze may serve to disconfirm the learning disabled person's language and cause others to view him as shifty, untruthful, unaffectionate, and untrustworthy.

Linguistic Features

Linguistic competence subsumes a vast array of skills, primarily developmental but also heavily influenced by the linguistic competence of family members. As a result, social/linguistic competence must really be measured in relationship to family linguistic competence, just as the communication style must be related to the subculture.

Pragmatic Language. By the time a child enters kindergarten, he is able to follow verbal directions, can count, and knows the days of the week and the months of the year. He can listen to and remember a story, describe an experience, and process increasingly complex language. The language learning disabled child mishears or forgets what people say, cannot remember what he is supposed to do, and loses the thread of verbal information if language is complex or extended. He may have trouble with descriptive language, particularly if he is not able to look at the object he is describing. He may forget words or relate a story in so disorganized a fashion that it is incomprehensible. His auditory imperception causes him to misperceive linguistic material, thus relating it to the wrong schemata and creating erroneous inferences. The most noticeable social consequence of pragmatic incompetence is the anxiety and insecurity that it engenders, which reduces one's willingness to use language for social encounters. However, deficits in the comprehension or utilization of interactional language have direct impact on social adequacy as well.

Cooperative Interaction. Recent studies have demonstrated that even very young children have a sophisticated repertoire of conversational skills (Bates, 1976; Donahue, Bryan, and Pearl, 1980; Donahue, Pearl, and Bryan, 1980; Dore, Gearhart, and Newman, 1978; Erwin-Tripp and Mitchell-Kernan, 1977; Keenan, 1974). These studies suggest that the ability to be a cooperative conversational partner depends on social as well as linguistic knowledge. Mutual conversants enter into an elaborate social contract, in which both follow established conventions governing conversation. These include the ways of initiating and terminating a conversation, managing the orderly exchange of conversational turns, knowledge of when to interrupt or change the topic, ways of introducing and monitoring topics, ways of repairing communication breakdowns, and ways whereby background knowledge and novel information are shared. An adequate conversationalist attempts to ensure that his interactor comprehends the information when required. He is adept at including or excluding others who appear on the scene and, by the form of his inclusion and the degree of courtesy afforded, signifies the role of the third person. He knows with which types of strangers he can initiate conversations and to whom and in what circumstances he should apologize, even when he is not at fault. He is aware of the requisite length of a conversation and the number of times that repetition is reinforcing. Both the situation at hand and the quality of his relationship with his interactor dictate the degree of intimacy permitted in the interaction.

He is able, as well, to provide minimal reinforcement to conversations when he wishes them to terminate, or to indicate that the conversational message is unclear, so that his interactor will change the topic of conversation. He can use conversation to do favors for others, to enhance his self-image, to enhance others, and to accentuate the similarity between himself and others, thus effecting conformity (Jones and Wortman, 1973). He learns to comprehend and produce humor, puns, metaphors, sarcasm, and alliteration.

Many learning disabled persons appear to be unaware of some of the rules governing interactional language. Some appear not to realize that one interrupts language at the end of clauses, at pauses, or at lowering of the voice. Some feel that all conversational pauses should be filled in (Bryan, Sherman, and Fisher, 1980). Some fail to select topics of conversation that are mutually interesting or to notice their interactor's boredom and change the topic; neither do they appreciate the importance of avoiding similar topics of conversation with that person or class of person in the future. Some are uncertain as to the juncture at which a conversation should be initiated and when to persist. Some are unable to differentiate between repetition that is reinforcing and that which is perseverative and irritating; therefore, they are unable to exercise judgment about the number of times to repeat a statement in immediate succession or over time. Some possess limited, stereotyped conversational possibilities which appear appropriate on first encounter but wear thin after several exposures.

Bryan and Pflaum (1978) found that learning disabled children, possibly because of their linguistic limitations, appeared less able than controls to take the perspective of their interactors into account when formulating their messages. Garvey (1977) determined that young intact children in the role of listener request additional information about an unclear message; but Donahue, Pearl, and Bryan (1980) found that learning disabled children in grades 1 through 8 were less likely to request additional information when presented with a confused message. Pearl, Donahue, and Bryan (1980) found that children with internal locus of control for failure were more likely to request clarification than those who were external for locus of control. Pearl and associates felt that, to some extent, the learning disabled children failed to differentiate informative from uninformative messages; but, more important, these children failed to understand what the role of listener entails—that is, that conversational rules obligate listeners to take responsibility for initiating the repair of communicative breakdown. There is evidence that teachers' evaluations of children's cognitive abilities are affected by the students' understanding of the rules which govern classroom discourse (Shuy and Giffen, in press). Donahue, Bryan, and Pearl (1980) suggest that the failure of learning disabled children to understand the rules of conversational turn-taking also seems likely to add to their social rejection by peers.

Bryan, Wheeler, Felcan, and Henek (1976) found that children who ask for assistance receive it, that children who are cooperative also are helpful, and that rejection and competitiveness elicit rejection and competitiveness. The learning disabled children in their sample, especially males, made negative comments about their peers 33 percent more often than nondisabled children; they also received more negative statements. They asked the same number of questions of peers but their peers, in turn, did not solicit their assistance as frequently or speak to them with the same consideration as they demonstrated when addressing age mates who were more competent learners. The intact children challenged the learning disabled children with competitive statements, such as "I can do this better," more frequently than they dared their other classmates. Learning disabled males were the most likely to be ignored by peers; and learning disabled girls were the greatest recipients of mildly nasty statements from peers, whereas nondisabled females were least likely to receive such statements.

An important linguistic task is that of persuading others to adopt one's point of view. Bryan, Donahue, and Pearl (1980) found that learning disabled children in grades 3 to 8 were less persuasive than controls. Despite having had persuasive interactions modeled for them, they were less effective in convincing others to choose gift items and more frequently made "oddball" choices of items they deemed desirable. The authors found that learning disabled children failed to play dominant roles in conversation and were less likely to be group conversational leaders or to keep the group on task, and that learning disabled children across grades and sex were less likely than the nondisabled to be involved in group discussions. They noted that older learning disabled children could be more disruptive to the group process because they engaged in more off-task behavior. Learning disabled males, in particular, were discrepant from controls in their expressions of affect, such as amount of laughing. Some learning disabled persons appear to be unaware that communication can be used to bring about concordance in point of view; therefore, they do not state their case in a manner that would result in a complimentary response or agreement from their interactor.

Some learning disabled persons also tend to interpret language in a literal fashion. They take words at face value and ignore contextual cues. Although the literal interpretation of language and events in the learning disabled has not been researched, such literal behavior has been traced to brain damage in adults. Winner and Gardner (1977) found that adults with acquired damage in the right cerebral hemisphere comprehend metaphor literally.

Linguistic Complexity. Opie and Opie ([1959] 1976, 1969) describe the complex linguistic facility of British school children. They note that children use rhymes to regulate peer relationships and games. Rhymes allow them to save face in unexpected situations, to overcome awkward interactions, to fill in silences, to hide emotions, or to express excitement. Children use rhyme to underline the absurdity of the adult world, to mock danger and death, and to savor language. The Opies ([1959] 1976) suggest that oral rhymes which children inherit from other generations of children are essential to the regulation of their games and their relationship to each other. They note, as well, that the use of wit and parody affords children opportunities to demonstrate independence without having to rebel. The Opies suggest that business is conducted with peers through verbal declarations and that children assign nicknames to other children and adopt a common language of words, such as "neat." Wolfenstein (1955) found that when verbal humor, such as puns, becomes more prominent at the beginning of adolescence, jokes become subtler and employ more elaborate disguises for the expression of tabooed ideas. He observed, as well, that brighter children laugh more frequently, especially at absurd and incongruous situations, than do children of normal intelligence. It appears that children, through the use of linguistic complexity, are enabled to work through some developmental tasks in an acceptable and safe fashion as well as enjoy a rich and shared form of expression.

The child or adolescent who is friendless will miss the exposure to peer linguistic codes and lack opportunities to practice the language forms used by his age mates. The child who has difficulty with language memory may not remember the rules of games and will forget others' names, nicknames, and the peer "lingo." Children who lack linguistic versatility will be unable to use language as a developmental tool; or to express wit or humor; or to formulate rhyme, parody, riddles, puns, jokes, and wise sayings; or to engage in verbal dueling. Children who do not notice the linguistic patterns used by different ages and classes of persons or who are uncertain of what constitutes ages and classes may use inappropriate forms of conversation. Thus, a preadolescent or adolescent male might converse with a male peer in the manner of a female adult addressing another female adult—producing a litany of family members' diseases instead of engaging in a topic of interest to adolescents. Conversely, such a person might address adults in a communication style that is appropriate only for child-to-child interactions. Children who do not realize that language is used for personal gain—be it reinforcement to the self or winning an argument or point of view—and who do not realize that one's choice of language, tone of voice, pitch, or body stance produce a reaction in others will not use language in a directed fashion. Similarly, children who do not recognize the situations in which specific topics of conversation or particular words are and are not taboo will not honor the sanctions of the group by selecting acceptable euphemisms or alternate topics of conversation.

Learning disabled persons who have not learned the many possible behaviors that one might use in a social situation tend to resort to the same greeting or topic of conversation whenever they encounter someone. For example, one man's acquaintances knew that he had a phrase that he used whenever he met them, regardless of how many times a day he saw them. Such stereotypical behavior irritates interactors who generally avoid the perseverative person. It also tends to elicit a similar response from interactors time after time. As a result, the learning disabled person who already has a sparse interactional repertoire reduces his exposure to alternative behaviors. Furthermore, his knowledge of others is confined to the behaviors they use in relationship to him. We never can know others completely; however, the more varied the behaviors we can bring to others, the more varied the responses we will elicit, which results in more comprehensive knowledge of them.

By approximately the age of four, intact children have mastered most of the complexities and rules of their native tongue. In a few more years, they possess the entire linguistic system (Farb, 1973). Consequently, when one encounters persons from early childhood onward, the expectation is that they will be linguistically adequate. When persons violate the rules of language, we presume that the violation is purposeful and take the content of their language less seriously, become impatient, or devaluate their status.

Attention

Social involvement refers to the capacity of an individual to devote his concerted attention to an activity, conversation, or collaborative work effort. It implies a commitment on the part of the interactor. Adept interaction requires the interactor to form judgments as to which involvements are dominant and which subordinate (Goffman, 1963). He must note and appraise the shift in cues that signifies the demotion of a dominant involvement to a subordinate position. At a party he may be conversing with someone (dominant), yet still process key words from surrounding conversations (subordinate). Once his current conversation seems to have run out of interesting material, he terminates it (subordinate) and joins a group of speakers who sound more promising (dominant). Similarly, persons who have reached the level of automatic functioning in many of their activities can divide their attention between main and side involvements. They can tie their shoelaces while conversing, knit while watching television, and listen to a conversation on the telephone while attending to other social cues.

Warr and Knapper (1968, p. 17) describe the importance of selective attention in social processing: "It is manifest that in making judgments of our physical or social environment we do not process all of the information available to us. Indeed, we probably learn to select only certain aspects of other people [and events] . . . [and] to discard less relevant stimulus information. . . . [There needs to be] some form of 'input selector' which governs the information which is in fact processed. . . . Some aspects of the stimulus will be sufficiently salient to warrant selection, whereas others will not be noticed." Mackworth (1976) posits that selective attention becomes relatively efficient and stable by about seven years of age.

The learning disabled person who has had to pay disproportionate attention to remembering what people are saying, who has to hide the fact that he cannot remember the name of a relative or well-known acquaintance or conceal his poor memory for faces, will have less energy to devote to the salient features of his interactions. Therefore, problems in selective attention are compounded by embarrassment and anxiety. In a similar fashion, the learning disabled person who must concentrate on finding his way around the city or who is ashamed because he cannot find his classroom or locker will have little surplus energy to devote to interaction. The child who must focus on tying his shoe cannot attend to conversation at that moment.

When we listen to language, we typically phase in and out but manage to attend to a sufficient number of significant words, inflections, and gestures so that we can extract meaning. The child who phases in on inconsequential words such as "the" and "is" or who is poor at effecting closure will have poor comprehension. The learning disabled person who attends to extraneous rather than salient features of interaction—be they visual, spatial, or auditory—or who fails to make speedy shifts from subordinate to dominant as social cues change will be socially inappropriate. The person with a short interest span will fail to notice some social modeling.

Bryan and Sherman (1980) found that the negative perceptions that adults had of learning disabled children accrued from their briefness of gaze and smiling behavior. Emery (1975) found that learning disabled children demonstrated difficulty in the processing of moving visual stimuli. Bryan (1979) reported that learning disabled males and nondisabled males were equally likely to model prosocial behavior but that the learning disabled boys had greater difficulty in remembering the actions and words of the models. Mercer and associates (1975) found learning disabled children's modeling performance to be positively correlated with academic achievement. Parrill-Burnstein and Hazan-Ginsburg (1980), in an experiment in which learning disabled children verbalized about a pictured social theme, found that children with heterogeneous learning disabilities integrated the social situation less adequately, had more trouble inferring thoughts and feelings, and attended to more peripheral details. Bryan, in her 1979 monograph on social inadequacy in the learning disabled, comments: "In no study did the results support the stereotype of learning disabled children as hyperactive, emotionally labile, or disruptive. Rather, the results find differences between learning disabled and nondisabled children to fall in categories related to attention. Learning disabled children appear to learn to look reasonably busy, not be disruptive, not get into trouble, and not work. Even when nondisabled children with similar academic achievement show wide ranges in attending behavior, learning disabled children are still found not attending as much" (pt. 1, p. 20).

Three pieces of research relate to some extent to social attention. Schumaker, Sheldon-Wildgen, and Sherman (1980) noted that learning disabled adolescents were more disruptive than controls in the classroom. Parrill-Burnstein and Hazan-Ginsburg (1980) found that children with language learning disabilities recognized fewer faces than those with heterogeneous learning disabilities and controls and also demonstrated the greatest difficulty in discriminating faces previously seen, and spontaneously formulating and using appropriate strategies for face recognition. When they were taught strategies, recognition improved, although not to the level of controls. However, it did improve with age. Lund and colleagues (1980) found differences in learning disabled children's response to visually presented material, although whether the differences are attributable to attention, memory, or judgment has still to be determined.

Interpersonal Cognitive Problem Solving

Flavell (1974) delineates four developmental stages in the acquisition of sophisticated social perception:

Stage one (prior to five years of age). Child has only a rudimentary understanding that others can have a different visual experience from his own. He is able to identify a few simple emotions in others, such as happy or sad.

Stage two (approximately five to seven years of age). The child begins to have an awareness that others may have thoughts that differ from his. He is able to discriminate others' actions as being accidental or intended.

Stage three (eight to eleven years of age). The child is able to view simple social episodes from the other individual's perspective. He is able to infer the feelings of others, even when they are in situations that are largely unfamiliar to him.

Stage four (twelve years of age). The child begins to make less use of surface characteristics in describing others and pays more attention to inferred inner experiences and social relations between people.

Selman, Jaquette, and Lavin's (1977, pp. 264–274) stages of interpersonal awareness deal, as well, with perceptions of friendship and interpersonal behavior:

Stage one (five to eleven years of age). The child realizes that it is intentions, not just physical abilities, that determine whether a friend is trustworthy. Trust is equated with convincing a friend to do one's bidding. He defines loyalty as unilateral obedience to the dictates of a leader or other members of the group.

Stage two (seven to fourteen years of age). The child sees trust as an equalizing reciprocity between the self-interests of friends. Group loyalty is seen as an exchange of favors or "liking one another."

Stage three (twelve years of age to adulthood). Trust is perceived as a sharing in and supporting of each other's intimate and personal concerns. Group loyalty is seen as an individual contribution to an ongoing communal whole, an all-for-one loyalty.

Stage four (adolescents and adults). Friendship is viewed as an ongoing process, in which trust means an openness to change and grow, as well as stability in a relationship. Group loyalty is seen as a contractual agreement to relinquish one's personal pursuits for the sake of the group's collective goals.

Piaget (1926) suggests that the child must progress from a "one-track" mentality to one in which he is able to operate flexibly and reversibly from one perspective to another. The realization that an object and a person may appear differently if viewed from a different perspective is a critical feature of both cognitive and social development (Light, 1979). Spivack, Platt, and Shure (1976, pp. 5, 6) suggest that there is a grouping of interpersonal cognitive problem-solving skills (ICPS) that mediates the quality of our social adjustment. These skills are described as "an awareness of possible interactional problems and sensitivity to the potentiality for or existence of a problem; the willingness to notice that an interaction has soured; the capacity to generate alternative solutions to problems; an articulation of the step-by-step means necessary to arrive at a solution; and a consideration of the consequences of one's social acts in terms of their impact upon oneself and others, an ability to visualize consequences."

Competence in interpersonal cognitive problem solving requires an ability to assess one's interpersonal skills and to examine oneself in relation to others. One must be able to generate a variety of possible solutions from different categories of options and select the most appropriate. One must be able to organize one's imagery and behavior sequentially, project possible obstacles and reactions, and devise alternative behaviors as well as imagining alternative consequences. Finally, there is an understanding that one's own feelings and actions may have been influenced, and, in turn, may influence how others feel and act.

Spivack, Platt, and Shure suggest that a deficit in ICPS could occur as part of a general deficiency in intellectual stimulation or as a consequence of family dynamics. However, anyone can experience episodic lapses in ICPS as a result of stress.

Although there has been some research on the relationship between social cognition and impulsivity, hyperactivity, and frustration tolerance, the social cognitive ability of learning disabled persons has been largely unresearched. Muus (1960) and Ojemann (1967) demonstrated that the ability to relate social behavior to social outcomes relates positively to frustration tolerance and to tolerance of ambiguity. Ten- to twelve-year-old boys who were taught alternative ways of handling frustration improved in ability to cope with frustration over those who did not receive instruction. Luria (1959) reported that hyperkinetic, impulsive children lack proficiency in verbal control tasks. Meichenbaum (1977); Bates and Katz (1970); Harrison and Nadelman (1972); and Constantini, Corsini, and Davis (1973) demonstrated that impulsive children exert significantly less verbal control over behavior than reflective children do. Meichenbaum further found that reflective preschool children manifest significantly more outer-directed and self-regulatory speech than impulsive preschoolers. Moreover, he noted that the private speech of the reflective children was significantly more responsible to situational demands. Parrill-Burnstein and Hazan-Ginsburg (1980) found that children with heterogeneous learning disabilities changed hypotheses regardless of feedback. They continued to eliminate hypotheses when the correct response was to retain the hypothesis. Neither the heterogeneous learning disabled nor the language learning disabled children sampled other hypotheses from the stimulus array following negative feedback. Difficulty in responding appropriately to feedback hindered the experimental group's ability to solve problems.

Wiener (1978) found that the learning disabled children with conceptual disabilities in her sample frequently disrupted classroom routine. They created more disturbances than the children with visual/spatial disabilities and were more impatient and defiant than children with other types of learning disabilities. They appeared inattentive and withdrawn and demonstrated little initiative in contributing to the overall functioning of the classroom. They tended to quit easily and exhibited poor comprehension and low creative initiative. They manifested major difficulties in acquiring positive peer relationships and generalized strategies less than children with visual/spatial or sequencing deficits.

Those learning disabled persons who demonstrate problems in ICPS exhibit difficulties in planning and social judgment, whether on the level of choosing a friend, selecting an appropriate comment, joining in an activity that will have a comfortable outcome, or devising alternative courses of action when the current one proves to be less than optimal. Conceptual disabilities also can be manifested as gaps in knowledge and the persistence of misconceptions that are normally not seen in a person of that age. The concepts are applied in contexts where they are not applicable. Thus, some learning disabled children assume that, since eating results in growth, adults will continue to grow as long as they continue to eat. They may judge an acquired attribute, such as manners, to be an intrinsic attribute in which a specific amount is allocated to each individual; Susan believed, for example, that if a person uses manners indiscriminately they will run out before one's life is over. They may conclude, as Richard did, that when a person works overtime the day has more than twenty-four hours, or they may decide that bread and butter must be nourishing because one works hard to obtain them. The literal interpretation of language and auditory imperception may cause the learning disabled to create erroneous inferences, or they may assume relationships based on incidental rather than salient features. These conceptual distortions contribute to uncertainty, rigidity, and social imperception, which, in turn, creates further distortions in social processing. At times, harmless information is judged as being hostile or rejecting because it is taken literally or not seen from the interactor's perspective. Thus, the youth who was told that swimming would not hurt his blisters felt betrayed when they hurt in contact with the water.

Sequential Disabilities

Wiener (1978) found that many of the learning disabled children in her sample who had sequential disabilities behaved inappropriately in the classroom. They worked slowly and tended to create disturbances and demonstrate poor impulse control. They tended to blame others for their actions or errors. However, their social skills appeared good, and they exhibited fewer problems in developing positive peer relationships than the other learning disabled children.

Occasionally one happens upon a learning disabled person who exhibits a singular deficit that is manifested solely in one area of processing. More typically, one encounters learning disabilities in which the deficits are manifested in a number of areas of functioning. As a result, a learning disabled person's social disabilities typically reflect deficits in several areas of capacity.

Temperament and Other Personality Factors

Notwithstanding the presence of primary social disabilities, the learning disabled person's temperament and resultant behavior will exert considerable influence on his social competence. Many temperamental factors—such as quality of mood, degree of flexibility, length of interest span, ability to persist with a task, and activity level—appear to be congenital (Thomas and Chess, 1977). In addition, the learning disabled person's behavior will represent, to some measure, his family's and culture's reaction to his temperament and disability and his unique ability to cope with stress, to forgive, to enjoy life and friendships, and to persist in the face of failure. Some learning disabled children have been allowed to maintain socially unproductive behaviors because parents and teachers have been reluctant to upset them by correcting them. Similarly, they have found it easier to allow such children to persist in using these behaviors than to cope with rigid responses to suggested changes.

Learning Disabled Person's Interactions with the World

A number of studies have found that the immediate and sustained impressions of learning disabled children by parents, teachers, peers and strangers of different ages tend to be negative, particularly in response to nonverbal cues (Strag, 1972; Bryan and Sherman, 1980; Bryan, Sonnenfeld, and Greenberg, 1980; Bryan and Perlmutter, 1979; Bryan, 1974a, 1974b, 1975, 1976; Bryan, Wheeler, Felcan, and Henek, 1976). Perlmutter (1980) noted that observers form impressions about children in ten to twenty-five seconds.

One of the impediments that the learning disabled person has to altering the behavior to which others respond negatively is the absence of direct feedback. Most persons in our culture respond to social awkwardness with silence, avoidance, and subtle, implicit disapproval. The learning disabled person, in his possible oblivion to some forms of implicit social information, may not notice the disapproval. This may explain why he overrates his social status. Similarly, it is difficult for the learning disabled person to interpret his interactor's withdrawal, since withdrawal might signify aversion to his behavior, a need to be alone, or an indication that he just is not that person's "type." We tend not to clarify our withdrawal, particularly with disabled persons, so that the learning disabled person has little explicit accessible information for the creation of more acceptable social skills.

Friendship. Davis (1973) suggests that people seek friendships for stimulation, for sharing the surplus emotional residue of private experience (griefs, joys, fears, hopes, suspicions, anger), and thereby increasing enjoyment and decreasing one's discomfort. He posits that we use friendships to prove ourselves against others and to participate in activities with others. The boring, perseverative learning disabled person may be a poor source of stimulation. If he is egocentric, does not process others' expressions of emotions accurately, or share his own feelings, he will not be someone with whom feelings can be mutually exchanged. He will not reinforce positive behavior or relay compliments. If he is not versatile linguistically, a competent game player, or academically proficient, he may not be considered to be someone with whom one might compete. If he has been sheltered and his experiences limited, he may not be aware of the recreational possibilities available in his community and unskilled in availing himself of them. If he is constricted, he may not generate exciting possibilities for mutual activities.

When persons respond to our overtures of friendship, they confirm our concept of self. As a result, it is more difficult for the low-status person to acquire friends because his peers and their families seek high-status friendships as confirmation of their own personal worth. However, Siperstein, Bop, and Bak (1977) found that learning disabled children who were athletic or attractive were valued for those attributes. The child who appears to lack peer-valued attributes may find that the early adolescent years are particularly lonely. That is the age at which his peers and siblings strongly feel that their friends and relatives are a reflection of their own worth as others perceive them and therefore make extra effort to avoid the contamination of his friendship.

Hartup (1979), in researching children's social behavior, found that the peer system involves complex structures and hierarchies. The ranking of an individual within the system often determines how other children relate to him. A child who is low in the peer hierarchy may have little or no opportunity to develop leadership skills. As a result, a learning disabled child's status may influence his ranking, and his ranking position itself may affect the acquisition of social competence and peer acceptance.

In order to initiate a friendship, one must know how to (1) establish an encounter, (2) initiate a conversation, (3) pick up on verbal or nonverbal information that could be of interest, (4) arrange successive encounters, (5) select appropriate meeting places and activities, (6) share intimate material, (7) carry out partings. One must be able to differentiate behavior that is permissible with an acquaintance from behavior that one might indulge in with an intimate, such as silence, reading, sleeping, daydreaming, and burping. One must learn how to recognize the cues from others that signify a willingness to achieve increased increments of intimacy. One must be able to differentiate between behavior that is suitable for initiating a friendship and that used to sustain a friendship.

As we become increasingly familiar with others, we construct an image of them from information accrued over time. We develop assumptions about their physical appearance and its meaning to them, their behavior such as face-saving and protecting others' sensitivities, interactional style, quality of mood, and reactions to stress. We learn social information such as age, address, birthplace, ethnicity, socioeconomic status, place and kind of employment, educational and marital status, and information about family members. Friends learn each others' biographies by fitting the anecdotes that are randomly related into an ordered temporal sequence.

The learning disabled person who is a poor observer or one who has a sparse store of information will not make many assumptions about others. The person who fails to notice the informational possibilities that arise in conversation limits himself to a narrow format, thus losing opportunities to learn to know others comprehensively. For example, he might ask where an item was purchased and merely reply "Oh" when told that it was bought in Spain. A more expansive person might query when his interactor was in Spain, what made him go, what he saw, what his impressions were, whether he has traveled to other countries, and the ways he typically spends his summers when he is not traveling. The learning disabled person who is poor in the sequencing of time or in knowledge of life stages will have difficulty in ordering an acquaintance's anecdotes into a sequential biography and developing an imagery of them occurring throughout his friend's life span. The learning disabled person who is lost in space and does not know the state in which he resides; the location of that state in his country, or the country's position in the world will be unable to infer much about a friend's personal history from knowledge of his place of origin and current residence.

Wilchesky (1978) found that his experimental group of nine-year-old learning disabled children at a specialized camp, when asked with which friend they would share activities, selected the same child, regardless of activity. However, the control group selected different children, depending on the activity they wished to pursue. This suggests an immaturity in the learning disabled campers' selection of friends, because they failed to take the differential interests and skills of their cabinmates into account. This impreciseness in selection is likely to result in increased rejections by peers who are approached to engage in activities in which they have neither skill or interest.

Undoubtedly, learning disabled persons desire and need friends just as their peers do. Bader (1975) refers to them as "unsuccessful extroverts." Bryan (1974b) found that learning disabled children in a laboratory setting were more generous than controls. She suggests (1979) that their generosity may reflect an attempt to repair their image. Bryan, Donahue, and Pearl (1980) found that learning disabled children are more likely to agree to others' suggestions and less likely to disagree with others or argue against others' choices than controls.

Nonetheless, it appears that the learning disabled may be less skilled in ingratiating themselves with others. Bryan, Donahue, and Pearl (1980) found them to be more disruptive than controls. Similarly, Bryan (1978) found that learning disabled children tried so hard to be helpful in teaching a game to others that they intrusively interfered with and obstructed the other children's attempts to play the game.

Intimacy. The issues of intimacy and sexual behavior essentially have been ignored as they relate to the learning disabled. This is unfortunate because there are many learning disabled persons who will not know how to choose a possible intimate, approach him or her, recognize signs of interest or disinterest, create increasing increments of intimacy, or know when to suggest a long-term commitment. Similarly, they may not know how to convey interest in and be sympathetic to the values, accomplishments, failure, fears, aspirations, and identifications that their partners project. They may not be skilled in negotiating differences or in compromising their position. They may share little of their feelings, their language may not convey caring and sharing, and their actions may not support their intimate's saving of face or protect his secrets.

If they lack friends, they also will lack knowledge of possible sources of dates, dating dress, and behavior. They will be exposed to few models of appropriate expressions of intimacy. The clumsy person or the one whose body image is uncertain may experience considerable embarrassment and ineptitude in physical expressions of love. The person with language processing problems may not remember information from conversations that his boy or girl friend considers important and may not have the language of courtship in his repertoire.

Extent of Our Knowledge

Empirical research and clinical anecdotal material appear to support the hypothesis that persons with some types of learning disability evidence social ineptitude. However, Deshler and others (1980) found that learning disabled adolescents differed from low-achieving adolescents only on two of fifteen variables related to peer relationships in self-reporting and parent reporting instruments. They reported being asked to go out with a peer less frequently, although their parents reported that they asked their peers to go out more frequently than the low-achieving and normally achieving youth. Both the learning disabled and low-achieving students reported having younger friends than the normally achieving adolescents. Some of the social inadequacies noted with preadolescent children may be compensated for by adolescence. However, since delineation of learning disabled populations differs in research studies, and Deshler and associates did not look at subclusters of disability, it is possible that their experimental group contained socially adequate adolescents, or adolescents who did not assess their social adequacy with accuracy. Since they did not examine the quality of the interactions in their experimental group, it is possible as well that some differences might have emerged in those contexts. In any event, the persistence of social inadequacy into adulthood has been reported (Anderson, 1972; Siegel, 1974; Gordon, 1969) but has yet to be researched.

Virtually no research on the manifestations and etiology of social ineptitude in the learning disabled occurred before the 1970s. In many instances, the selection of an experimental group as being learning disabled appears to have been somewhat arbitrary, which is understandable in the absence of a universally acceptable definition of the disability. In other instances, the research design appears questionable. The subgrouping of disability clusters in the examination of specific social attributes and the differentiation of male and female social behavior appear to be particularly promising, but greater homogeneity of cluster assignment must be attained. More sophisticated and careful research is needed on behavioral manifestations of social ineptitude, types of disabilities associated with specific areas of social disability, environments in which the ineptitude occurs, and conditions in which improvement is noted. However, there is a sufficient research base on which programs can begin to be built.

Chapter 7

�֎ ✖ ✖ ✖ ✖

Planning, Implementing, and Evaluating Remedial Programs

✖ Until the past decade, remediation of social inadequacy in exceptional persons was oriented almost solely toward those with considerable intellectual limitations, such as the mentally retarded, or those with profoundly maladaptive behavior, such as the autistic. Of necessity, such programs focused on basic living skills and gross social behavior, such as wiping one's nose with a tissue. Only in recent years have persons with subtle social ineptitude and adequate capacity to acquire high-level social/cognitive strategies been included in social remedial programs. Therefore, it is reasonable to expect that they will respond to carefully conceptualized programs with considerable improvement in social adequacy, although the extent of improvement still cannot be predicted. The remedial premise for the learning disabled is that the client has not learned or has inadequately learned certain age-expected social behaviors, which must then be taught, generalized, and reinforced.

At the same time, inappropriate behaviors that have been used as substitutes, and reinforced by peers and adults, must be eliminated.

Since the remediation of interactional deficits in the learning disabled is so new, research into its effectiveness is in its infancy. Wiener (1978) studied the gains in social competency made by eight- to twelve-year-old children at a six-week therapeutic summer camp which incorporated several generalized and individual remedial approaches in teaching social competency. She found that the eight- to nine-year-old children demonstrated a significant increase in skill between pretest and one-year posttest ($t = 6.2, df = 16, p < .01$), and they lost an insignificant amount of social skill between posttest and six-month follow-up. The ten- to twelve-year-old children did not demonstrate such dramatic gains in interpersonal problem-solving skills ($t = 2.6, df = 13, p < .05$), but they did not show a skill decrease between posttest and follow-up. Wilchesky (1980a) found that learning disabled children ages eight to twelve who were deficient in the processing of affect achieved comparable competence to that of controls after a five-week training period. Wiener's research seems to indicate that the extensiveness of response to social remediation is related to cognitive competence.

Program implementation is hindered by the lack of clarity surrounding definitions of social competence, particularly in relationship to children; the absence of standardized tests to assess social skills; the nonexistence of a body of social psychological literature describing children's interactions in our culture; and the paucity of research on the relationship between social skill building and increased social acceptability in the learning disabled. Whereas boards of education are funded to provide academic remediation, there is not, as yet, funding allocated for the teaching of social skills. There is also some confusion about which professionals— educators, social workers, or others—should undertake or supervise this task. Nonetheless, there is an emerging realization that such training is needed (Bader, 1975) and that program development must precede research and manage, for the present, without a research base. Social skill program planning for the learning disabled in North America has concentrated primarily on the building of more adequate social skills and secondarily on sensitizing peers to empathic and friendly attitudes toward the learning disabled, both being important foci. In either event, it is necessary to involve peers, family, and other significant persons in remedial planning and goal setting, so that they can act as reinforcers.

Remedial Priorities and Goals

Human social behavior is so complex that the task of teaching social adequacy may overwhelm the remediator. Just as in academics, remediation should address itself to a circumscribed number of deficits at a time, so that one must establish priorities. It is important to include the learning disabled person, his nuclear family members, and his teacher in delineating social remedial priorities. They certainly are aware of the social behaviors that are particularly nonproductive and irritating, and they should be able to articulate specific remedial goals. Once the initial remedial goals have been met, a new set of priorities can be established.

Bryan (1979) suggests that remediation should progress from the simple to the complex, from the concrete to the abstract, from the observable to the invisible. She points out that one should keep in mind the elements of a social interaction. This will entail the analysis of the message one communicates to others, verbal and nonverbal communications of others, and other situational constraints. For instance, it is insufficient to cue a child into other people's facial expressions without also instructing the child to examine the face he presents to the world. In the same vein, it is insufficient to teach the child to engage in social chit-chat if he chooses to do so when people wish to be left alone.

Remedial goals should be fourfold: (1) remediating social deficits, (2) altering the learning disabled person's environment to one where more adequate social skills are modeled and healthy environment promoted, (3) teaching of skills—such as motor coordination, grooming, and knowledge of games—that increase social acceptability, (4) teaching the client what the city has to offer recreationally.

It seems reasonable to assume that a program consisting solely of peer modeling will enjoy limited success, since, if learning disabled persons learned social skills through modeling, they already would be socially adequate. However, peer interaction should play a role in remediation because the goal is the acquisition of more adequate peer social skills. Consequently, a program model that promotes peer interaction and minimizes alternative uses of time, such as seeking adult attention, should be considered. In designing a program, one should include the following elements:

1. Determine whether the child has the prerequisite skills in his cognitive and behavioral repertoire before skill building is initiated.
2. Build skills in small increments with considerable repetition and generalization of material learned to real-life situations.
3. Include an informal component, such as a club group, where the emphasis is on peer interaction, but also incorporate a highly structured component that deals directly with social skill learning.
4. Relate training materials to the client's experience and problems. The more the program emulates the client's actual life experience, the greater the probability of success. Bryan (1979) suggests a life experience approach similar to that used in reading.
5. Do a task analysis of each client's deficit areas, in which concepts, processing, and affective knowledge are probed.
6. Choose a program model that will permit the greatest amount of social remediation. A model that also includes activities such as dancing or photography considered prestigious by the peer group is beneficial.
7. Clarify all language that is complicated, embedded, or ambiguous.
8. Make explicit all subtle, implicit interactional cues.
9. Place emphasis on rectifying deficits in the organization and planning of the client's social/temporal world.
10. Extinguish undesirable behaviors, with concomitant probing to determine whether the client is aware of alternative behaviors and knows how to use them effectively.

11. Supervise staff extensively to ensure that behaviors that should be discouraged are not reinforced; that staff make optimal use of situations that present themselves to promote social learning; that staff receive feedback on quality of job; that the supervisor models social behaviors that he wants utilized by staff; and that materials are used as jumping-off points rather than as ends in themselves.

A variety of remedial models have been reported to be effective. It appears that many possible vehicles can be utilized to achieve interactional improvement, as long as they allow clients to relate to their peers instead of overwhelmingly to an activity. Three types of models have been used: those in which the entire program emphasis is on a highly structured approach to social remediation; those that combine a structured component with a recreation component; and those in which the program is recreational but social deficits are corrected when they appear. The structured approaches have included the following models, used singularly or in combination: a highly structured, sequential coaching program; role playing; drama; puppetry; behavior modification; cognitive behavior modification; and interpersonal cognitive problem solving. Social/recreation models have included club programs, day and summer camps, film-making groups, clubs in which older learning disabled persons were leaders along with intact persons, and "Big Brother" or "Big Sister" programs.

If social/recreation models are used, they should promote knowledge of a variety of recreation possibilities, awareness of what the community has to offer recreationally, and ways of determining future recreation possibilities. They should also encourage clients to learn how to use public transportation. Clients should be involved in planning and hosting activities in which the group participates, in contacting group members by telephone to facilitate arrangements, and in critiquing programs later. Whichever model is utilized, the clients should be aware of the purpose of the program and the goals for each of the participants.

Group Goals. Notwithstanding the importance of an individual task analysis of social deficits, there tend to be several deficits that socially deficient learning disabled persons have in common.

Therefore, the program for the group as a whole can be addressed to the following shared needs:

1. Learning how to plan, execute, and evaluate a social encounter, whether it be a casual encounter, such as inviting a friend to one's house or to play outside, or a more structured one, such as going roller skating.
2. Determining how to handle a social situation and devising alternatives when one's approaches do not bring about the desired results.
3. Using the telephone to contact peers and adults (greeting, small talk, message conveyed, response to other's message, termination); telephoning for a specific purpose, such as ordering a pizza.
4. Planning the use of one's free time.
5. Learning how an isolated person can find activities in which to participate and socialize while avoiding traps for the lonely.
6. Sharing one's feelings when appropriate and being attuned to others' needs; using language to bring others around to one's point of view; keeping one's language on target rather than veering onto tangents.
7. Seeking friendships by being caring, interested in others and interesting to others, and being pleasant and well groomed rather than buying friendships, having others befriend one through pity, or agreeing to join activities against one's better judgment in order to curry friendship.
8. Developing sensitivity to others' social cues and providing the appropriate response; picking up on comments or pieces of information by which one can explore others' interests.
9. Reading body language.
10. Relinquishing unproductive behavior that often results from rigidity, disorganization, and poor judgment and replacing it with a more flexible and productive approach.

Individual Goals. Prior to the remediation of social deficits in learning disabled persons, it is important to have the remediator observe same-age persons in the neighborhood and work toward the shaping of similar behaviors. It also is essential to remember that the learning disabled person's social deficits probably are manifestations of several areas of disability, which must be taken into account in remediation. Someone who makes an erroneous inference as a result of auditory imperception may need remediation in both auditory discrimination and in taking social cues into context and account in determining a situation's meaning. In addition to direct teaching of social alternatives, therapeutic improvement can accrue when well-motivated clients are made aware of their deficit areas and of the principles of compensation. For instance, the person who does not notice visual detail can remind himself to be more observant of the visual/spatial facets of interaction as well as the nonhuman aspects of the physical world that convey social information and to take note of unusual features to assist memory. He can remind himself to associate visual features, such as a person's hairstyle or use of a pipe or cigarette holder, with other information that he has. He can also learn gracious methods of limiting embarrassment when he fails to recognize a close acquaintance. The person who forgets people's names can remind himself to say the name to himself, to visualize it as written, and also to make associations. Finally, it is helpful for the remediator to be able to determine the extent of the client's knowledge in his area of social deficit and the situations in which his inadequacy is manifested.

Stages of Social Functioning

Trower, Bryant, and Argyle (1978) have conceptualized a model of social functioning that can be useful for task analyses of deficit areas:

> *Stage one: Motivation and Social Goals.* These goals may include behaviors such as "making friends" and "influencing people" or more immediate and specific objectives, such as conversing with a neighbor.
> *Stages two and three: Perception and Translation.* These are the processes whereby the individual attends to and interprets relevant social information from the environment and translates the social precepts into plans of action through problem solving and decision making.

Stage four: Response. Once different courses of action have been evaluated and one alternative chosen, the individual then engages in an overt behavioral response. This implies that he has a number of possible responses within his behavioral repertoire which enable him effectively to implement the plan of action he has chosen.

Stage five: Feedback from the Environment. Based on the information received about the consequences of his actions, the individual may alter his original goal, change his perceptions and/or plans, and/or ultimately modify his behavior.

Remediation of Specific Deficit Areas

Organizational Ability. The disorganized learning disabled individual may rigidly persist with his inefficient methods of planning the use of time, tasks, and social encounters. When this is the case, his inflexibility must be dealt with, and he must become aware that his chaotic systems prevent him from reaching social, academic, and vocational goals. Organization itself can be taught through the development of an understanding of the ways whereby people plan their use of time and activities and work toward more distant goals.

Specific exercises might be the researching, planning, and executing of outings, activities, and parties for the group, with a sequential critique of the activity at termination. The telephone, telecommunicator, videotape, or role playing can be used to practice the organization of social encounters, be they job interviews, asking a girl for a date, or telephoning a friend to chat about school. Parrill-Burnstein and Baker-Ward (1979) found that children who were taught organizational strategies retained information better. Bryan, Donahue, and Pearl (1980) found that learning disabled children are less persuasive, more submissive, and less dominant in interaction; and Bryan, Wheeler, Felcan, and Henek (1976) found that their instructions are unclear, incomplete, confusing, and excessive. Training components therefore could include instructing others on execution of a task, on traveling to a destination, on preparing food, or on dressing for a date; leading a group discussion; and persuading others to adopt one's point of view.

Role Organization. Role organization can be taught through exposure to visitors or outings whereby prediction of the salient characteristics of people is attempted by noting the color, style, and condition of their clothing, as well as their hair styles, jewelry, makeup, stance, and language. Their probable age, vocation, mood, marital status, and sexual preference can be conjectured. Characters in moving pictures or television dramas can be used as illustrations of the primary roles and subroles assumed by individuals (when, for instance, a husband or wife is behaving as a spouse, parent, or child). The participants can use language in role playing to project momentary needs to make others responsive to those needs, as well as notice and respond to the needs that others project. Perception of affect can be taught through movies, television, photographs, outings, and videotapes of peer expressions of emotion. Sharing of one's own feelings can be role-played or dealt with in a discussion. The leader can respond to comments made in the course of activities with "How did that make you feel?" or ask participants how they suppose others feel in specific situations.

Intensity of Social Experiences. Social interactions vary in intensity from cursory to intimate. In a cursory interaction, participants are prepared to expend minimal energy, and the interaction deteriorates if one interactor exceeds the energy demands or introduces unexpected and uncomfortable information. So, if the learning disabled child climbs through his hostess's windows, or if the learning disabled person talks too long or repetitively about a topic to a casual acquaintance or in a cursory encounter, or if he introduces information of too personal a nature, he will have exceeded his interactor's preparedness to invest in the interaction, thus rendering it invalid. This also will happen if he misjudges his instructor's momentary willingness to become involved in an interaction. Role playing, drama, and real-life situations can be used to enable the participants to practice determining the social demands of situations—for example, appropriate topics of discussion with a teacher or a neighbor or a stranger on a park bench or in line at the supermarket; ways of responding to a query about what grade one is in, without creating anxiety in the interactor; the information one should and should not offer about one's disability and in which context; the behavior one should use in someone's home, based on the type of furnishing, decorating, and cleanliness (Is the furniture delicate antiques? Are homemade afghans and toys scattered around?), which provide clues to interests; ways of determining the type of social situation one is in, or will be in, and the probable expectations that one's interactor will have in regard to behavior; and the body language that signifies the extent to which an interactor is willing to invest in one.

Visual/Spatial Processing. Learning disabled persons who have difficulty in expressing themselves verbally often have equal difficulty with nonverbal expression. Activities such as charades, pantomime, and silent meals where gesture is substituted for speech may assist in nonverbal expression. The participants can state a message silently to themselves while the others guess its content from body language; one participant can state the message while another supplies the gestures; the television can have the sound turned down and the messages determined by the visual features; and the participants can provide feedback to one another on the appropriateness of their body language. The participants can engage in outings during which they guess the conversations of persons not within hearing distance, and predict the features of stores, restaurants, and neighborhoods. They can go into individual rooms in homes and generate predictions about the inhabitants by the features observed. Visual/spatial observation should be taught concomitantly with selective attention and role prediction.

Facial and Body Expressions. Minskoff (1980) suggests that children who are being taught to discriminate facial expressions initially should discriminate faces as being similar or dissimilar. Parrill-Burnstein and Hazan-Ginsburg (1980) suggest that the client should be taught to notice distinctive facial features. Imitation, mirrors, instant photographs, videotaping, filmstrips, and movies can reinforce teaching. Participants can label expressions, practice correct and incorrect facial expressions, and discuss the effectiveness with which their affect matches their intended message; they can act out situations in which body stance and facial features convey one message and the words suggest another message—for example, sarcasm—and determine the actual message. Their own facial expressions, gaze, and smiling behavior can be role-played and reinforced through behavior modification.

Gestures can be taught through contrasts, mime, silent role playing, shadow acting, and one person verbalizing while the other gestures. Clients can analyze and predict partial and complete situations portrayed through gesture.

Modeling, imitation, and the aforementioned modalities also can be utilized in the teaching of postures. The spatial arrangements of interaction and the meaning of proximity and distance can be taught through acting, role playing, pictures, movies, movie making, and naturalistic observation and discussion.

Linguistic and Paralinguistic Features. Wit, parody, rhyme, and puns can be learned to a lesser or greater extent through practice and through humor. Families can develop traditions of making their own greeting cards and using social opportunities for wit and punning. Literal interpretation of language can be reduced if the client is taught to consider the context before responding. Pontification, perseveration and the tendency to digress onto tangents can be reduced by practice conversations and by making the client aware of his tendency to emote, be repetitive, or lose the main point of the conversation. Various linguistic patterns of approaching and interacting with people can be modeled and practiced through drama and use of the telecommunicator both to achieve linguistic versatility and to learn to recognize the impact of one's behavior on others. Tactful use of language can be role-played and discussed. Cooperative interaction can be modeled and practiced, so that the client learns, for example, when to interrupt, when to allow pauses, when to ask for clarification, and when to reinforce an interaction. Clients can practice overtures to others that are positively reinforcing, rather than rejecting, and flattering, rather than demeaning; these interactions can, in turn, be reinforced by praise from the leader and peers. They can use language to convince others of the validity of their position, such as winning an argument, to have someone agree to join them in an activity, or to purchase something from them. Participants can learn to notice aspects of an interactor's demeanor or conversation that might indicate an area in which that person is interested and, thus, a possible topic of conversation. Initially, this observation can be practiced by study of newspaper and videotape interviews and then through role playing of meetings with peers at school, on the street, and at parties. Clients need to develop an appreciation of the acceptable ways of probing for information and the cues that signify an unwillingness to discuss a topic.

Participants can try to judge one another's mood and intent through assessing voice tone, pitch, and loudness and noting the junctures in language at which the voice is lowered or raised. They then can listen to their own voices on tape to determine whether their own tone, pitch, and loudness was consistent with the message they wished to convey. Yawns, sniffs, burps, and throat clearings can be interjected in the leader's and participants' role playing so participants can guess the messages that such gestures convey. In their wanderings around town, they can smell various odors— the perfumes that people wear, unwashed bodies, and cooking smells—and discuss the social information that they glean from these.

Attention and Memory. An interactor first must attend to the salient features of a social situation before he can understand it. Drama, the creation of films and videotape sketches, and role playing can be used to assist clients in learning to focus on those auditory and visual cues that are meaningful to his current social situation; he also can learn to shift those cues into the background and focus on other cues as his social situation changes. He might practice entering a room in which a party is in progress, stopping at the door to scan the furnishings and objects in the room and noting the age, dress, and degree of formality of the guests so that he has the information from which to select the behavior that is most likely to be acceptable. He then scans the room to determine whether he knows anyone, and, if not, whether anyone is alone and can be joined for a conversation. Once in a conversation, he relegates the surrounding conversations and sights to the periphery of his attention. However, when he nears the point where he wants to end his present conversation, he begins to listen to snatches of the other guests' conversations and watch their movements in order to select another interesting person or group to talk to.

Incidental social learnings that complement the party scene include the stage at which to join a person or group, methods of determining the host's and guests' interests through nonverbal and verbal cues, and the use of small talk directed to those interests. On another dimension, if the client's disability occupies his attention unduly so that he has less energy to devote to social encounters, he may need help in learning ways of solving problems in such situations as they arise. He would be able to adopt such short cuts as wearing loafers rather than cope with shoelaces, asking for assistance when he cannot read, or requesting help in finding his way around a building. Such tactics ensure that one's energy is not disproportionately directed to attempted mastery or to dealing with feelings of anxiety about failure and the feelings that failure evokes.

Just as it is important to differentiate the salient and extraneous features of social situations, it is equally important to select the visual, spatial, and auditory features that should be remembered and thus develop memory strategies. If the client has a deficit in auditory memory, he could practice tricks such as repeating aloud the name of a person he meets ("How do you do, John Jones?"), visualizing the name, asking himself what the name rhymes with or reminds him of, or associating the name with some feature or some known fact about the person. Because no memory trick is perfect, it is equally important for the client to learn gracious or humorous methods of informing someone that he has forgotten their name.

Practitioners typically remember their remedial failures even more than their successes, particularly if they have an amusing outcome. For example, at the camp for learning disabled children which I directed, Angie approached me countless times each day with the identical query, "What did you say your name was, anyway?" Possibly to preserve my sanity as much as to teach her a memory trick, I encouraged her to associate my name, Doreen, with other words in her vocabulary. I succeeded only too well, and was referred to as "doorknob," "doorpane," and "doorstop" for the remainder of the summer.

Those clients who forget the content of conversations can practice listening to conversations, selecting the key words and phrases, and reiterating a summary of the conversation after it has terminated; this selection of key words and reiteration should be practiced aloud initially, then silently. Clients also can be taught to be alert to their mind wandering and to bring their attention back to the interaction at hand. Those persons who do not notice or remember visual detail can practice looking at pictures and at people and then draw them from memory or describe as much about their posture, facial expression, clothing, and accessories as they remember. In a similar fashion, they can delineate the aspects of shops, restaurants, and exteriors and interiors of homes that indicate the product or service offered or the tastes and interests of the occupants. Such exercises can culminate in entering a store to determine whether the clients' judgments about the probable quality and price of the merchandise were accurate and a discussion of the cues inside the store that furthered that judgment or a meal in a restaurant where the dress and demeanor of the participants is consonant with their prior assessment of the type of restaurant it might be by the layout of its window, the quality of paper and printing of the menu, and the interior appointments.

Since deficient memory systems often interfere with learning disabled persons' recall of the rules of games, from cards to baseball, it is helpful for them to learn the general format that games follow and the reasons that such rules have been formulated. Then the rules of specific games can be related to that format, and rhymes and other memory strategies associated with those rules to increase the likelihood of remembering. The participants should practice the rules by playing the games, possibly creating their own table and field games, and also critiquing their games either verbally or through videotape replays, to discuss the adequacy of the rules, the ways they would alter them, and the effectiveness with which they implemented such rules. They could also learn ways of determining which side of the field one's goal is on, how to welcome someone who joins one's team, what to say and do when one's team wins, loses, or scores a point, and ways of being a gracious winner or loser of a board game.

Interpersonal Cognitive Problem Solving. By ages eight to eleven, a child is able to view simple social episodes from the perspectives of others (Flavell, 1974). A twelve year old begins to make less use of surface characteristics in describing others and pays more attention to inferred inner experiences and social relations between people. The child generates alternative solutions to interactional problems, basing them on his interpretation of the social situation with which he is confronted; he also predicts alternative consequences, evaluates the options available to him, and selects a plan of action that seems most appropriate for that particular social situation. If a child appears inefficient in interpersonal cognitive problem solving, the three-stage process described by Stone, Hinds, and Schmidt (1975) involves the teaching of the following ICPS skills: (1) information seeking, (2) generating alternative solutions, (3) setting personal goals. Spivack, Platt, and Shure (1976) suggest that ICPS might be enhanced through training in the following skills:

* An awareness of the possibility that interpersonal problems can occur in interaction and recognition of an actual problem when it occurs.
* Generation of alternative solutions, the development of a step-by-step plan to solve the problem at hand, including an appreciation of possible obstacles as well as the complexity and length of the process.
* Recognition of the consequences both for oneself and others of one's actions.
* The ability to imagine several alternative consequences.
* An appreciation of the influence that past events have on one's own and other's motivation and social behavior.

Clients can practice ICPS in a wide variety of contexts—for example, in selecting a friend; dealing with scapegoating or rejection; breaking into a closed group of friends; improving relationships with educators, bosses, fellow workers, or family members; or determining why an interaction has deteriorated. There are some excellent program suggestions in *The Problem-Solving Approach to Adjustment* (Spivack, Platt, and Shure, 1976). ICPS can be practiced through group discussions, pictures, videotapes, films, and role playing.

In the learning disability field, there is increasing recognition that one of the commonest and most disabling deficits shared by the learning disabled is their defective ability to analyze a task in their deficit areas of functioning and the consequent disadvantage in evolving productive strategies for their problems. Hallahan and

Reeve (1980) support this position in their summary of studies of selective attention in the learning disabled. They suggest that deficits in attention are not as handicapping as are deficits in analyzing tasks and selecting strategies. However, there is evidence to suggest that those persons who verbalize perceptions are able to achieve functional adequacy despite perceptual distortions (Miller and Rohr, 1980). Consequently, the self-instruction model proposed by Meichenbaum (1977) seems promising for those persons who do not analyze social situations and select appropriate strategies. He suggests the following training sequence:

- An adult model performs a task while talking to himself out loud (cognitive modeling).
- The subject performs the same task under the direction of the model's instructions (overt external guidance).
- The subject performs the task while repeating the instructions aloud (overt self-guidance).
- The subject then whispers the instructions while performing the task (faded, overt self-guidance).
- The subject performs the task while guiding his performance via private speech (covert self-instruction).

Over a number of training sessions, the package of self-statements is modeled by the teacher and rehearsed by the subject, initially aloud and then silently. In the thinking-out-loud phase, the model demonstrates the following skills: (1) what is it I have to do? (2) focusing attention; (3) self-reinforcement ("Good, I'm doing fine") and evaluation of one's strategies and corrections if necessary; (4) relaxed acceptance of errors when they occur and recognition that errors do not prevent continuance of the interaction ("That's okay, even though I made a mistake, I can proceed slowly").

A critical aspect of teaching learning disabled persons that each social situation has a predictable organization with outcomes that they can influence is their consequent realization that they are in control of their own successes and failures. They become aware that their own behavior evokes predictable responses in others and that alterations in their behavior will alter the behavior of others. Bryan (1980) suggests that behavior modification and modeling might be effectively used to create understanding in children that they can determine their successes and failures. She suggests that children observe a model who adapts his strategies to success and failure, paces his way through the task, and praises himself upon completion.

Remediation of Moral Conceptual/Deficits. Moral maturation can be encouraged through an ICPS model exploring (1) the moral implications of specific social situations; (2) alternative behaviors that one can bring to the situation; (3) probable outcomes; (4) the advantages and disadvantages of each outcome for us and for others; (5) the projected effects of one's plan on one's immediate circle, community, nation, and the world; and (6) the extent to which behaviors vary in morality in a variety of circumstances. If the client group consists of adolescents who still are excessively dependent on their parents' moral decisions and rules, are absolutist in their beliefs, or are breaking the law, the following areas could be included in programming.

1. Alternative moral decisions, their probable consequences, others' likely reactions to them, and the reaction of the members in the therapeutic group. For example, if Jimmy's mother has told him that he must never again steal money from her purse but one of his classmates needs a loan to purchase a textbook and his parents are not available, should the boy take money from the purse if the classmate assures Jimmy that he will repay the loan before Jimmy's mother misses the money? What are Jimmy's alternatives? What will happen if he doesn't buy the text today? What would the group members do in these circumstances?

2. Benefits and detriments of each decision to the person himself, and to his family, peer group, fellow students, teachers, subculture, and culture; the probable way that each of these groups perceives his behavior. For example, if Tom decides to smoke pot with his girl friend, what would the immediate benefits be to Tom and to her? What might the longer-term effects be? Will his decision to smoke or to not smoke alter the impressions that his friends, family, subculture, and culture have of him? In what ways will they think differently of him?

3. The equal acceptability of one's moral decisions to others who will be affected by the decision, as well as to oneself. For example, if Susan ignores her curfew in order to stay at the party longer, what effects will the ignored curfew have on her parents? If she has intercourse with a friend, what might the short- and long-term consequences be? How will her act affect her partner, his family and his friends? What might she have done instead of having intercourse? If Susan has intercourse, how might she avoid pregnancy and venereal disease? If they occur, what might her options be?

4. The likely consequences of enacting a moral decision that opposes one's family's moral beliefs or the peer group's values. What will the reactions of your family be if you shortchange someone with whom you are doing business, marry someone of a different religion, beat someone up, or have a party in the nude with friends? How will their reactions affect you? If your gang decides to rob a storekeeper and you decide not to join them, what will they think of you?

5. The extent to which erroneous decisions have short-term and long-term consequences; ways of minimizing or reversing negative consequences. For example, if a boy became involved in any of the behaviors just mentioned, what will the consequences for him and others be, in terms of his family, peer, and intimate relationships, job possibilities, and feelings about himself? Would he want to change people's judgments that resulted from his behavior? If not, why not, and if so, how would he do so?

6. The varying moral acceptability of behaviors in different contexts. For instance, is stealing always wrong? Suppose a person is starving and stole food from someone who had an abundance. Is stealing from someone affluent as bad as stealing from someone who is poor? Are cheating on one's income tax, taking soap and towels from hotels, robbing a bank and robbing a home equally immoral? Is stealing more justified if you avoid being caught? If you decide not to steal, on what would you base your decision?

7. Methods of altering a situation linguistically rather than through action. Consider the example of Jimmy and the textbook cited earlier. What might he have said to his classmate, the bookstore owner, or his mother instead of stealing the money? If Tom's

friends smoke pot one evening and he prefers not to, what might he say to them that still would retain their respect yet not involve him in something that he would rather not do?

The Learning Disabled Person in the Community

Making and Keeping Friends. LaGreca and Mesibov (1979) outline seven social skills that seem to contribute to positive peer relations in children and suggest that these skills be training goals for intervention: (1) smiling and laughing with peers; (2) greeting others; (3) initiating interaction with peers and responding to initiations from others; (4) conversational skills such as those involved in sharing materials or in deciding who goes first; (5) validation and support of other children; and (6) physical grooming. As the child matures, the following skills can be added:

- Learning to notice what the peer group wears, how they act, and the phrases they use so that one can model one's behavior on theirs.
- Deciding who one wants to befriend and being able to verbalize the reasons why one has selected that person as a potential friend. The subject should be able to articulate the attributes he seeks in a friend, determine which friends he seeks to meet particular needs, explain the attributes that he brings to a friendship, and learn to seek friendship from persons who are likely to appreciate his attributes and be prepared to accept his deficits.
- Learning the ways whereby one establishes acquaintanceship with someone and the behaviors that one uses to bring about increasing increments of intimacy, such as standing close to potential friends, carrying objects that could serve as conversation starters and commenting on some positive aspect of the person's appearance, behavior, or reputation, and—to increase intimacy—the use of more familiar language, nicknames and endearments, and physical closeness such as holding hands and hugging.
- Noticing the behavior by which others signal that they would like a more intimate relationship, such as confidential tones in speaking and extended eye contact.

- Changing an acquaintanceship to a nonsexual friendship, which would involve more contact by telephone and in person, increased suggestions for mutual activities, increased questions about the friend's experiences and feelings, and willingness to be helpful, supportive, and interested.
- Learning a friend's life history, aspirations, and beliefs without intruding into areas he prefers not to share.
- Sharing similar aspects of oneself and concealing other aspects, both in ways that will be positively received.
- Selecting topics of conversation that will be mutually reinforcing and suggesting activities that have a high potential for being acceptable to one's friend and mutually enjoyable.
- Recognizing and respecting the cues whereby others signal their need for silence and solitude.
- Ingratiating oneself with persons in authority such as teachers, bosses, police, and judges without being obsequious; ingratiating oneself with persons casually encountered, such as librarians, salespersons, and receptionists.
- Altering others' behavior through one's personal presentation of self.
- Assessing the benefits and detriments of a relationship so that one can decide whether to maintain the relationship at the present level of intimacy, make an increased commitment to the person, reduce the commitment, or terminate the relationship.
- Ending a relationship so that the termination is understood yet not perceived as an overwhelming failure by one's friend.

These goals can be worked on through group discussion, role playing, drama, the making of movies and videotapes, the use of the telecommunicator, outings to observe behaviors and other features of interaction such as clothing, attendance at fashion shows, and looking at clothing stores and catalogues.

Some learning disabled persons need to be taught the sequences of dating and sexual behavior: the choosing of a possible date, the approach and signals that denote the other party's interest or disinterest, appropriate clothing for dates, possible topics of conversation, and when one might suggest sharing expenses. They need to learn to gauge the rate of expression of increasing verbal and physical intimacy and the stage of intimacy at which a long-term relationship can be suggested—so that they do not propose marriage to a casual friend. They need to explore what alternative relationships they might suggest if a marriage proposal is rejected. The responsibilities and expectations that people have toward one another, including parents, siblings, same-sex and other-sex friends, neighbors, and fellow employees—should be discussed.

Although there has been little literature on the sexual knowledge or ability of learning disabled adolescents and adults, Rothenberg, Franzblau, and Geer (1979) found that their learning disabled subjects aged sixteen to twenty-two were, in many instances, unable to distinguish or label body parts and were confused or had incomplete knowledge about menstruation, reproduction, pregnancy, birth control, and venereal disease. Some had grossly incorrect notions about reproductive processes and all were anxious and uncomfortable about sexuality. They suggest that the discomfort coupled with lack of knowledge rendered the learning disabled unprepared for the assumption of sexual responsibility. Rothenberg, Franzblau, and Geer utilized a seven-session workshop format to desensitize their group to the discussion of sex and street language. They found that parent-teacher meetings in which both groups were encouraged to view their offspring and students as young adults with sexual needs and concerns were beneficial. In addition, I feel that the use of sex as an expression of respect and affection and the consequent desire of both parties to keep the details of their sexuality confidential could be discussed. Such a discussion might prevent a situation in which a learning disabled college student publically recited a list of all the girls with whom he had had intercourse.

Intimacy is modeled by family members, but it is first practiced extensively when we become friends with a same-sex "best buddy" in preadolescence or adolescence. Within these relationships we practice sharing secrets, compromising in use of shared time, protecting our friend's self-image and reputation while learning to trust him. Although some intact persons may be able to become intimates as adults without having had a same-sex buddy in their earlier years, learning disabled persons probably would find it more difficult to bridge that gap. Consequently, training programs need to encourage the participants to contact one another between sessions to plan mutual activities that might lead to friendships. If this does not occur, the group leader could have the participants arrange outings with one another with him along, gradually reducing his participation. Specific goals, such as meeting with a friend once a week, must be set for some youth, or they will avoid interactions.

In the process of becoming mutually sensitive to one another's needs, youth in the "best buddy" stage of development learn to control expressions of anger. Random expressions of anger or anger that is aroused by the most innocuous of precipitants threatens others' feelings that they are in control of their own anger; potential friends will disapprove of and avoid excessively aggressive people. Training programs should include exercises that direct aggression to the source of the anger. Participants also can practice negotiation, compromises, and arguments in which the language deals solely with the contentious issues and one's case is presented reasonably and convincingly while the other person's point of view is considered. Those participants who continue to be profoundly or randomly angry should be referred to psychotherapy.

The Learning Disabled Person as Scapegoat and Victim. One of the overwhelming obstacles to the learning disabled child's and adolescent's acquisition of friendships is the loss of face that their peers expect from their other friends if they befriend the learning disabled youngster, who lacks status and is often a scapegoat. This difficult problem can be alleviated to some extent through sensitizing peers to the learning disabled member's behavior, needs, and feelings, through teaching the learning disabled person ways of behaving that are least likely to provoke teasing and ignoring teasing when it occurs, and through arranging structured social experiences for the learning disabled member so that he is able to anticipate the requisite behaviors, execute them competently and confidently, and thus appear in a positive light to his peers.

Few program materials are addressed to making intact children empathic to their learning disabled peers; they primarily deal with making students aware of the learning disabled students' academic deficits and virtually none are geared to creating an understanding and tolerance of social deficits. One of the typical approaches to sensitizing peers to the learning disabled has been to create an appreciation that all of us have disabilities of some type—ranging from defective eyesight to difficulty in singing on key. But this method of making children aware of learning disabilities has limited merit. Such deficits as a need for eyeglasses or poor singing ability are not stigmatizing, but deficits in esteemed areas of functioning such as athletics, academics, and social activities consequentially devalue a person in his own and others' eyes. As a result, when an adult suggests that we all have deficits because "Johnny has freckles and Kathy wears glasses," the danger is that the children will feel that they are being misled.

A more promising approach might be to create an understanding of the learning disabled person's deficits to reduce the discomfort that the learning disabled person's social ineptitude arouses. This discomfort stems from their learning disabled peer's unclear role projection and the consequent confusion as to what to make of him—he has not learned to signify that he is intact or that he is learning disabled. He presents himself as a composite of many possibilities, some of which are intelligent, mentally ill, alert, mentally retarded, insensitive, boring, irritating, and shifty. Peer awareness can involve the development of an understanding of the abilities that the learning disabled child has, as well as his deficits in social behaviors, and encouragement of the learning disabled member's acquisition of more appropriate interactional skills.

Learning disabled children in recreational or athletic activities are often scapegoats because the other children are afraid that the learning disabled member will cause their team to lose, that he will absorb a disproportionate amount of the leader's attention, or that others will perceive the group as being odd. The group members need to recognize the learning disabled child's right to engage in recreational pursuits of his choice. Concomitantly, they need assurance that his membership in the group will not impede the group's involvement in activities or rob them of their share of the leader's attention. If they are concerned about what will occur when the group engages in an activity that the learning disabled member cannot handle competently, the leader can suggest examples of the ways in which he would involve the learning disabled member, such as playing basketball on a court in which baskets are hung at graduated lengths so that all of the players have a chance to score points. The group members should be afforded opportunities to express their concerns, discomfort, and impatience and feel that they will receive a sympathetic hearing. The leader's behavior will influence the attitudes of the group members, and a leader who treats participants with respect is likely to elicit respect. Similarly, a leader can be condescending, resentful that a child with special needs is in his group, or so eager to win the group's favor that he, too, scapegoats the learning disabled child. Leaders of integrated recreation groups should be supervised by persons who are knowledgeable about learning disabilities and able to suggest strategies, alternatives, and possible supports, such as the use of volunteers.

If group members do engage in scapegoating, the leader should advise the children that such behavior is unacceptable and determine the reasons underlying the scapegoating so that they can be addressed with speed. Activities that stress pleasure rather than competition are less likely to result in scapegoating. The reduction of scapegoating also should be an active goal of all educators. They need to create an expectation in their schools that their students will treat one another with kindness and respect and reward those students who do not bully vulnerable children. The following examples illustrate possible approaches to the problem of scapegoats.

Joe directs a summer camp in which learning disabled and other handicapped children are integrated. He heard that the twelve year old boys were talking derogatorily about Sammy, who was to join their group for the second period of camping. They were calling him a "retard," "klutz," and "queer." Joe met with the boys and asked each camper why he had come to camp and what he hoped to get out of the summer. He then told them about Sammy's goals and his right to an enjoyable and productive summer at camp. Joe expressed hope that the boys would ensure that Sammy's holiday would be pleasant. When the boys did treat Sammy kindly, Joe praised them and invited them to his cabin for cookies and hot chocolate.

The nine year old girls at camp were teasing and picking on Nancy. Joe met with them and listened to their concerns. He worked out a compromise in which Nancy agreed to try not to talk so much and not to awaken her cabinmates early in the morning, if they would stop picking on her. He reminded Karen, the ringleader, that she had been picked on the summer before, and she told the group how that felt. Joe solicited the group's support in making Nancy feel wanted and part of the group.

Some older campers, the thirteen year old girls, were picking on Elizabeth. Joe realized that nothing in Elizabeth's behavior was irritating and that the girls were sufficiently mature to comprehend the effects of scapegoating. Consequently, he told the group what his standards of expected behavior were, the kinds of behavior that he would not tolerate in his camp, and informed them that campers in that cabin who created scapegoats following his talk would be sent home.

In many instances, children who are scapegoated either set themselves up as scapegoats or reinforce the position by their responses to being teased. Children are likelier to choose as scapegoats others who are fearful or unlikely to retaliate. Parents, club leaders, and teachers can teach the learning disabled child and adolescent to minimize bullying by altering his behavior. He can be encouraged to dress in the same fashion as his peers, carry his books in the same way, have the same lunch box, the same expressions, and similar habits; special treatment—such as having mother meet him at school—should be avoided. An observer can note the behaviors with which the learning disabled child sets himself up to be teased, work with him to eliminate those behaviors, and substitute ones that will be more acceptable. The learning disabled child can be rewarded for ignoring teasing, taught assertiveness, and helped to avoid being self-centered. Parents should encourage use of the strategies to eliminate teasing that are being followed in the recreation group or classroom and empathize with their offspring's feelings about being teased.

As learning disabled persons age, scapegoating decreases because other adults are less concerned with peer response to their behavior than they were in childhood and adolescence; they no longer need to bully others in order to curry favor. However, some learning disabled adults, by virtue of their gullibility and loneliness, are victimized in another fashion. They may be sold valueless merchandise, be asked for loans that are not repayed, join singles or dating clubs that fail to provide the promised activities or dates, or be sold a verbal bill of goods from erstwhile friends who default on their promises. Such learning disabled adults need to be involved in role playing skits and discussions to practice dealing with salespersons, real estate agents, and telephone solicitors. They must learn to differentiate sales pitches and conversations that are genuine from those that are suspect by noting voice tone, gaze, body stance, and content of the appeal. Similarly, they need to learn how to check the reputation of companies and tradespeople and seek restitution when a product or service has been unsatisfactory. For example, a group's reputation can be examined by determining how long it has been in business, by speaking to several customers, and by attending some of the group's functions before becoming a member. It is helpful if learning disabled adults know how to obtain advice from a bank manager, lawyer, or accountant for aid with contracts, investments, and credit.

Adult Life for the Learning Disabled. The majority of learning disabled persons will function competently as adults. For many, the most consequential obstacle of their lives is the school system. Once they no longer have to cope with physics, geometry, or sports or be penalized for their spelling errors, residual disabilities become sources of amusement rather than impediments to functioning. Actually, such persons no longer are disabled since a disability is a deficient ability to perform expected activities. However, three groups of learning disabled persons require ongoing services. The first group of adults needs academic remediation to retain their jobs, advance in their fields, or reach realistic vocational goals. The second group needs access to counselors who will assist them with coping skills when their social ineptitudes, rigidity, disorganization, poor frustration tolerance, deficient judgment, and propensity to perseverate result in unsatisfactory and unproductive situations. Since they are immature, many will not have a vocational or life plan, regardless of their actual age. Most such adults do poorly at establishing short- and long-term social, vocational, and recreational goals, setting priorities, and allocating time and energy toward realization of any goals they may have. The third group, which represents a small but previously ignored percentage of the learning disabled, will always require sheltered living situations, or program models that offer gradual increments of independence. Such persons will be so impulsive, so deficient in judgment, and so socially inept that an independent life style is not feasible.

Selecting Program Models for Building Social Skills

Recently there has been an intensive thrust toward mainstreaming disabled or handicapped students into "regular" classrooms; its counterpart, *normalization,* is the integration of such persons into "regular" recreation, jobs, and living situations. The normalization principle, which originated with Wolfensberger (1972), stresses the overwhelming importance of integrating the mentally retarded into recreation programs established for intact persons. He encourages recreation leaders to offer developmental activities to their mentally retarded participants. However, rather than the emphasis being on the retarded participants to acquire the social skills that intact persons have, Wolfensberger stresses the importance of creating an atmosphere that minimizes the external differences. Group leaders are encouraged to treat mentally retarded adults in the same fashion as they treat intact adults in the group. For persons whose handicaps are too severe for integration to occur, he suggests that their sheltered program be situated in a residential district, in a building that blends in with surrounding buildings, and that the program have an adult name, not a cute or childish one, that does not mention mental retardation.

In the learning disability field, the considerations in regard to enrolling a person in sheltered or integrated recreation and the ways to achieve normalization have differed from those articulated by Wolfensberger. The decision of whether to enroll a mentally retarded person in a sheltered or integrated recreation program is based, in large measure, on the extent of the retardation while, for the learning disabled, the decision is predicated on his social adequacy as well as the types of programs that are available. If a learning disabled person needs to learn more adequate social skills, he may well be enrolled in a sheltered program in which there is an emphasis on intensive, personal, social remediation. A sheltered program that provides companionship and feelings of accomplishment often is the program of choice.

The goals of sheltered recreation for the learning disabled are: intensive remediation of social deficits; incidental learnings that will enhance social acceptability, such as learning game skills and rules or how to ice skate and ride a bicycle; becoming acquainted with recreational possibilities in one's town; and promotion of success and fun. Integrated recreation for the learning disabled strives to increase participation in activities with intact peers. Developmental activities—those that draw other participants' attention to their learning disabled peer's differences—are avoided. Rather, leaders are encouraged to familiarize themselves with the learning disabled member's strengths and interests and to incorporate these areas into his program, so that the learning disabled person's competencies are stressed. Although an integrated program does not include intensive remediation of social deficits, the leader can encourage socially acceptable interactions and discourage nonproductive behavior.

As expectations change throughout the stages of life, a learning disabled person's ability to cope may change, especially when the complexity of expectations increase. The need to return to a sheltered program from one that is integrated does not necessarily mean that a person has regressed; it may simply indicate that the sheltered program offers possibilities for the learning of more sophisticated social skills, companionship without competition, and less anxiety about appearing strange to intact peers. Greenberg (1970) found that learning disabled adolescents and adults remembered a sheltered group that they had attended in childhood as the one positive social experience they had enjoyed.

Many communities have no sheltered programs for the learning disabled, and those that do may have programs for the learning disabled child but none for the adolescent or adult. Therefore, if learning disabled persons want to join a recreation program, in many instances the only one that is available is integrated. For some, the companionship that they enjoy in such a group may represent the only social contacts that they have with peers. Consequently, the groups they join must be selected with care. If a learning disabled person has a particular talent or interest, he might join a group that specializes in that interest. Otherwise, a structured club group that offers a variety of activities (none requiring a high degree of competence) and that avails itself of the community's recreation facilities often is a good choice. If none of the group's members know the learning disabled newcomer, he can make a fresh start without being hampered by his reputation.

Ideally, the program director should have a background in human development and some knowledge of disabilities. The group leader should be mature, secure, empathic, and flexible. The group members' interests should complement the learning disabled participant's strengths and deficits—a clumsy person should not join a group that is absorbed with sports, for example. Group leaders should be provided with information about the client that relates to the demands that he will meet in the group. If Billy is expected to tie scout knots, the leader should know that his fine motor coordination and spatial memory are poor; he should try to tie a less difficult knot, have the task broken down into several steps, or have an alternative task assigned. Similarly, the leader does not need to know the grade level at which the participant spells if the program does not include writing. The goals of integration for the client should be articulated prior to enrollment and evaluated periodically.

Planning Social Skill Building and Adjunctive Programs. Some interactional skill development programs are carefully conceptualized whereas others are so imprecise and diffuse that little, if any, gain results. There are programs in which the planners do not determine the most critical needs of their client population and so gear the program to superficial or nonexistent needs, such as providing a gross motor program for well-coordinated clients or offering academic remediation to children who already receive sufficient remediation in school but need social skill remediation. Some programs have goals that are overly ambitious when one considers the frequency with which the program occurs, the competence of the staff, the availability of supervisors and consultants, the program design, or the extent of the disabilities of the enrollees. Thus a program might have an articulated goal of remediating the academic, physical coordination, and social deficits of the participants, yet the program meets one evening a week and uses untrained adolescent staff who are not evaluated on the job. The children, who are severely disabled, move from component to component every twenty minutes, and no component is directed to individual areas of deficit. Parents and teachers are not informed of program goals so that they can reinforce learnings throughout the week. How can such a program succeed?

Some programs are geared to the remedy of social deficits, but the staff, in their eagerness to correct as many deficits as possible, forget the persistence with which people retain social behaviors that they have spent their lives rehearsing. They therefore do not allow sufficient time for the practice and generalization of each new behavior that is learned. Nor is there time for the client to recognize that the reactions he elicits for new behaviors are more gratifying than the reactions provoked by his inappropriate behavior. Clients also need sufficient opportunities to practice newly learned behaviors in actual situations, such as in school, at parties, or in restaurants. Finally, some program designs have been carefully conceptualized, but the needs of the persons who have enrolled in the program are not compatible with program goals; their likely improvement will be modest, and they may end up being disappointed.

When one plans a program for disabled persons, one either decides on a program model and then solicits a population that can benefit from that model or one is aware of a specific population with unmet needs and designs a model that addresses those needs. In either instance, the following questions should prove helpful in program planning and evaluation, regardless of whether the program is directed to the social or other deficits of learning disabled persons or to the counseling needs of family members:

1. Have the total remedial needs of the proposed client population been assessed and a determination made of which needs were and were not being adequately met by other programs?
2. Of the unmet or inadequately met needs, which are the most critical? For example, if the clients all have academic, linguistic, and social deficits, what is the most disabling of the three?
3. What are the goals for the program as articulated by the board and director of the agency, workers, clients, parents, and teachers? Are they consistent? Are they likely to be realized

when one takes into account the program approach, amount of personal attention, staff's knowledge and ability, frequency of meetings, population served, and opportunities to generalize the skills learned outside the program? Is there a written program plan?

4. Does the client value the skills being taught? If not, is the client's attitude valid and are alternatives being considered? Did the client and family choose goals that represented the client's most critical needs or goals that reflect parental anxieties or that are the least threatening? What rationale underlies the goals that were selected? Does the program function in a fashion that implements stated goals?

5. Does the program serve the population it purports to serve? Is the program geared to the actual population that is enrolled or the population that is described in the agency's brochure?

6. If programmed material is used either with clients or other family members, is it strictly followed or utilized as a "jumping off" point? Do workers pick up on situations that occur? Are materials used correctly and for maximum effectiveness?

7. Are community human and physical resources, media, or audiovisual material used to augment the program?

8. Is there a concept of what client growth should occur at each juncture of the program and a means of ongoing program evaluation? Are clients included in the evaluation? What procedures do workers use to elicit client and community feedback? Are workers able to handle client criticism? Is the program orientation able to change as clients' needs change and new information becomes available? What are the vehicles for access to, evaluation, and implementation of current research into the program format?

9. How do workers provide support and direction? Do they encourage the client to solve problems, or do they tend to provide answers? How is the material generalized? Is the program coordinated with other programs that the client receives and with other facets of his life?

10. Do the workers appear to be trusted and respected by clients? What behaviors do the workers use that might encourage or discourage these responses?

11. What records are kept and how are they used? For example, are they utilized to effect program adjustments, chart client growth, effect a more refined therapeutic approach, or as a basis for supervision?

12. Are workers observed and supervised? How effectively do they utilize the supervisor and supervision? What is the supervisor's background and strengths? What other resources are made available to workers or do they seek them themselves? What do workers want to learn? Has there been a provision in the program to increase their knowledge in the desired areas? Are workers encouraged to solve difficulties and develop creative program approaches? What benefits do they feel that they are acquiring from the program?

13. If there is a concomitant parent program, do workers share with parents what is being attempted with their children, why and how it is working, and ways of reinforcing the newly learned skills outside of the group?

14. Does the worker model the attitudes and behavior that he would like the client, parents, and other family members to assume? For instance, if peer-to-peer interaction is being promoted in the children's group, are the parents encouraged to interact with one another rather than direct their comments to the worker? If the children are being encouraged to express their feelings appropriately, is expression of feeling similarly allowed and fostered in the parents' group?

15. Have sequential, carefully conceptualized education and counseling been incorporated into the parents' group? Are siblings and extended family members included? Are affective and educational issues dealt with simultaneously?

16. Is the parents' group perceived as secondary to the children's group? (In other words, is the attitude one of keeping the parents amused while they are waiting for their children?) If, however, the parents' group is deemed equally important, has a program been designed that deals with parents' most critical needs? Has the optimum number of sessions been determined, regardless of the number of sessions the children meet?

17. Have the workers', clients', and parents' expectations—such as arriving on time and staying until the end of the sessions—

been articulated? Are they accountable for lapses?

18. Does the program format or staff attitudes imply that the parents have done a poor job of childrearing?

19. Is a component built into the program whereby experienced clients and parents assist new clients and parents?

20. What human, physical, and financial resources are available? Are they sufficient to offer an individualized program in the selected areas of concentration? If resources are qualitatively and quantitatively insufficient to permit personal task analyses and incorporate individual remedial components, how can the model be reorganized to promote increased effectiveness? Are additional untapped resources available?

21. Do the allocation and use of time and space promote achievement of the program's goals? For example, if the program occurs once a week, is there sufficient repetition to encourage consolidation of material learned? If more frequent meetings are impossible, should goals change or components outside the group be coordinated with the model to ensure sufficient exposure? Is time within the program used effectively? Does the physical space promote the desired atmosphere?

22. Has the format been conceptualized for each session, including methods of greeting clients or parents, reviewing previous sessions, establishing tasks for time between sessions, introducing content of following session, and concluding sessions warmly?

23. Is the program model sequential, so that clients registering part way through the program experience difficulty understanding the content? If so, is there a provision for orienting them? If there is considerable fluctuation of participants enrolling and leaving, would an open-ended format be more appropriate? Is the program model the most effective for the size of the group?

24. Is the program content consistent with the clients' educational and intellectual levels?

25. What consultants are available to the program?

26. How will disruptive, uncooperative, or nonresponsive client behavior be dealt with?

27. What expectations for client improvement have been expressed, and what protection do the staff have if they fail to

effect the desired improvement? What vehicles are included for periodic feedback to parents and educators?

When the program is designed before the clients are selected, the following questions also should be asked:

- Have the planners selected a program design, goals, staff, facilities, and a client population that are consistent with probable goal implementation? Have they defined the subcluster(s) of learning disabilities that the program is designed to serve? For example, is it geared to language disabled persons, those with motor coordination problems, those with visual/spatial problems, or to children who are inattentive or hyperactive?
- If applicants have handicaps in addition to their learning disabilities, such as controlled or uncontrolled epilepsy, emotional disturbance, or sensory handicaps, which handicaps can be accommodated? Will handicapped persons who are not learning disabled be served?
- What expectations exist about the parents? Will clients with uncooperative parents be enrolled?
- After clients have been enrolled in the program, what will your criteria be for determining that a client is unsuitable for the program? What behaviors would cause you to terminate a client's involvement?

Careful planning is essential but insufficient to ensure adequate programming. Programs also need periodic evaluations in which administrators, staff, clients, parents and outside consultants contribute to the critique; outsiders provide the objectivity that those close to the program lack.

Chapter 8

�֟ �֟ ✤ ✤ ✤

Techniques for Enhancing Social Skills

Judith Wiener

✤ The traditional treatment for children with emotional or social problems has been psychotherapy. Most psychotherapy is characterized by a nondirective open-ended approach and involves verbal expression and abstract thinking. Not surprisingly, this sort of counseling with learning disabled children (most of whom have short attention spans, are disorganized, and have problems with verbal expression and abstract reasoning) has been less than successful. Recently, a number of alternative interventions have been utilized with learning disabled children. Remedial programs that are effective tend to have twelve essential elements (Cruickshank, 1975; Griffiths, 1970-71).

1. *Structure.* Most teachers and psychologists agree that learning disabled children need a structured classroom

and curriculum. In a structured environment, everything has its time and place, all events are planned carefully, a set routine or procedure is followed consistently, expectations are communicated to the child clearly, and individual choice is introduced gradually.

2. *Concrete Formulation and Materials.* Some children with learning disabilities cannot deal with abstract principles. In mathematics, for example, they may need counters for a longer period than other students. To learn social skills, they may require numerous and frequent demonstrations or examples of a particular rule before they are truly able to comprehend it.

3. *Use of Various Sensory Modalities.* By definition, learning disabled children have information-processing deficits. Some learn better visually, others auditorally, and others motorically. Many students have problems retaining information unless it is presented through several modalities. Since affective education is taught in a group situation and the learning styles of the children in the group presumably vary, it is necessary to present information through as many modalities as possible.

4. *Cues for Attention.* Many learning disabled children have an attentional disorder. Consequently, they often do not attend to instructions given to the group. Cues for attention include saying the individual child's name, giving a previously arranged nonverbal signal (flicking lights, playing a musical note), physical touching, and asking children to repeat the instruction.

5. *Reduction of Distracting Stimuli.* Some learning disabled children, particularly those with figure-ground problems, find it difficult to learn in a stimulating environment (Cruickshank, 1977). These children are so distractible that they cannot concentrate on the information they are to learn when there are competing noises or visual stimuli. Although it is probably not necessary to set up the extremely stark classroom environment advocated by Cruickshank, minimizing external noises and the amount of visual clutter is certainly recommended. Some children should sit close to the teacher for group lessons and sit in a quiet corner or cubicle for independent seat work.

6. *High-Interest Materials.* Curriculum materials that are of interest to learning disabled children help motivate

them. This principle holds true also, of course, for children who are normal learners. Unfortunately, many learning disabled children are subjected to the teaching of skills in a dull, repetitive manner and are forced to read material at their instructional level rather than at their interest level. A structured environment does not preclude the use of games, colorful concrete material, high-interest–low-vocabulary books, good films, and the like. An endless series of blue dittoes is not appropriate. The same principle apples to affective education programming.

7. *Programming by Small Increments in Difficulty.* Tasks should be analyzed carefully and each of the component parts sequenced and taught separately. Most learning disabled children can learn quite complex concepts if taught in this manner. Task analysis is particularly important for teaching role-taking and interpersonal problem-solving skills.

8. *Modeling of the Appropriate Response.* Since learning disabled children need as many cues as possible to process information, modeling the appropriate response or behavior is important. When the teacher (or another student) models the response, the student's anxiety is relieved when he is not sure of the answer.

9. *Immediate Feedback.* Feedback is an essential element in all learning. Most normal learners can wait a considerable amount of time before receiving feedback. Most learning disabled children, however, need feedback very close to the response. Since they frequently make mistakes, they tend to be quite anxious and to believe that their answer is wrong. Immediate feedback sometimes reduces that anxiety.

10. *Positive Reinforcement.* Learning disabled children receive more negative reinforcement in the classroom than normal learners do (Bryan and Wheeler, 1976). They tend to believe they are wrong unless told otherwise. It is important to reinforce some of these children for behaving according to expectations—to reinforce them for doing what the teacher believes all children can do easily.

11. *Spaced Practice.* Since many learning disabled children have attentional disorders, they cannot concentrate on a single task for a long period of time. The length of a les-

son should be matched to the child with the shortest attention span in the group. Frequent short sessions on a topic are
more efficient than one long session.

   12. *Opportunities for Overlearning.* Since many children
with learning disabilities have problems with memory, teaching a concept until it appears to be learned is not sufficient.
It is likely to be forgotten quickly. Frequent review of the
concept is essential. Review need not be in the form of dull,
repetitive drill. The same concept may be reviewed through
games, role playing, films, a field trip, or a story read to
the group.

These twelve elements are equally essential in facilitating the success of an intervention in the affective and social domain.

   In this chapter various intervention approaches will be discussed. For each approach, a method of adapting the traditional
techniques to make them suitable for learning disabled children by
incorporating the twelve elements will be described.

Biological Intervention

   Biological intervention, including dietary modifications and
psychostimulants, is frequently used for hyperactive children or
those with attentional disorders (Feingold, 1973; Whalen and
Henker, 1976). The objectives are to increase attention span and
decrease distractibility, impulsivity, and hyperactivity. These interventions do not purport to remediate social perceptual or social
cognitive problems, modify family dynamics, or develop a more
positive self-concept. Since the subject of this chapter is enhance-
ment of social skills, the research on diet and psychostimulants will
not be discussed.

Individual Psychotherapy

   Prior to the general recognition of learning disabilities as a
separate problem in the 1960s, individual psychotherapy was the
treatment of choice for children with academic difficulties (Golick,
1977). It was postulated that the reading problems were a result of
unresolved oedipal conflicts (Miller and Westman, 1964). The psy-

chotherapy was usually not effective in teaching children to read and often increased anxiety, since the goals of treatment were not reached and the problem was defined by the child and family as an emotional disturbance. Furthermore, many of the children could not make progress in unstructured, nondirective play therapy or verbal counseling.

In spite of the foregoing, psychotherapy has some validity for some children with learning disabilities. Individual counseling may help a child identify and express his feelings, understand his learning problem, develop a more positive self-concept, become more adept at interpersonal problem solving, work through his feelings about his family, reduce anxiety, and learn how to function in crisis situations. Effective therapists with learning disabled children modify their approach to incorporate the twelve elements listed in the introduction.

The one-to-one aspect of psychotherapy has specific advantages for children with learning disabilities. If the office is uncluttered, it is easy to minimize distractions. In instances where play therapy is being used, it is important to have only one or two toys visible at one time instead of exposing the child to a whole room of toys. The therapist can develop a treatment mode specific to the child's needs. Role playing, visual aids, and puppets can be used to make concepts more concrete and appeal to two sensory modalities. Vocabulary can be tailored to the child's level of understanding. Immediate feedback and positive reinforcement can be easily provided, and points can be reviewed frequently. Although there are no peer models, the therapeutic relationship often leads to an identification with the therapist and modeling of the therapist's behavior. Two examples of adaptations of traditional psychotherapeutic approaches for learning disabled children are discussed below.

The Mutual Story-Telling Technique. Richard Gardner, a child psychotherapist, has developed the mutual story-telling technique (Gardner, 1971). His patients are provided with cassette tapes and asked to make up a story for a "television program." The rules are that the stories should not be repetitions of ones the children have heard or an account of a true event. The children are then asked to add a moral or lesson at the end of the story. Gardner analyzes the stories in much the same way as psychoanalysts analyze dreams. He then relates stories which involve the same characters, settings, and initial situations but have more appropriate or healthy resolutions of the most important conflicts. If the children wish, the tapes are played back.

Gardner's objective, with learning disabled children, is to treat the secondary psychogenic problems—the emotional problems that result from being disabled. He tries to help children acquire a more positive self-concept, reduce their anxiety, become less angry, or cope with family conflicts that may or may not be related to the disability. When working with learning disabled children, he reminds them frequently of the rules and procedures and provides a great deal of positive reinforcement. The mutual story-telling technique involves considerable modeling, since Gardner always responds to a story with one of his own. In order to assist children who have difficulties with verbal expression, he provides prompts. The following is an example of Gardner's structuring of the verbal task: "I'll start the story and when I point my finger at you, you say exactly what comes into your mind at the time. You'll then see how easy it is to make up a story. Okay, let's start. Once upon a time, a long, long time ago, in a distant land, far, far away there lived a ____" (p. 27). Gardner then points. If the child says dog, Gardner replies "and that dog" and points again. When the child stops, Gardner follows with connective statements such as "and then," "the next thing that happened was," and so on. Gardner is an active therapist when working with learning disabled children. He often interrupts them to ask them to clarify their point or correct the sequence. The tape-recorded playback facilitates overlearning.

Thus, a psychotherapeutic process which is inherently open-ended and nondirective can be beneficial for learning disabled children if the therapist structures it appropriately.

The Life-Space Interview. The second technique is the life-space interview (LSI), which is adaptable for children with learning disabilities (Redl, 1966; Morse, 1971). The essence of the LSI is that it always centers around an issue or a crisis at or close to the time of its occurrence. As a result, the situation is concrete and meaningful to children. The therapist is usually a teacher, child care worker, or guidance counselor, and the therapy is undertaken wherever the event occurred—at school, camp, home, or elsewhere. Possible issues include loss of self-control, provoking scapegoating, fighting, stealing, running away, and frustration due to failure. A group interview may be held when the problem involves more than one child.

The beginning of the LSI is unstructured and nondirective—children who are in a crisis state are encouraged to "ventilate." At this stage the therapist wants to determine how the children see the situation—not to obtain "objective truth." In the course of talking, children may provide cues that the situation is not an isolated one but is symbolic of their lives as they see them ("Everybody picks on me," "I'm bad," "I can't do anything right"). The therapist probes to find out more about their view of themselves (since it may provide data that can be used to alter the environment and facilitate self-acceptance) and reflects their statements back to them to encourage elaboration. The therapist should demonstrate empathy by sitting at the children's level, attempting to achieve eye contact if that does not cause discomfort, using vocabulary children understand, and reflecting their feelings back to them.

Once the children's point of view is expressed, the interview becomes more structured. The therapist tries to determine what happened in logical sequence—a descriptive account with no implied value judgments. Several techniques may be used to help learning disabled children with this, including returning to the place where the event occurred, puppetry, role playing, and reverse role playing. Since it is not assumed that behavior will change as a result of insight, the therapist tries to explore the internal mechanics for change. He needs to learn whether children recognize the importance of being compassionate toward another person or of following rules, or whether they believe that what is right is what they can get away with. The therapist tries to determine whether the children wish to change their behavior, what their goals are, and what they find reinforcing. Children who have problems with self-expression may find it easier to choose from a list of items the therapist articulates. Again, role playing and puppetry are sometimes helpful techniques.

The resolution phase is the most important part of the LSI. In this phase, the therapist assumes the primary role in trying to find a solution that is realistic for particular children. In some instances, the therapist suggests that on the basis of the previous discussion there is a different way they can act in that situation, and helps them articulate the alternative. Role-playing the alternative may facilitate social learning. For many learning disabled children, a behavior modification program is an appropriate solution. If only simple management techniques are required, the therapist should explain the program immediately and role-play what will be done. If the problem is more complex, a second interview should be held in which the focus is a structured explanation of the program.

Behavior Management/Modification

Behavior management is frequently effective with learning disabled children because the principles are consistent with the twelve elements. By definition, the approach is structured; and modeling, immediate feedback, and positive reinforcement are built in. The goals of behavior modification programs are to eliminate or decrease maladaptive behaviors and to teach or increase appropriate behaviors. Although children may be taught to perceive or discriminate specific cues which should stimulate specific behaviors, they are not taught problem-solving skills which generalize to other situations.

Most children are motivated to try to behave according to expectations if promised concrete rewards or privileges (positive reinforcement) on an appropriate schedule. However, more mature adolescents capable of abstract thinking generally respond to praise, encouragement (social reinforcement), frequent feedback, and logical discussion. They often resent the use of tangible reinforcers, since they see themselves as being motivated by higher principles.

The basic principles of behavior management will not be discussed here. In this section, three prototypes of behavior modification programs that I have found to be successful with learning disabled children will be described. The three programs can be implemented by teachers on their own without taking elaborate baselines. Parental support facilitates the effectiveness of the programs.

Child's Name _____   Date _____

Period	Comments	Homework	Teacher's Initial
1			
2			
3			
4			
5			
6			
7			
8			
9			
10			

Signature of Home Room Teacher _____

Signature of Parent or Guardian _____

General Comments:

Figure 1. Daily Report Chart

Daily Report. This program is suitable for students who tend to be disorganized, have difficulty attending to task, and often engage in acting-out behavior in order to get attention. Students who may benefit from this program have a negative self-concept and thrive on frequent social reinforcement provided systematically. It is not an appropriate program for students who are not concerned about social reinforcement and require tangible rewards. I have used it with students aged eight to sixteen.

The teacher divides the day into periods according to the work schedule. For young children, the chart in Figure 1 is taped to their desk. Older students on a rotary system are responsible for carrying it from class to class and showing it to the teacher at the end of the period. In that instance, a guidance counselor, home room teacher, or resource room teacher coordinates the program.

The advantage of this program is that it helps students to remain organized and provides them with feedback on their behavior. Their parents have the opportunity to praise them on good days and are aware of problems and homework. With older students, the program should be discontinued if they consistently lose the chart and/or forget to present it to their teachers for comments at the end of the period. For students of all ages, the program should be discontinued when the number of positive comments does not increase and the number of negative comments decreases over time. Teachers can phase out the program by increasing the length of the periods for younger children, and using the comment sheet only for problematic periods for older students.

A positive feature of the daily report system is its simplicity and the minimal amount of teacher time required. Tangible rewards are not introduced when they are not needed. The structure and positive reinforcement may teach organizational skills, decrease attention-seeking behavior, and help a student acquire a more positive self-concept.

Simple Contingency Contract. Some students are not motivated by social reinforcers and need more structure than that provided by the daily report. They may benefit from a simple contingency contract (shown in Figure 2), as a means of reducing or eliminating attention-seeking behavior or behavior resulting from the students' disorganization and impulsivity. Examples of targeted behaviors include:

- Come to class on time and prepared (pen, notebooks, correct books).
- Follow the teacher's directions.
- Do not disturb others.
- Speak in a soft voice.
- Do not play with toys during work time.
- Complete assigned work.

I,___(student's name)___ , agree to follow the school and classroom rules listed below:

1. (List
2. targeted
3. behaviors)

I,___(teacher's name)___ , together with the rest of the staff, agree to give___(student's name)___ one point for following each of the above rules during every period according to the attached timetable sheet, which ___(student's name)___ is responsible for carrying from class to class and giving to the teacher at the end of the period.

During the week of___(date)___ ,___(student's name)___ will be allowed to choose one of the following daily rewards if he gets_____ points during the day:

1.
2. (List
3. daily
4. reinforcers)
5.

At the end of the week,___(student's name)___ will be allowed to choose one of the following weekly rewards if he gets_____ points:

1. (List
2. weekly
3. reinforcers)

(Include   At the end of each week,___(student's name)___ will bring
if   home a copy of the chart to his parents, who will give the weekly
appli-   reward if earned.
cable)   On___(date at the end of month)___ ,___(student's name)___ will
have the privilege of___(major reward)___ if he has earned
_____ points.

_____   _____
(student's signature)   (parent's signature)

_____
(teacher's signature)

Figure 2. Model Contingency Contract

The vocabulary should be adjusted according to the students' level of sophistication.

Figure 3 contains a sample timetable sheet on which the points and rewards are recorded. During the first week, children should obtain rewards for receiving 60 percent of possible points. If they achieve the weekly reward, the criterion should be raised to 75 percent the next week and 90 percent thereafter. If the criterion is not met the first week, the criterion should be lowered to the points obtained and then raised gradually each week if the children are successful.

Most children are able to inform teachers what they find reinforcing. Those who cannot express any desires or name unavailable items can be asked to choose an item from a list of reinforcers read to them by the teacher. Table 1 is a list of rewards or privileges that most children find reinforcing at school.

Since it is important to ensure that students understand the operation of this program, teachers should role-play and reverse role-play it with them. When playing with the child, the teacher should act out the inappropriate and appropriate behavior and the consequences of such behavior. The child should then follow suit. Praise or feedback should always accompany the rewarding of points or rewards.

The following steps should be taken to phase out the program:

1. Change targeted behaviors if a new behavior is more problematic than the one listed.
2. Increase the interval required to earn points.
3. Eliminate the daily rewards.
4. Switch to a daily report system with weekly and monthly rewards.
5. Eliminate weekly and then monthly rewards.
6. Phase out system completely.

Most mainstream teachers have the resources to design and implement the aforementioned program, and it is well within the range of a special education teacher who has a self-contained class

Child's Name _____   Date _____

Points

Period	Monday	Tuesday	Wednesday	Thursday	Friday
1					
2					
3					
4					
5					
6.					
7					
8					
9					
10					
Total					
Reward					

Total Points _____   Weekly Reward _____

Parent's Signature _____

Contract Summary Sheet

Child's Name _____

(date) Week	Total Points	Weekly Reward	Week	Total Points	Weekly Reward

Monthly Rewards _____   _____

Parent's Signature _____

Figure 3.   Contract Chart

Table 1. Reinforcement Chart

Daily Reinforcers	Weekly Reinforcers	Monthly Reinforcers
Primary Students (age 6–8)		
Scratch and Sniff stickers	Medal or button	Major excursion
Reward cards	Popcorn making	Larger toy
Free time	Happy Grams	
Treats (cookies, candy)	Small toy	
Sit near teacher	Outing with family	
Show work to principal		
Be first in line		
Present at Show and Tell		
Write on blackboard		
Special job		
Games		
Junior Students (age 9–12)		
Extra time in library	Extra gym time	Major excursion
Help in the kindergarten	Help run house	Larger toy or
Listen to music	leagues	equipment
Games	Certificate	Lunch at McDonald's
Treats	Small toy	with teacher
Special jobs	Outing with family	
Choose own seat	Popcorn making	
Speak on PA system	Cooking	
	Allowance	
Secondary Students (age 12–16)		
Edible prize—donuts	Bonus marks	Take a desired
Free time (spare)	Sports activities	course
Lunch with friends	Allowance	Major excursion
	Outings with friends	Clothing or
	Extra shop time	equipment
	Lunch at McDonald's	A specific grade
	with teacher	

of learning disabled children. This program is structured, concrete, highly motivating, and interesting; and it involves programming by small increments of difficulty, modeling, immediate feedback, positive reinforcement, and overlearning. It is not effective with children who are so angry or depressed that they have no interest in the positive reinforcers that could be offered. This is best illustrated by the following case.

> May is a fifteen-year-old severely learning dis-
> abled girl who was adopted at the age of ten. Her
> sixteen-year-old brother was also adopted by the same
> family but had to be placed in a group home because
> of his uncontrolled behavior. The agency responsible
> for the placement was insensitive and initially did not
> inform May of her brother's whereabouts. May had
> always been impulsive and disorganized and had pre-
> viously responded to the above program. After her
> brother's removal, she became angry and violent. The
> only relevant reinforcer for her was to be reunited
> with her brother. When she was placed in the same
> group home, her violence subsided, and she was
> once again motivated by the more common tangible
> reinforcers.

This program is also not effective with more sophisticated adolescents who find a system of this sort demeaning. It seems to be successful with most disorganized, impulsive learning disabled children with negative self-concepts who tend toward acting out attention-seeking behavior and who are not motivated by social reinforcers exclusively.

Teasing Program. Many children with learning disabilities have difficulties with peer relations (Bryan, 1974a). In a group of learning disabled children, teasing, name calling, and bickering can be almost constant. One child is often the scapegoat. The teasing program reduces the amount of such conflict in a contained special education class or recreation group.

The first step is assessment. The teacher must take a baseline to determine how much teasing (name calling, bickering) occurs in a day. A golf counter worn on the wrist can be used to compute the number of teases per day for a three-day period, and the average can be calculated. With this data the teacher can explain the program to the class. As part of the explanation, the teacher should act out the various negative interactions that have been counted.

The chart in Figure 4 is placed in a prominent position in the classroom. Whenever a tease occurs, the teacher marks an X on

	No. of Teases	Monday	Tuesday	Wednesday	Thursday	Friday
Reward	1 2 3 4 5 6 7 8 9 10					
No Reward	11 12 13 14					
Punish-ment	15 16 17 18 19 20					
Total						
Conse-quence						

Weekly Reward _____

Figure 4. Teasing Chart

the chart below the appropriate day. Three ranges are set: (1) from
no teases to a number 20 percent below the average from the
baseline data, (2) from the 20 percent below the baseline average to
the baseline average, (3) above the baseline average. If the children
score in range 1 on a given day, they receive a privilege (such as free
time or a special game or activity); if they score in range 2, there is
no consequence; in range 3 there is a mild negative consequence
(such as a fifteen-minute detention or a small amount of extra
homework). At the end of the week, there is a weekly reward (such
as a special Friday-afternoon activity) when the children in the class
score in range 1 every day of the week. A monthly reward (major
class excursion) is given when they have received four consecutive
weekly rewards.

At the end of each successful week, the teacher adjusts the ranges by lowering (by about 10 percent) the number of Xs permitted for the daily privilege or required for a negative consequence. The program can be eliminated when the class consistently obtains less than five Xs per day for four weeks.

Like other behavior modification programs, the teasing program is structured, concrete, appeals to various sensory modalities, programs by small increments in difficulty, and provides for immediate feedback and positive reinforcement. Done in isolation, it does not teach children alternative ways of interacting with peers and may prove ineffective. This program should be implemented in conjunction with some of the affective education and social skills training activities discussed in the next section.

Affective Education/Social Skills Training

Affective education and social skills training programs for learning disabled children have received increasing attention during the past few years. The programs generally work toward two main objectives. The first objective, compensating for the social perceptual and social cognitive deficits which interfere with healthy interaction with adults and peers, involves the following specific subskills: (1) learning role-taking skills, such as inferring the feelings of others from a situation and perceiving nonverbally expressed emotions and cues; (2) labeling and communication of feelings; (3) acquiring interpersonal problem-solving skills; (4) increasing attention span and organizational skills and decreasing impulsivity, distractibility, and hyperactivity; (5) learning life skills involving self-care and skills that facilitate peer popularity. The second objective, helping the learning disabled child accept his disability and see himself in positive terms, involves these specific subskills: (1) developing a more positive self-concept and (2) understanding the nature of the disability.

Learning Role-Taking Skills. Many children with learning disabilities cannot readily perceive nonverbally expressed emotions and cues, or infer the feelings of others from a situation, or act on the basis of the perceived cues (Wiig and Harris, 1974; Bryan, 1977). Minskoff (1980) has developed a social skills training program to remediate these deficits. The program has the following four objectives:

1. Discriminating visual and auditory social cues in the behavior of oneself and others.
2. Understanding the meaning of these cues.
3. Building the specific social responses into a response repertoire.
4. Discriminating negative nonverbal social cues in persons with whom one is interacting; relating these cues to specific responses one has made; and then modifying such responses in similar future situations.

Students are taught to use appropriate body-language cues—including facial expressions, gestures, and postures (Minskoff, 1980a)—as well as spatial cues, vocalic cues, and such artifactual cues as clothing and cosmetics (Minskoff, 1980b).

The teaching methods include training selective attention with the use of descriptions and explanations and guided problem solving through role playing. Structured, concrete cues involving a variety of sensory modalities are presented, and the programming involves small increments in difficulty and overlearning. Modeling, immediate feedback, and positive reinforcement are essential features.

Labeling and Communication of Feelings. Many children with language disabilities have problems with labeling and communication of feelings. Some become withdrawn, and others tend to act out angry feelings physically instead of expressing themselves verbally. The Magic Circle program (Palomares, Ball, and Bessell, n.d.) can be modified to help learning disabled children express feelings more effectively. The basic structure of this program is that the children meet daily for about thirty minutes, sitting on the floor in a circular arrangement. The curriculum lists discussion topics sequenced from kindergarten to grade 12, with a different topic discussed each day.

To commence the session, the leader states the five rules: everybody has a turn; no one is allowed to "put down" another person; no one is forced to talk (If a student does not want to talk, he says "Pass"); no one talks out of turn; and everybody listens. The leader makes sure the rules are enforced and contributes to the discussion as a group member.

Several modifications of the Magic Circle program are required to conform to the twelve elements. To facilitate sitting in a circular arrangement, children may be asked to sit around the edge of a carpet or on a line drawn on the floor indicating the circumference of the circle (structure). The rest of the room may be darkened, or the activity can be performed in a screened-off area to minimize distractions and focus attention. Ten- to fifteen-minute sessions with eight to twelve children are adequate. The sessions should be ended before the children become restless. In addition to the leader's stating the rules at the beginning of the session, the children might be asked to repeat them (cues for attention and overlearning).

Discussing a new topic each day (as suggested in the Magic Circle program) is inappropriate with learning disabled children. Instead, the same topic might be discussed for a week, in order to help the children learn the vocabulary and concepts and feel confident about expressing themselves (programming by small increments in difficulty and overlearning). The following topics might be utilized to teach labeling and communication of feelings:

1. Something that happened today that made me feel happy, sad, frustrated, angry. (About a week should be spent on each feeling. Positive feelings should be introduced first because they are less threatening.)
2. A "warm fuzzy" I gave today—how I felt and how the other person felt.
3. A "warm fuzzy" I received today—how I felt and how the other person felt.
4. A "cold prickly" I gave today—how I felt and how the other person felt.
5. A "cold prickly" I received today—how I felt and how the other person felt.

The teacher can introduce the concepts of "warm fuzzy" and "cold prickly" by reading the story in *T.A. for Tots* (Freed, 1973) to the children and by having them make "warm fuzzy" and "cold prickly" objects in art class (appeal to various sense modalities, high-interest materials).

Teachers who work with learning disabled children must be more active leaders than the usual Magic Circle leader. During their turn, they should model an answer which is one step more sophisticated than that of most of the children in the group. Relatively competent children should be chosen to begin the discussion and reinforced for their contribution (modeling and vicarious reinforcement). It is important to praise children for sharing their feelings, help them label their feelings more accurately (for instance, more precise words for *happy,* depending on the context, might be *proud, contented,* or *excited*), and ask leading questions when children are having difficulty (structure, immediate feedback, and positive reinforcement).

To conclude, the modifications of the Magic Circle program should make it suitable for small groups of eight- to twelve-year-old children with learning disabilities. The program described above should take about ten weeks, depending on the capability of the group.

Acquiring Interpersonal Problem-Solving Skills. An important aspect of social competence is the ability to solve interpersonal problems. Learning disabled children's difficulty in this area is a factor in their lack of acquisition of positive peer relationships (Bryan, 1976). Consequently, teaching them to solve interpersonal problems should be an objective of social skill training programs. According to Spivack, Platt, and Shure (1976), socially competent children have the following four problem-solving skills:

1. They are able to conceptualize several alternative solutions to an interpersonal problem (such as how to persuade another child to relinquish a toy).
2. They can engage in step-by-step planning (or means-end thinking) to reach a goal (such as becoming captain of a team).
3. They are capable of predicting the consequences of a specific course of action (such as grabbing another child's toy).
4. They are able to understand cause-and-effect dynamics in human relations (such as when a child is upset after being yelled at by the teacher and takes it out on another child).

Role playing is an effective technique for teaching interpersonal problem solving (Sarason, 1976). Its success can probably be attributed to the fact that it is concrete, appeals to several sensory modalities, and is highly interesting. Two role-playing programs are discussed here. The first, a program that I have used, is suitable for eight- to twelve-year-old children. The second, devised by Sarason (1976), is suitable for learning disabled adolescents.

In order to make a role-playing session a learning experience, it must be structured by the teacher; and cues for attention, modeling, positive reinforcement, small increments in difficulty, and opportunities for overlearning should become part of the process. The following steps to structure a role-playing activity are suggested:

1. Choose an interpersonal situation which is a problem in the group (such as teasing or fighting).
2. Plan at least two scenarios involving the interaction of two or three characters centered around the interpersonal situation. The first should be as nonthreatening as possible. The "Peanuts" characters tend to interest children and make the situation seem less applicable to them. The second scenario should be similar to the first, except that the members of the group become the characters. If a third scenario is planned, a situation that has actually occurred might be role-played.
3. The children should be asked to sit on chairs set up in a horizontal line or lines, as in an audience (structure). Before the session begins, a nonverbal signal for them to be quiet and come to attention should be arranged (for instance, flicking lights, a whistle or tone, hands on head). If possible, two adults should be involved in the session. The teacher may be joined by a parent volunteer or older mature student.
4. The teacher presents the initial problem to the group (for example, Lucy calls Charlie Brown a nasty name out in the school yard). If the goal is to teach consequential thinking, the class can be asked to predict what might happen next. The teacher and assistant act out the suggestions (modeling), and the group discusses how the participants feel and evaluates whether the consequences are true to life. The children are then asked to

think of alternatives that would result in a friendly resolution of the problem. After they are acted by the adults, those who have been listening quietly have the opportunity to role-play the alternatives (positive reinforcement for appropriate behavior). Again, the feelings of the characters and the practicality of the solution are discussed by the group. The same procedure is repeated (overlearning) using a parallel situation involving particular children in the class.

5. If the audience or actors get out of control, the nonverbal signal is employed.

6. Depending on the teacher's objectives, the problem for the group to solve may require consequential, alternative, means-end, or cause-and-effect thinking. Means-end thinking may be taught by providing the children with the beginning and ending of a story and asking them to fill in the middle (for example, a new child moves into the neighborhood and has no friends. At the end of the story, she has three new friends). The story is then role-played. Younger or less capable students should work on consequential and alternative thinking; older or more advanced students should learn means-end and cause-and-effect thinking.

7. At the end of the session, the teacher may say what he has learned from the experience. Then the children might be asked to say what they have learned (modeling and overlearning).

8. Some students of ten years of age and older may find the sessions more interesting if they are videotaped. The teacher's modeling of role playing may be less necessary with this group. Videotaping permits immediate feedback to the actor on his behavior and provides another opportunity for overlearning.

Sarason (1976) has devised a role-playing approach for teaching adolescents interpersonal problem solving. He has employed it with delinquent boys in a detention center and with students in a vocational program in a secondary school. The procedure incorporates all the twelve elements and is appropriate for learning disabled adolescents.

Sarason used a small-group social skill training format. Each group had four to ten adolescents (the small groups were needed in the detention center) and two trainers. In the detention center the trainers undertook the role playing and were male graduate students. In the secondary school dramatic arts students videotaped the scenes. The trainer was a teacher or guidance counselor.

The topics of the role-playing sessions are very relevant for learning disabled adolescents. They included:

1. Dealing with authority (police, a difficult boss).
2. Becoming part of the group.
3. Resisting peer pressure (showing off, skipping school, drinking).
4. Handling anger (avoiding fights and arguments).
5. Taking responsibility.
6. Performing effectively in a job interview.
7. Coping with school problems.
8. Asking for help.
9. Coping with boredom.
10. Planning ahead.
11. Making decisions.
12. Dealing with difficult parents.

A consistent format was used for each of the sixteen modeling sessions. Sarason (1976, pp. 77–78) describes the procedure:

> Following the first day's orientation, which included a short example scene, each subsequent meeting adhered to this format: One of the models began the session by introducing and describing the particular scene to be enacted that day. The introductions for each of the scenes had been memorized by the models. These introductions served to orient the boys to the group's work for the day and to afford them a rationale for the particular scene. After the boys had been briefed concerning specific aspects of the modeling to which they should pay special attention, the models role-played the particular scene for the day while the boys observed.
>
> Most of the scenes employed are divided into parts. In some cases the first part depicts an undesirable way of coping with the problem and the second a more desirable

way. Following the model's enactment of the situation, one boy is called on to summarize and explain the content and outcome of what had just been observed. The group is not told at the outset which boy will be called on. This procedure helps ensure that each boy attends carefully to what is going on in the group. After this, models and boys comment on and discuss the scene briefly. A short break then takes place, during which soft drinks are served and an audio or video role-playing tape is played. After this, the remaining boys enact the situations, so that each boy participates in each session. Each meeting ends with final summaries and comments concerning the scene, its most salient aspects, and its generalizability.

In the procedure employed, comments and questions by the models are aimed at sustaining the group's interest in and attention to the scenes being role-played. Responses made by the models are brief, specific, and not projective. Lengthy discussion by group members is not encouraged. The models attempt to get the boys thinking about related and similar situations in which the modeled contents of the scene could possibly apply at some point in their lives. An example of this is provided by the "Job Interview" scene, which was followed by an enumeration of the many situations in which boys would be required to make a good impression on somebody in authority.

The modeling sequence consisted of fourteen sessions. Pairs of boys in the groups made up and enacted their own scenes during the fifteenth session. These scenes were subsequently role-played by the other boys. The boys were informed of this procedure a week in advance, were given adequate time to develop an appropriate scene for the session, and were given the opportunity to use the models as "consultants." This homework assignment aroused the interest of most of the boys, who clearly endeavored to do a good job in the development and presentation of their scenes. Although most of their modeling sessions were elaborations or extensions of aspects of previously modeled materials, some of the boys produced highly original and relevant situations. The final session, the sixteenth, served as a review and summary of the work conducted during the previous fifteen meetings.

In Sarason's (1976) empirical evaluation of this procedure with the delinquents, he found that the modeling group was more positive toward the state's system of dealing with young offenders than controls, recalled and applied the contents of the sessions better than students in a discussion group, and had less recidivism in a three-year period. Sarason speculated that the reason for the effectiveness of the modeling was the degree of structure, the provision of an alternative model from home or peer group, and the fact that "observational opportunities provide an individual with information about the world, how it works, and how to survive in it" (p. 87). In Spivack, Platt, and Shure's (1976) terms, the adolescents acquired the interpersonal problem-solving skills of alternative, consequential, means-end, and causal thinking.

Increasing Attention Span and Organization and Decreasing Distraction. Some children with learning disabilities have a short attention span and are disorganized, impulsive, distractible, and hyperactive (Bryan, 1974). These problems affect their classroom performance. Although most interventions to change these behaviors are ecological in nature, several investigators have used cognitive training to decrease the impulsive behavior of hyperactive children (Meichenbaum, 1977). The self-instructional method is described by Meichenbaum (1977, p. 32) as follows: "(1) An adult model performed a task while talking to himself out loud (cognitive modeling); (2) The child performed the same task under the direction of the model's instructions (overt, external guidance); (3) The child performed the task while instructing himself aloud (overt self-guidance); (4) The child whispered the instructions to himself as he went through the task (faded, overt self-guidance); and finally (5) The child performed the task while guiding his performance via private speech (covert self-instruction)."

As training progressed, the statements modeled by the trainer and repeated by the child were expanded through response chaining and successive approximation procedures. Meichenbaum and Goodman (1971) found that the impulsive children who were trained through modeling and self-instruction improved on the Porteus Maze test, Wechsler Intelligence Scale for Children performance IQ and Kagan's measure of cognitive impulsivity. The self-instruction procedure is structured and incorporates all of the twelve elements. For further discussion of it, see Chapter Seven.

Learning Self-Care and Life Skills. Due to motor problems, difficulty with verbal reasoning and expression, or a restricted environment, many children and adolescents with learning disabilities do not acquire some basic self-care and life skills. Most intact children have learned to eat and dress by themselves with limited assistance and have been toilet trained by the time they enter school at the age of five. By the end of third grade, they are independent in all of these skills and have acquired some basic housekeeping skills such as making beds, doing dishes, and setting the table. During later childhood and adolescence, most of the other skills required for independent living (cooking, shopping, grooming, housekeeping, and use of transit) are learned.

Most children learn these skills without systematic instruction. Many learning disabled children, however, require direct instruction at home and school to learn these life skills. They also benefit from instruction in activities that facilitate integration into the peer group (activities such as bicycle riding, skating, swimming, and dancing). The self-help training programs that are available tend to be prepared for moderately mentally retarded children and adults (Baker, Brightman, Heifetz, and Murphy, 1976). They are very structured and involve fine task analysis. To adapt them for learning disabled children, some steps can be omitted, and more reliance on verbal instruction and social reinforcement is permissible. In general, learning disabled children and adolescents should be able to acquire these life skills quite quickly with direct instruction.

Developing a More Positive Self-Concept. Self-concept and self-esteem are generally acquired as a result of daily interactions with the environment. Consequently, ecological intervention tends to be the treatment of choice. Nevertheless, there are some specific exercises which may help students develop greater awareness of their own strengths, weaknesses, and interests. The numerous books on values clarification are excellent sources of material that can be adapted for learning disabled children by incorporating the twelve elements. The method of adapting exercises is illustrated by showing how the *20 Things I Love to Do* strategy (Simon, Howe, and Kirschenbaum, 1972) may be modified. Normally, in the "20 Things I Love to Do" activity, the teacher asks the class to divide an 8½ x 11 inch sheet of paper in half and write the numbers 1 to 20 down the left margin. The students are allowed five to ten minutes to list, on the left half of the page, twenty things they love to do. They are then asked to draw five columns on the right-hand side of the page (see Figure 5). In column 1 the students are asked to write a $ sign if the activity costs more than $10 each time. In column 2 an *A* is put if the activity is done alone, a *P* if done with people, and an *AP* to indicate that either is possible. In column 3 they are asked to write an *M* if they believe the activity might be on their mother's "20 Things I Love to Do" list, an *F* if it might be on their father's list, and an *MF* if on both lists. In column 4 the five most important items to them are rank-ordered. Finally, in column 5 the approximate date when they last engaged in the activity is written. Once the page is filled out, the students are asked to look at it carefully and decide what they have learned from the exercise. This may be communicated to the class if the student wishes.

Modifying this activity for learning disabled children involves reducing the spatial complexity, writing demands, and session length; making the concepts more concrete, and providing opportunities for modeling, positive reinforcement, and overlearning.

One method of adapting the activity is to have learning disabled children make a "10 Things I Love to Do" scrapbook. For each of ten days they are given an 8½ × 14 inch piece of paper resembling the righthand side of Figure 5 and are requested to draw a picture of one thing they love to do. A checkoff system is used to help them indicate whether they do the activity alone or with people, whether it is active, whether it involves money, and whether they are adept at it. Before the scrapbook is begun, the teacher may engage the class in a brainstorming session in order to create a master list of things children love to do. The teacher should show the class a scrapbook as a model. It may be necessary to praise students who do not copy the model precisely. During the class, the teacher moves among the children, reinforcing them for their ideas. Thus, the procedure is concrete and structured and involves modeling and positive reinforcement.

The same procedure is practiced for ten days (spaced practice, overlearning). Once ten pictures are completed, the children bind them into a scrapbook. During the next few days, all the

Picture of one activity the student enjoys					

Name _____ Title _____

Alone ◯	Active ◯◯
People ◯	Quiet ◯◯
Both ◯	Good at it
$ Yes ◯	Yes ◯◯
No ◯	No ◯◯

10 Things I Love to Do

1 Go to concerts	$	P	MF	3	5/80
2 Eat ice cream		AP	M		Mon
3 Swim in lake		AP	F		8/80
4 Teach		P	F	4	To-day
17 Work with children		P	F	5	3/6
18 Have intimate conversations		P		1	5/6
19 Make a party	$	P			12/80
20 Play the piano		A	M	2	March

20 Things I Love to Do

Figure 5. Modifications of the "20 Things I Love to Do" Activity

children discuss their scrapbooks with the teacher individually, in order to help the children verbalize what they have learned about themselves from the experience (concrete formulation, immediate feedback, small increments in difficulty). The final step is for the children to meet in a group, show their scrapbooks to each other, and state what they have learned. (See the section on labeling and communication of feelings for an appropriate structured format.) Teachers should reinforce the children for sharing, assist with verbalizing concepts, and point out how children differ in their preferences and values.

The "10 Things I Love to Do" activity takes ten to fifteen days to complete and is appropriate for eight- to twelve-year-old children. Both the teacher and the children can gain insights into the children's self-concept. The information may help the teacher find reinforcers to motivate students. For these reasons, the "10 Things I Love to Do" activity is a valuable strategy for children with learning disabilities.

Understanding the Nature of the Disability. Many children with learning disabilities do not understand the nature of their problem, and their fantasies about their disability may be worse than the disability itself. Consequently, helping them understand the nature of their disability is an important objective.

The Tuned-In, Turned-On Book About Learning Problems (Hayes 1974) is written for learning disabled children and adolescents. Most children above age ten comprehend the vocabulary in the book or on the cassette tape. An excellent method of using this book is for teachers to read it aloud with groups of learning disabled children and discuss the material with them. Some of the activities in the book may be done as a group, with students sharing their perceptions, feelings, and experiences. To assist with overlearning, students may read the book or listen to the tape independently (appeal to various sensory modalities). A valuable adjunct is the opportunity for students to contract with the teacher to try some of the compensatory strategies discussed in the book. If learning disabled children adequately understand their problems and can discuss them openly, it is possible that the reactions of denial, depression, and anger that are common when they are confused about their problems may not be as severe.

Ecological Intervention

Individual psychotherapy and affective education are forms of intervention that focus on the child. The emphasis in the behavior management approach is on changing environmental contingencies in order to modify children's behavior. In an ecological intervention, treatment is directed at the child, the environment, and the interaction between the child and the environment. Frequently, a variety of other approaches—including psychotherapy, behavior management, and affective education techniques—are utilized as part of the ecological intervention.

Two types of ecological interventions—special education settings and a remedial summer camp environment for children with learning disabilities—are discussed in this section.

Special Education Settings. Learning disabled children are frequently placed in contained special classes or resource rooms in order to increase the intensity of remedial programming in academic subjects. According to Bryan and Wheeler (1976), the changes in the environment resulting from special education placement go beyond remedial programming. In a resource room with a special education teacher, the children spend more time on task-oriented behavior and much less time on waiting than in the regular classroom. They receive a larger proportion of positive reinforcement and a smaller proportion of negative reinforcement and generally interact more with the teacher. Bryan (1974b) concludes that the attentional deficit of learning disabled children can be altered when the educational environment is changed.

Bryan and Wheeler (1976) compared the behavior of teachers in regular and special classes for the mentally retarded and learning disabled. They found that the special-class teachers related to the children primarily as individuals and that the children had a high rate of responsiveness, whereas the regular class teachers communicated mainly by addressing the class as a group.

The studies completed by Bryan (1974b) and Bryan and Wheeler (1976) indicate that more of the twelve components of an effective remedial program tend to be incorporated into special-class settings than in the regular class. Further investigation is required to determine whether classroom environments that are more structured and have less distracting stimuli and teachers who provide more cues for attention, immediate feedback, and positive reinforcement tend to help learning disabled children attend to tasks and develop a more positive self-concept. Also needed are studies comparing regular classes, special classes, and resource rooms for the learning disabled in terms of the presence of concrete and high-interest materials, the appeal to various sensory modalities, programming by small increments in difficulty, modeling of the appropriate response, spaced practice, and opportunities for overlearning. Bryan and Wheeler (1976) concluded that the school experiences of learning disabled children are different from the experiences of average achievers. If the children are to be kept in the regular classroom, the classroom must be studied in a systematic way to separate the environmental variables from the subject variables contributing to any child's problems.

The Remedial Summer Camp. Camp Towhee, sponsored by the Integra Foundation and subsidized by the government of Ontario, is a remedial summer camp for children with learning disabilities. Sixty children, from eight to twelve years of age, live at the camp for six weeks each summer. They obtain an individualized remedial program for about two hours per day in two of the following areas of functioning—reading, spelling, mathematics, language, writing, gross motor skills, arts and crafts, music, drama, and nature—depending on their needs. The remainder of the day is spent in normal camping activities, such as swimming, hiking, or boating. Camping and remedial activities are usually combined, and the natural environment is used as much as possible in remediation. Emphasis is placed on children's acquisition of social skills, interpersonal cognitive problem-solving skills, and a more positive self-concept.

Although behavioral techniques are frequently employed, Camp Towhee is primarily an ecological intervention. The following factors are central to the milieu:

1. Removal from home and school and the dynamics of these settings for a short period of time.
2. A natural rural environment, with woods and fields to run and play in, a lake, aesthetic beauty, and camping facilities. These stimulate the curiosity of the child and a will to learn.

3. A warm, supportive, mature staff.
4. Daily life with peers, necessitating learning skills of cooperating in a group.
5. A task analysis of each camper's social deficits and direct and indirect remediation.
6. A structured day, with planned activities for all but half an hour.
7. Carefully planned success experiences within an individualized program. The twelve elements that are essential in an intervention with learning disabled children are adhered to when activities are planned.
8. Remediation, including social deficit remediation, through games and camping.
9. An atmosphere in which every possible means is utilized to structure the program and the environment to facilitate the children's use of language, mathematics, and movement.
10. Emphasis on informing parents and teachers of the children's activities at camp and helping them develop appropriate programs at home and school.

The effect of the camp environment on the children's interpersonal cognitive problem-solving skills, self-concept, and classroom behavior has been studied (Wiener, 1978). The results indicated that the children were more adept at interpersonal cognitive problem solving after the six-week camp program and maintained these gains over a six-month period after camp. Similarly, they acquired a more positive self-concept, which was not transitory, since they continued to respond positively during the followup testing. They learned to behave more appropriately over the summer and continued this modified behavior in the classroom for the six-month follow-up period. Specifically, they were less anxious about their achievement, less likely to blame others for their errors or to quit easily, and less bothered by changes in plans after they attended camp. One of the limitations of the study was that there was no control group of learning disabled children who would have met the criteria for admission to camp but did not attend. Consequently, controlled pretest, posttest, and follow-up comparisons were not made.

To conclude, children's home, school, and recreational environments have an effect on their affective and social development. More research is required to isolate the relevant environmental variables so that appropriate ecological interventions for learning disabled children can be planned.

Biological intervention, individual psychotherapy, behavior management, affective education, and ecological intervention all have the potential to facilitate social adjustment and the acquisition of social skills in children with learning disabilities. Effectiveness of any single approach seems to be governed by appropriate matching of the children's needs and the approach employed, and by the degree to which the twelve essential elements of a remedial program for learning disabled children are incorporated. A combination of approaches may be used with one child simultaneously or at different points in time.

Most of the specific practical techniques discussed in this chapter are based on my own clinical experience or on the experiences of others. Clearly, more empirical evaluative research is required to assess the relative effectiveness of the various interventions.

Chapter 9

✣ ✣ ✣ ✣ ✣

Education, Counseling, and Therapy for the Learning Disabled and Their Families

✣ There is growing recognition that family environment is a critical component in the short- and long-term adjustment of learning disabled persons. For example, although the learning disabled adults in Anderson's (1976) sample suffered from negative self-images, low tolerance for risk, and poor social relationships, four of these adults—those with strong family support—were motivated despite records of poor performance. Again, noting that social background significantly affects the progress of learning disabled students, Koppitz (1971) suggests that children's families and community agencies should be involved in programming for learning disabled children. Therapeutic intervention with learning disabled persons and their nuclear and extended families may, in some instances, be as important as academic remediation. Similarly, parents of the learning disabled possess unique educational needs that must be addressed in a systematic fashion.

Indications for therapeutic intervention are: (1) a learning disabled child, adolescent, or adult who suffers from concomitant emotional problems, who copes poorly with demands, or who has become unduly stressed and discouraged by his difficulties; (2) family members for whom the learning disability compounds stresses other than those stemming from the disability; (3) parents who are upset by having produced and having to cope with a learning disabled child; (4) family members with emotional problems that predate the discovery of their relative's learning disability but that are exacerbated by the behavior of the learning disabled person or of family members toward them; (5) family pathology in which one of the presenting features is a member with a learning problem that would not necessarily be a primary learning disability. Regardless of whether or not a family needs psychotherapy, every family of the learning disabled has education and counseling needs that can be addressed through counseling the learning disabled individual, the parents, the nuclear or extended family, or through groups drawn from several families.

Parents' Educational Needs

It has been my experience that few parents of the learning disabled comprehend what the disability is and the principles whereby it is remediated. When they are asked why their children find spelling, reading, writing, speaking, or motor coordination difficult when other children handle these functions with ease, they frequently are unable to reply. Since they do not understand that the disability is a disorganization in the processing, planning, and execution of events, they are unclear about the treatment approaches that are applicable to their particular child. As a result, they are vulnerable to the anxieties engendered or hopes raised by each chance remark, lecture, or newspaper article. They also are poorly equipped to be their child's advocates in ensuring that his remedial needs are met and evolve both within the school system and through other resources. Therefore, the first priority in the planning of a parent education program should be to develop an understanding of learning disabilities, and relate that understanding to the reasons for their child's ineptitude. They need to realize that, just as he fails to apply a strategic approach to tasks, whether those tasks be spelling, doing arithmetic, planning the use of time, preparing a meal, or handling a social encounter, in a similar fashion, he fails to evaluate his production and to modify subsequent production in response to his evaluation. Since he finds that simple tasks in his deficit areas are difficult to execute and, hence, produce anxiety, complex tasks in those areas are even more confusing and stressful for him. He probably also has difficulty holding all the facets of a complex procedure, such as learning the multiplication table or a folk dance, in his memory system in order to execute the task successfully.

Once parents understand what learning disabilities are in general terms and what their child's specific disability is, they need to match remediation to the presenting disability. If a child's problem is clumsiness, remediation of his motor coordination is appropriate. If the youngster has trouble remembering what he has heard or expressing himself, language remediation is indicated. To a large extent, remedial approaches utilize a child's strong areas of functioning, while attempting to bolster his deficit areas. Thus, if a child forgets much of what he hears, he will have to be taught to read by the sight method, although phonics may well be introduced at a later stage to obviate the need to remember how every word in the language looks. Similarly, if a child forgets what he sees, his remedial program might lean heavily on phonics, with a sight approach augmentation so that he does not have to sound out every word he sees. If a child performs poorly in a number of processes, a multisensory approach frequently is indicated. In all instances, remediation will involve learning the organization of written language, such as rules of grammar, and the patterns that language follows, such as word families. Most importantly, an eclectic teacher tries a variety of approaches, and selects those to which the child is most responsive. Any remedial clinic, school, or teacher that promotes solely one approach, regardless of the excellence of that approach, does not offer learning disabled children optimal chances for therapy. Other premises of remediation that parents should be aware of include the need to segment difficult tasks into components so that the child can master each successfully and repeat material that has been learned so that it is reinforced in a variety of forms numerous times.

Parents who understand their child's disability and the principles of remediation may be able to incorporate some remediation into everyday life. For example, parents might play word memory games with a child who demonstrates language retrieval problems. Other parents, whose child has a limited vocabulary, might expose him to new words in a variety of contexts, as well as being used in rhymes and riddles. Some parents might leave notes under the dinner plates of their reading-handicapped children, attach poems to the refrigerator door, place riddles on their children's pillows, or organize family scavenger and treasure hunts; they might leave written clues over a period of time that hint at an upcoming outing. Parents whose children are uncoordinated might have them walk on raised curbs, figure out how to fit their bodies over, under, and through obstacles created out of furniture, swim with the family, and bake cookies to improve dexterity. Parents whose children have trouble with mathematics might have them plan how they will spend their allowances, double or halve recipes, determine the quantity of food that should be cooked for the number of people eating, change miles to kilometers, and find shortcuts to figure out 15 percent gratuities. Some guidance may help parents judge the appropriate times when remediation can be incorporated into daily living and when all of their energies should be devoted to other areas. If parents are able to handle tutoring in a relaxed manner, they should determine the times of the day in which they relate best to their child. If tutoring results in frustration or impatience, parents need to find someone who can handle it better or learn to live comfortably with the fact that their child does not receive formal tutoring at home.

After parents comprehend the facets of their child's particular learning disability and how they interact with intelligence, temperament, and talents, they can be selective in seeking information on the disability and in relating it to their child. In other words, parents whose child has language disabilities would not pursue information on motor handicaps or compare the prognosis of one learning disabled person to their child when they share few attributes.

Parents need to learn what types of medical, psychological, and educational testing yield useful information, the indications for retesting, and the age at which testing should end. They should also know what to tell the child before and after testing. Before the testing session, the child should have the testing explained to him as a procedure for determining the reasons for his difficulties in specific areas of functioning, so that a course of action that will make him more competent in his deficit areas can be formulated. If possible, the physical layout of the testing room, the types of questions to be answered, and the length of time of the testing should be described to him. Once the parents learn the test results, they should share them with their child. They might say, for example, "The reason that you have trouble reading and spelling is that you forget the way the words look. We will find someone who will help you to remember how words look and teach you to read and spell by sounding out words."

It is important that the child have a medical assessment to investigate the possibility of conditions that might exacerbate the learning disability such as hearing or vision impairment, allergies, nutritional deficiencies, and subclinical epilepsy. Unless the disability has had a sudden onset in a previously intact child or there is evidence of sudden deterioration, there seems to be little practical usefulness in neurological investigations; neither the knowledge of the location of the brain dysfunction or speculation as to cause is useful for remedial planning. Presently, the most useful guides to remediation are tests that suggest a child's abilities and disabilities, such as an educational and psychological assessment undertaken by an examiner who notes the manner in which a child approaches a task, the contexts in which he is able and unable to perform specific tasks, the types of errors he makes, and the levels of complexity that he can handle. Similarly, educational tests that provide total scores tell us little, whereas tests that indicate the level at which a child errs and the types of errors made provide useful indications for remediation.

There is little purpose in having a child retested if his previous testing describes his learning style. However, if he is having difficulty that cannot be explained by his last testing, if there is a sudden alteration in his behavior, or if his previous testing did not describe him as parents and teachers see him, successive testing might help. Once the learning disabled youth reaches middle adolescence, testing should be terminated unless a deterioration in functioning is noted; generally, there are few changes in test results after midadolescence.

Just as parents must determine when to stop testing, they must grapple with a more difficult decision—when to stop remediation. This decision must be faced both for the child who has not appreciably responded to remediation and for the child who has. At some time the parents and child must weigh the amount of remediation he has received over the years, the extent to which he has responded, and the price of his remediation to date in terms of energy expended, financial outlay, and activities forfeited. These issues should be balanced against his current coping level, the skills needed to reach vocational and other goals of living, and the demands made on the child's and family's time and energy. These factors will determine whether or not to terminate remediation. When the family has decided to forfeit remediation, this decision should be shared with educators so that their energies can be redirected from remediation to helping their student with coping strategies. If the learning disabled person finds that he needs additional remediation at some point in life in order to reach a goal, the decision can be reversed. It is comforting for parents to realize that their offspring probably will continue to improve in his deficit areas after remediation has stopped. As long as he does not avoid tasks in his less-competent areas of functioning, the combination of maturation and practice will increase competence, although rarely to the point of perfection.

Some tasks need to be simplified and taught sequentially. For example, if a child cannot tie his shoelaces, he could practice with a bathrobe sash under his knees while sitting and learn to knot the sash; he would progress to tying the sash into a bow and then knotting and bowing a shoelace. Parents need to plan the steps to help the child learn a skill. Consider a child who runs around his host's house all night when invited to sleep over; he needs to build up to a night's sleep in short increments. Initially his friend could be invited to his house for brief, structured, supervised play periods, which become increasingly longer and less structured. These practice sessions should include a meal and occur at different times of the day. The child could then practice sleeping in rooms in his own house other than his own bedroom and visiting his friend's home for a play period, a meal, an evening, and finally sleeping overnight.

Through observation, parents can note the areas in which the child is disorganized; they can observe whether the manifestations of disorganization arise from a lack of strategies and planning in a facet of functioning, minimal productivity, chaotic execution of tasks, anxiety generated in anticipation of tasks, or stubborn insistence that nothing be changed in that area of his life. The child who is disorganized spatially might have a locker, desk, or room in which everything is in disorder or in which he demands that nothing be moved. He may be unable to find clothing, resist going to new places, or to familiar places alone, always leave his belongings behind, never remember where they have been left, and forget how people's faces look. In a similar fashion, the child with temporal disorganization may plan his time so inefficiently that he accomplishes little, insist that routines occur at the same time each day, and become unduly upset by changes in schedule. Once parents are aware of their child's area of disorganization, they must organize that facet of his life externally, while teaching him to structure that area for himself.

The child who has difficulty organizing space needs parents who teach him how to sort and store toys, clothing, and books into categories. They should discuss with him the categories they have chosen, suggest the possible categories one might select, and be firm about storing everything in its proper place. When he has achieved a degree of order, he can assume increasing responsibility for sorting and storing his belongings. A person whose language is disorganized needs to learn how to describe an experience sequentially and how to return to the central topic if he has veered onto a tangent. In a similar fashion, parents must realize that their children do not preorganize tasks in their deficit areas; they approach tasks that they feel will be difficult with anxiety, rather than using a problem-solving approach, which should be modeled and practiced, as suggested in Chapter Seven. Just as parents initially provide structure for their child, and increasingly teach him to organize himself, in a child's early years parents must explain his behavior to relatives, friends, neighbors, educators, and others while teaching him how to explain the adjustments he requires in the briefest, most direct fashion possible. This explanation should be limited to the difficulties he experiences or anticipates in a situation; whenever possible, he should request assistance without elaborating on the reasons why he requires help.

A child's comment or confusion may signify that he has not acquired a concept that a child of that age is expected to know. Parents need to recognize the level the child has reached and teach him successive levels of complexity from that point, as well as correct erroneous ideas of how the world functions. For example, a parent who discovers her son does not know when his birthday is should probe other aspects of temporal knowledge, such as the times of the day, days of the weeks, months of the year, and so on. Parents also need to learn how to encourage their child to conceptualize, and to select alternatives. One way to do this is by asking questions: "Is there another way that you could have done that?"; "Where will you get the wood to build your boat?"; "Why do you suppose she behaved in that fashion? What else might she have done?"; or "What can you tell your teacher that will make her sympathetic to your problem?"

Their child's frustration, hyperactivity, or disorganization should alert parents that he is overstimulated or anxious; they should provide him with expectations that are less complex or anxiety producing. Once they recognize the source of the stimulation, they can calm the child down by an arm around his shoulders, quiet language, a reduction of excitement, or removal to a less-stimulating place. Tasks can be restructured and the level of difficulty increased after he copes comfortably. A stable, low-stress household that is still flexible and enjoys change and growth will also benefit families with a learning disabled member.

A general understanding of child development and behavior will help parents cope with each stage of their own child's development. They need practice in distinguishing behaviors that are typical of youngsters or adolescents of their child's age from behaviors that might be attributable to the child's temperament or to the disability. It is critical that they appreciate the effects that environment has on these attributes. They should not become unduly alarmed at changes in behavior if such changes occur normally at junctures in development, such as puberty, when behavioral change is expected. Every behavior that their child produces should not be attributed to the disability, although they should be sensitive to the difficulties that the disability creates for their child. Neither should they credit every behavior that their other children exhibit to a possible learning disability. Moreover, the disability assuredly should not absorb all their time and thoughts, even if they feel that a lesser commitment will shortchange their child.

Parents must be encouraged to allow their child the independent experiences that he is capable of assuming, just as they must allow him to make the same errors in judgment and become involved in the same misbehaviors that his brothers and sisters are allowed. It is acceptable and often desirable to have parents plan an experience more precisely for their disabled offspring than they do for their intact children, but, in the end result, he must try it on his own. It is helpful for parents to articulate the expectations that they have for their child and the ways they achieve such expectations. They could discuss what children and parents do and do not owe each other.

Parents should set short- and long-term goals for themselves and for their learning disabled child. Counselors can assist parents in setting of goals that are realistic, given the child's capabilities, and using existing services to meet those goals. For instance, if one goal is to have the child learn the family's language of origin, the first question is whether his linguistic ability is sufficient to learn a foreign language. The second consideration is whether he can cope with the pressures of learning a new language in addition to his academic pressures. If he is likely to be stressed, the parents should decide whether they would prefer him to learn their language of origin and handle a less rigorous curriculum, not learn the language, or learn to speak it but not to read and write it. Would a private tutor provide less pressure than a class? If he can cope with a class, what alterations in approach should one ask of the teacher? What predictions can we make about his ability to cope with speaking, writing, and spelling another language from our knowledge of the ways he handles the English language?

In a similar fashion, parents should establish and work on short- and long-term social, recreational, and academic goals for their child. The setting of such goals focuses the parents on working toward improvement in those areas that they deem the most important. Since parents of the learning disabled become unduly anxious about distant possibilities, and the learning disabled become disproportionately anxious about upcoming events, exercises in parental goal setting and implementation should assist family members in adopting a planning approach to future goals and to success.

All family members need to be able to perceive the learning disabled member in perspective. It is easy to become overwhelmed by the disparity between his current level of functioning and that of his peers, but it is helpful to remember how far he has come. These exercises in perspective can be stimulated by particular professionals or lay persons in the community whose judgment parents have learned to trust. Therefore, one of the most critical tasks for parents is to find people who understand their child's abilities and disabilities and can suggest knowledgeable courses of action throughout childhood, adolescence, and early adulthood. Parents must learn to recognize the indications that they and other family members are experiencing problems that cannot be handled within the family and seek external assistance.

Counseling Issues

Before the inception of the volunteer organizations involved with learning disabilities, learning disabilities were widely attributed to family pathology. Parents of the learning disabled resented being blamed for their children's difficulties, when the difficulties were due, in large part, to intrinsic differences in the children. Nonetheless, the parental insistence that environment has no bearing on their children's functioning has assumed such an extreme position that family difficulties and pathology now tend to be blamed on the disabled child, rather than the other way around. As a result, learning disabled offspring have been the scapegoats for marital discord or breakdown, just as the disability itself has been the scapegoat for the child's misbehavior or delinquency. Regardless of how convenient a scapegoat the learning disabled child might be or how easy it is to blame the disability for all of one's child's behavior, learning disabled children rarely destroy a functioning marriage, although they will create stress. Similarly, the disability is not an explanation for antisocial behavior, although it might contribute to it. Family environment, on the other hand, is a critical component of the learning disabled person's adjustment. It influences the social and emotional development of learning disabled children more than it does their siblings (Kronick, 1976).

Since the learning disability itself is popularly perceived as being the only facet of family dysfunction requiring therapeutic intervention, it is popularly assumed that a therapist who works with a learning disabled person or his family must have an extensive background in learning disabilities. Actually, these individuals and families respond, in large measure, to their stresses in a similar fashion to other stressed individuals and families. It is essential, however, that the therapist believe that primary learning disabilities truly exist, and it is helpful for him to have some understanding of learning disabilities. In counseling essentially healthy families who are stressed by the disability, the emphases are on dealing with the feelings that the disability has created, teaching family members how to verbalize those feelings and encouraging other family members to express their feelings. Parents in such families must find or create services for the disabled member, and come to terms with the lack of optimal services, so that they alleviate their anxieties about their competence to provide adequate opportunities for their children. They need to be helped to appreciate the contribution that they are making toward their disabled member's ability to live a satisfying life. Of course, the emphasis in counseling pathological families is on a reduction of the pathology, with particular concern about the ways that the pathology perpetuates or exacerbates the disability.

Therapeutic Intervention with Pathological Families. Since learning disabled children are born into families within the entire range of mental health, from healthy to pathological, a child with a primary learning disability may be a member of a pathological family.

It is particularly important, in the provision of services for such children, to ensure that their learning disability is not attributed completely to family pathology and remedial services withheld. It is equally important that the child not be penalized or denied services because of a lack of parental cooperation or other undesirable parental behavior. The learning disabled member's disability needs to be taken into account both in therapeutic planning and in dealing with family members' reactions to the disability. One must be additionally alert to the ways the disability is exploited pathologically (Kronick, 1976).

In some pathological families, the injunction against separation and individuation of family members is so strong that one of the children is not allowed to attend school, or, if such a child does attend, he is not allowed to learn, since learning leads to independence. Such children demonstrate secondary learning problems. Unlike children with primary learning disabilities, they typically are able to process, to remember, and to produce information adequately and do not respond to remediation. Their families may blame their children's failures on the supposed ineptitude of professionals to diagnose and properly remediate what the parents insist is a learning disability. They use this illustration of professional incompetence to discount all professionals and thus avoid family therapy. Accordingly, the children continue to learn poorly because their families have proclaimed educators as bunglers. Furthermore, their families perpetuate the pathology by using their children's persistent learning problems as proof of the uselessness of utilizing professional help.

In counseling healthy, although stressed, families or disturbed families in which there is a learning disabled member, the counselor should be aware of the ways such families typically demonstrate their stress.

Counseling Healthy Families. All stress entails loss or threatened loss. When a loss or threatened loss is initially recognized, there is a period of preoccupation with the loss aspects—in this instance, the learning disability. As a result, the loss is perceived as encompassing all facets of the child's current and eventual life experience, and all of his behaviors are interpreted as relating to the disability. The stages that Kübler-Ross (1969) delineates in *On*

Death and Dying are transversed although not necessarily in sequence and can be experienced concurrently. Even when these stages have been adequately worked through initially, they can be reexperienced at times of stress, such as the learning disabled member's adolescence or approaching adulthood or the parents' middle age. Kronick (1974) describes the feelings and behavior of the learning disabled person and his nuclear and extended family members as they transverse each stage. Stress of any magnitude causes people to doubt their role effectiveness interpersonally and vocationally, so that they no longer perceive of themselves as agents of change, particularly with their learning disabled child. As a result, they may not provide problem-solving or other growth experiences for their youngsters (Kronick, 1976).

Reactions to stress can be: rigidity, regression, constriction of spheres of functioning, resistance to change, deterioration of communication skills, a view of people and institutions as malevolent and of the world as unsafe. Thus, the learning disabled person and other family members may behave rigidly and immaturely, although the inflexibility on the part of the learning disabled may represent, in part, his anxiety about his ability to perform adequately in strange or complex circumstances. His mother's inflexibility may result, to some degree, from her efforts to create a structured environment and to avoid changes that result in her child's misbehavior, even if capitulation to sameness means a loss of parental authority. Through these mechanisms the learning disabled child, who needs change in order to learn, tyrannizes a household into a stalemate position. Similarly, change and growth are further hampered by excessive maternal control (Humphries and Bauman, 1980). Mothers, in their efforts to assist their youngsters with difficult tasks and to avoid embarrassment in front of others, may assist their youngsters excessively and verbalize extensively, notwithstanding their children's noncompliance with their verbal requests. Similarly, the learning disabled member's immaturity may represent not only stress but a paucity of experience and delayed developmental processes. Since some outsiders are suspicious of or deny the existence of a disability that is not readily apparent, some learning disabled persons and their families isolate themselves from peers, neighbors, and relatives. In such instances, the parents may feel that no one comprehends their experience, and the learning disabled member may be depressed about his label. He may not want others to think of him as unintelligent or inept or to be labeled as "that kid in the dummies' class." The parents may conceptualize the world as a place where their child will be misunderstood, disallowed opportunities, and humiliated.

Stress can result in a narrowing of focus; facing the problem in its entirety is too overwhelming, so the problem and solutions are perceived in a restricted context. The perception of the disability is thus limited to one or two manifestations, with a simple treatment or remedial approach being embraced as a potential cure. Similarly, an isolated manifestation of growth or improvement may be generalized to total improvement. Such reductionist thinking enables parents to blame all the learning disabled child's difficulties on the omissions of one teacher's approach or on the failure of the education system to remediate the child more comprehensively, regardless of the current age of the learning disabled member. The anger of the learning disabled person or his parents at the person or system that ostensibly failed him may be so pervasive that it colors all their relationships.

Stressed families demonstrate a reduced ability to take risks or to allow separation, individuation, and growth. They may infantilize, overprotect, or rear their learning disabled child inconsistently. Their anger may be turned inward or misdirected. There will be concomitant difficulty around the handling of ambivalent feelings toward persons or situations.

The impact of the learning disability on family members is related to the number of stresses with which they are faced or have encountered in the past. Thus, single parenthood, a difficult marriage, inadequate housing or finances, several preschool children, illness, or threatened loss of job will compound the impact. The extent to which the learning disabled member and his relatives are devastated also will relate to their perceptions of the long-term threat that the disability poses to them—that is, how they imagine his adult life—and the extent to which meeting his needs will interfere with their aspirations. People with many outside interests will be less upset than those whose lives revolve around the disability.

Stressed persons overestimate their role in relationship to the stress; therefore, they magnify the importance of their parenting or their role as siblings and feel guilty for each failure to meet their personal expectations of adequacy. Consequently, they perceive themselves as unsuccessful parents and siblings. The pervasiveness of their guilt will relate to the extent to which they were made to feel guilty for past behavior. Parents and siblings may respond to imagined or real devaluation by demeaning family members, internalizing or displacing responsibility, or describing the learning disability to everyone that they encounter as their excuse for not creating a more acceptable product.

Some of the upset demonstrated by stressed families of the learning disabled is a realistic reflection of their experiences in society. Many have encountered ignorance, hostility, rejection, denial, fear, and withholding of information through misuse of confidentiality; and they have had their efforts to ensure services for their children labeled as "neurotic," "unrealistic," and "pushy." They have discovered that there is a severe shortage of adequate services and no services for some age groups or some facets of functioning such as recreation. They have been made to feel, on occasion, that they are the cause of their child's problems, or are delusional in imagining that there is anything the matter with their child and unrealistic in their demands.

Some families become so invested in the disability that it offers them too many satisfactions to relinquish. The disability may have become family members' primary mode of communication, become one of the few spheres in life where one of the parents can feel a sense of accomplishment (through volunteerism or providing remediation). Some parents define themselves as parents of the learning disabled, and in some families the preoccupation with the disability allows them to disregard other family problems. Similarly, the learning disabled member may be so invested in his ability to control or in the attention that he receives that he is reluctant to forgo being disabled.

The experiencing of the Kübler-Ross stages is healthy and functional. Intervention can hasten their passage, cushion their intensity, and create change in families where a member persists in one stage or uses it pathologically. We all have encountered parents who spend their lives denying the disability or their role in it at great cost to their spouses and children, parents overcome with guilt, those who are martyred to the disability, those who are envious of or furious at the entire world, and those who pursue magic cures. In instances where an offspring has a heterogeneous learning disability, a severe disability, or a learning disability coupled with low intellectual functioning, a degree of chronic parental depression may be expected and realistic. The parents must continuously reconcile the discrepancy between a society that views learning disabilities as reading and spelling disorders with an offspring who exhibits behavioral extremes; is forgetful, disorganized, gullible, clumsy, and stubborn; and lacks social and instrumental judgment. Parents of such children suspect that they will lead marginal lives in adulthood, yet no one shares their perception.

Each family member's reaction to the disability will be related to his understanding of it and its implications. The therapist can explore each member's perception of the disability, its etiology, manifestations, and prognosis, and each family member's concerns, fears, and frustrations. It is helpful to determine the behaviors and situations around which they become the most upset, frustrated, and angry and the type of help they are seeking. If they are looking for remediation or pragmatic assistance with the handling of behavior, they will be unresponsive to counseling until their more immediate concerns have been alleviated. If remedial or other services are unavailable, parents need to be taught the ways of creating such services before their feelings can be dealt with. Once the family's beliefs about the disability have been explored, the place of the learning disabled member and of the disability itself in the family system can be examined.

Some parents suspect that were the therapist to be aware of what happens in their family, he would realize that the child is emotionally disturbed rather than learning disabled. It is important that therapists not reinforce that belief. Some learning disabled persons believe that they are mentally retarded or disturbed or that they possess special properties such as unusual sensitivity. Some families have achieved a fine balance between attending to the disability and other facets of living, whereas others utilize the disability as a preoccupation; as an escape from marital, parental, or other responsibilities; or as a scapegoat for family ills. Parents can become blamers, rescuers, or martyrs. The learning disabled member can become blamer, victim, or dependent. He can behave irresponsibly, immaturely, manipulatively, or punitively.

Family members, including the learning disabled member, need to work through feelings of being cheated, feelings that they should have been rewarded by an intact child and that a just society should be more equitable in service provision. They need opportunities to mourn the loss of the intact person that they had hoped the learning disabled child would be, or the achieving child that they had expected to produce, while recognizing that life is not necessarily fair or just. Whatever justice ensues is likelier to reflect their efforts to explain the disability to outsiders or their creation of additional services than an allocation from a deity. It is helpful, therefore, to separate fate from destiny, and determinism from personal responsibility. Clients who have channeled their anger into constructive action, who feel that they have assumed control over their lives and future, feel less helpless, overwhelmed, and unjustly treated. They feel that they have greater control over their parenting and will model internal locus of control and expect age-appropriate control of the learning disabled member. The therapist who treats the learning disabled member as a responsible person will model appropriate behavior for parents and convey to him and them that he is capable of assuming control over significant aspects of his life, while being disallowed control over inappropriate aspects.

Recognizing that families of the learning disabled typically have experienced some uncomfortable, unempathic, and useless encounters with professionals, the counselor needs to permit the venting of anger, frustration, and feelings of worthlessness that such encounters engender. Family members need to learn to direct their anger to the anger-evoking situation or person rather than have it color their current experience or interactions with professionals who are prepared to be helpful. They need to learn how to seek professionals who can meet their momentary needs, to determine the expectations that are and are not reasonable to have of professionals, and methods of terminating an unsatisfactory relationship. Parents should learn how to recognize aggression so that it is not translated into infantilization of their child. In instances where parental trust in professionals has been impaired, an informal therapeutic approach has proved helpful.

Fathers need to be reinvolved in the childrearing process, perhaps by undertaking some of the roles that their wives previously have assumed; and mothers need to learn to empathize with their husband's difficulty in effecting a relationship with his child. Rather than berate or exclude him, wives need to validate their husband's feelings and develop nonthreatening opportunities for his inclusion. Fathers should be involved in interactions with educators and other professionals and in being their child's advocate in the community. Most important, they need to be encouraged to develop recreational pursuits that are mutually enjoyable with their child. Activities should not be chosen merely because they might improve the disability, and activities in which the child has to compete with his peers in areas in which he has difficulty should be avoided. There should be an assessment of the quality of support that the father affords the mother when she is stressed. It needs to be determined whether he takes over tasks until she has regained her equilibrium and provides opportunities for her to express feelings or whether he responds to her weakness by aligning himself with her or the child and demeaning the excluded one. Similarly, there should be an assessment as to whether the wife's involvement with her child is realistic or excessive, the gains she experiences by her involvement, and the feelings it masks. Family members may need to learn communication styles that express needs, reflect feelings, and encourage problem solving and change. Parents need to realize that the withholding of information from spouse or children in order to protect them is, in fact, harmful.

Families of the learning disabled need to relearn the premise that change can be pleasurable, that learning can be exciting, and that they have individual and collective rights to fun. They need to learn ways of minimizing their child's apprehension around change while avoiding the contagion of his disorganization and anxiety and succumbing to his controlling behavior. Similarly, they need to learn ways of minimizing and containing their anxiety so that it is not transmitted to their child. It is important for parents to feel that they and their children deserve enjoyment and that external demands that dictate a life primarily of work must be altered. They must learn as well to anticipate change with the expectation that change and novelty can be enjoyable and enriching rather than forboding. Parents who perceive the learning disabled child's behavior to be a reflection of their competence will feel that they are failures when his behavior is out of control. They may attempt to reassert control by eliminating change and need to distance themselves from behavior, set behavioral goals, and develop appropriate forms of control that allow for structured and conceptualized change.

Parents need to ensure that their child receives sufficient remediation that is directed to his areas of disability by a qualified professional while avoiding the impulse to avail him of every possible treatment. Children who spend all their spare time in remediation are fed an unusual diet, and swallow megadoses of pills; they experience a childhood in which their differences have been magnified rather than minimized. Learning disabled children and adolescents tend to live in a world of extremes. Their behavior, such as hyperactivity or hypoactivity and profound frustration, represents the extreme and evokes an extreme parental or educator response. These excesses may be augmented by a therapeutic regimen that replaces typical childhood pursuits and exaggerates the differences between such children's life experiences and those of their peers. Treatments that are geared to intellectual development absorb the child's time and prevent him from spending time in activities that are geared to social and emotional remediation. Similarly, such treatments demand so much of the parents' energy that there is little left to nourish their children's affective and interactional domains.

Parents need to learn to judge the appropriateness of a therapeutic program in terms of the demands it makes of the child and them and the extensiveness with which other life processes will be disrupted. A therapist who is prepared to function as a catalyst in assessing a client's remedial and therapeutic needs and can elicit parental trust tends to reduce parental anxiety sufficiently so that treatment seeking ceases. Similarly, a therapist who assists a family in weighing the issues that determine when remediation should terminate helps to free them from the compulsion to avail their child of each new treatment encountered. Excessive or prolonged seeking of treatments and cures masks ambivalence and denial. Isolation taxes parents of the learning disabled; they should mobilize extended family members and friends to provide some instrumental and affective support as well, as sources of direction and relief.

A sense of successful parenting helps to counteract guilt and feelings of failure. Accordingly, parents should be provided with childrearing techniques that are easy to execute and are compatible with their childrearing style so that they are likely to carry through with the program. In other words, permissive parents are unlikely to carry through with behavior modification but might enjoy an approach where the consequences that the child experiences for his behavior are related to his deeds. Verbal parents might respond to an approach whereby the child is coached through talking about his concerns. Whatever technique is selected, the parents must receive strong support in the initial stages of implementation to enable them to persist through the period in which the child tests his new limits. Regardless of the good quality of several childrearing techniques, all should be used as adjuncts to competent childrearing practices. The ideal childrearing environment is one in which the parents are eclectic in their approaches, tailoring their communications with their child to his developmental level, their communication style, and the situation at hand. The literature in the learning disability field stresses the importance of consistency in childrearing practices, but it does not mention the importance of the consistency of the covert messages that are conveyed in families. All family members should have a shared understanding of how they feel about one another and what they expect of one another. This is achieved through therapeutic intervention, not parent education.

In researching the permanence of change produced by parent counseling programs, Thomasen (1976) found that many of the changes were lost subsequent to termination. A follow-up component should be built into programs to maintain change and continue growth. It is particularly important to have contact with the family at junctures of probable stress, such as the learning disabled child's entrance into secondary school.

Idiosyncratic Issues in Counseling the Learning Disabled

Although I have stressed the similarities between learning disabled individuals and their families and other stressed individuals and families, there are alternative explanations for some of the behaviors that are observed in counseling situations. Some of the behavior of learning disabled individuals may be explained by traditional therapeutic explanations, and some behaviors may be more correctly attributed to the disability. Therapists should therefore consider the possibility of neurotic or organic etiologies for presenting behaviors or a combination of both. The following discussion briefly suggests some of the ways the disability might be manifested in therapeutic environments.

Linguistic/Conceptual Disabilities. The client with problems in auditory processing and memory may experience difficulty in understanding the language in a therapeutic session particularly if it is extensive, involves complex linguistic structures, is spoken speedily, or includes large words. He may misunderstand what is being said, process only part of it, tune out, or forget the content. Some of his knowledge or concepts may be illogical or literal and immature, and require exploration and clarification. The client may express himself with difficulty or embarrassment and lack the words and language to describe experience and feelings. He may perseverate on words, phrases, or content or may digress and ramble. The style as well as the essence of his language may require pragmatic intervention.

Attention. The learning disabled patient with problems in attention may not attend to the salient features or content of a therapeutic session. The length of the session, content, and presentations may have to be altered in order to achieve a more focused approach. In some instances, chemotherapeutic intervention might promote more directed intervention.

Visual/Spatial Disabilities and Disorganization. The client with visual/spatial disabilities may not notice the facial or body expressions of family members or the therapist or may inaccurately process their expressions of emotion. His own expressions may not represent his feelings or complement the content of others. Thus, he may not unconsciously mimic others' body movments or convey messages of concordance. The excessive space or lack of distance between him and others may reflect his deficient ability to judge distance or his ignorance of the rules of social distance. He may not maintain eye contact or smile at appropriate places; he may use atypical body gestures in communication and be egocentric in orientation. His difficulties in orienting his visual/spatial world may cause him to be reluctant to individuate, to use public transportation, or to learn to drive. The excessively disorganized learning disabled patient or family will be unable to consolidate therapeutic change and reach desired goals. Their disorganization may represent more than deficient motivation and may more properly belong to the disability; pragmatic assistance in structuring time and tasks may be required.

Boundary Setting. Enmeshment occurs when family members interfere excessively in each other's affairs and prohibit the development of individual life-styles, interests, and beliefs. Enmeshment may meet neurotic needs, but it may also be the end product of prolonged parental intervention with a child's tasks and his language in order to minimize interpersonal and academic failure and rejection. In similar fashion, a learning disabled person who demonstrates difficulty with the perception of social boundaries may be manifesting either neurotic or conceptual confusion.

Repetitive Behavior. Meticulosity, being bound to details, or repetition might represent perseveration, ignorance of the acceptability of repetition, deficient ability to structure change, or anxiety about one's capacity to handle change with competence. These repetitive behaviors can progress to obsessive behavior patterns, which may be suspected if the patient becomes anxious when the behavior is interfered with.

Splitting. The phenomenon of splitting is apparent in families of the learning disabled in which the disability is perceived as external to the essential self, as an evil appendage for which the key to its disappearance must be found. The "good" son or "good" daughter frequently is split from the "bad," "naughty," or "poor" student. Splitting also is noted within the dichotomous goals of intact adulthood and parental protection and infantilization combined with prevention of expressions of disloyalty to parents who have invested so extensively in their child.

Therapeutic Considerations with the Adolescent and Adult

Some learning disabled teenagers may be adolescents chronologically but not emotionally. They may be excessively dependent on their parents for support, assistance, and direction and have sparse contact with their peer group. Both the adolescent and his parents may be coping with the disappointment of residual deficits and the limitations that they dictate for further educational and vocational opportunity. They may have expected more comprehensive improvement than is apparent and be anxious about the future. They realize that the period of dependence is drawing to a close, yet they doubt that the adolescent or young adult is equipped to care for himself and are unable to imagine that he ever will do so. Alternatively, their aspirations might be unrealistically high. The adolescent or adult may still express his anxiety in a passive or hostile manner and his aggression through overt acts or withdrawal. He may involve his family members excessively in the anxiety he generates around complexity or change and in the consequences of his disorganization. Parents may discourage the adolescent from experiencing developmental tasks.

Counseling Siblings

The siblings of learning disabled persons rarely have been studied, nor have there been many programs directed to them. Observation, anecdotal reporting, and the literature on siblings of persons with other handicapping conditions suggest the following: The siblings will be particularly affected by the disability if they are close in age to their learning disabled brother or sister, the same sex, have no other or one other sibling, or are expected to achieve all that their sibling has been unable to accomplish. Parents may have unrealistic expectations of them and hope that the intact children will provide compensation for their sibling's shortcomings.

They will be at risk if their parents are overinvolved with their learning disabled brother or sister or inordinately angry, guilty, depressed, or unrealistic about the learning disabled child's abilities. Intact siblings may feel that they caused the disability or guilty that they are so much more competent than their sibling, or that they became angry at or teased or demeaned him. They may resent the attention that he receives and the demands that are made on them to assist him and include him in their activities. They may feel that their parents expect greater patience on their part than the parents themselves demonstrate. Just as learning disabled children wonder whether they will produce intact offspring, their siblings also fear that their children will be disabled. Siblings tend to be embarrassed about their brother or sister if he or she is clumsy, socially inadept, or in a special class. This embarrassment peaks in early adolescence, when youth want their family members to look and act like their peers' families. Their egocentricity around outward appearance leads them to suppose that their sibling's presentation of self reflects unduly on them. These feelings tend to diminish by late adolescence, when the sibling is sufficiently secure in his concept of self that it is not easily undermined. It is helpful for siblings to realize that other siblings of the learning disabled share the same feelings and that such feelings are not shameful. Counseling can occur in sibling groups, family therapy, multiple family therapy, and individual therapy.

Epstein, Berg-Cross, and Berg-Cross (1980) found that mothers of first-born learning disabled children had significantly lower expectations for their learning disabled children and significantly higher ones for their intact children than was the case in families where the learning disabled child was second born. In the latter instance, mothers adjusted their previously low expectations to more realistic appraisals.

Therapeutic Usefulness of Volunteer Organizations

Most volunteer organizations are unequipped to provide professional family counseling, and their educational programs tend not to be organized into sequential information systems. However, volunteer organizations provide the important function of exposing parents to other parents with similar problems, believing parents' descriptions of their children and experiences, and directing them to services. Parents are able to share their feelings and frustrations with patient listeners without encountering the discomfort or denial of outsiders or the limited schedules of professionals. Through constructive social action, parents learn that they can be agents of change, so that feelings of helplessness and powerlessness can be replaced by feelings of competency.

Volunteer organizations follow developmental patterns from their initial organization to maturity. They typically progress from an all-volunteer base, with extensive volunteer commitment and involvement and charismatic leadership, to dissent, to eventual professional leadership with much of the energies directed to organizational maintenance (Farber, 1968). Therefore, the quality and substance of the direction and support that parents receive will relate to the organizational stage. In the organizing stage of growth, the investment in parents tends to be accepting and extensive. The volunteers are likely to provide an honest appraisal of local professionals and services and dispense information liberally. The direction that volunteers provide will reflect the sophistication of their individual knowledge, the type and extensiveness of their own children's disabilities, the adjustments that they have made, the treatments or services that they feel have worked for their children, and their reasons for involvement in the organization.

In some instances, volunteers may direct families to inappropriate services or encourage them to invest in treatments that net disappointing results. This occurs because they lack access to psychological and medical information on the children of parents who seek their direction and are untrained in the interpretation of such information. Therefore, they make judgments about the child's disability, intelligence, and other attributes from parental accounts. Moreover, they may not be aware of the attributes that constitute an adequate service or appreciate which elements need to be considered in designing a service package for a child and family. They may be further limited in their ability to be helpful since most volunteer organizations are staffed by the small group of founding members who try to handle all aspects of the organization, in addition to parenting their own learning disabled children.

Some volunteers contribute to parental guilt by expecting parents to become far more involved in a treatment regimen or to be more active than they are able to be; they may also suggest that parents have used the wrong services to date. Conversely, they might represent the first caring insiders that a parent has encountered. They might be the only persons who have directed parents to useful services and provided the first honest appraisal of local services the parents have received.

Volunteer organizations experience their greatest crisis in the dissident stage, wherein there is a conflict of goals and an undermining of direction. This process usually occurs simultaneous to the original volunteer group's desire for retirement. The ability of the organization to be helpful to parents at this juncture depends on its success in mobilizing new volunteers who will perform a maintenance function and who can divorce themselves sufficiently from the dissent to remain effective.

The transition to professional direction and external funding tends to earmark more systematized and sophisticated service delivery. However, the alliances that are effected with other agencies and government and the professional background of the director, which could influence his willingness to criticize fellow professionals, might conflict with the organization's ability to provide parents with an honest appraisal of local professionals and services or the willingness to encourage some forms of activist behavior. In this final stage of growth, considerable organizational energy tends to be devoted to administrative concerns and the effecting of visibility through vehicles such as prestigious speakers and conferences. Goals of visibility can conflict with parental needs, which tend to be more effectively met by in-depth services that lack sparkle and mass appeal. The organization can be maximally effective at this stage if its professional direction is compatible with the parental goals of direction, support, extension of service provision, and social change.

In this book I have challenged the popular assumption that learning disabilities primarily are academic disabilities and have suggested, instead, that they are "living disabilities." Some of the deficits that many learning disabled persons evidence, such as social ineptitude, are more profoundly handicapping throughout a lifetime than are disabilities in reading, spelling, and mathematics, although these must also receive our attention. If readers share my hypothesis, they must share my perception that the learning disabled adult has been ignored, both in service provision and in the literature. It seems that as long as we pretend that the disability is limited to academic areas we also can pretend that it disappears once formal schooling is completed. I maintain that it is of utmost importance that we seriously consider the ways whereby interactional development programs for the learning disabled child, adolescent, and adult can be initiated and funded and staff training programs developed. I acknowledge the gaps in the knowledge base that should be the foundation of such programs but suggest that we possess sufficient information to begin. It is my hope that we will add to the research and to our clinical reporting while the programs are in operation.

Perhaps this book will encourage us to envisage learning disabilities as they interact with development and with personality attributes. I hope it will stimulate a view of the child and family in a dynamic fashion to encourage the generation of a psychology of learning disabilities. Once the importance of the family in the development of the learning disabled is accepted, just as the family is recognized as a critical parameter in the development of all children, I expect that programs will be directed toward families. Our failure to provide such services has been a serious sin of omission, because, unlike social deficits about which little is known, we know a great deal about families. We know how healthy and neurotic families function, and how families react to an illness, disability, or handicap in one member. I have attempted to add to that information base by describing the ways in which families of the learning disabled are similar to or differ from such families. Those of us who work in the learning disability field share the conviction that most learning disabled people, by virtue of their intelligence and areas of competent functioning, can achieve sophisticated and satisfying levels of living. The programs that we address to their needs must, therefore, be equally sophisticated, individualized, and carefully conceptualized.

I recognize the ease with which someone can become absorbed in his or her thesis and use it as a blanket explanation for all phenomena. I have certainly taken pains to describe the propensity of some parents to interpret every behavior that arises in their families as being attributable to the learning disability. Consequently, I make an added effort not to interpret all the social ineptitude that I encounter as representing, in part, a failure in social skill learning. Nevertheless, it is my strong impression that there are many people who, for a variety of reasons other than or in addition to emotional problems, have not acquired all the age-expected social skills. (One of the many possible causes for their gaps in social knowledge could be a deficit in social information processing, which is insufficiently severe to be labeled "learning disability"; since learning disabilities represent the extreme end of a continuum of processing that is common to all of us; such an explanation is highly plausible.) I feel that the alternative interpretations that I have proposed for behaviors that, to date, have been attributed to neuroses, may well be applicable for persons other than the learning disabled. I hope that this book will be useful in a far broader context than that of learning disabilities.

References

✽ ✽ ✽ ✽ ✽

Aberle, D., and Naegele, K. "Middle Class Fathers' Occupational Role and Attitude Toward Children." In N. Bell and E. Vogel (Eds.), *A Modern Introduction to the Family*. New York: Free Press, 1968.

Ainsworth, M. S. "Infant-Mother Attachment." *American Psychologist*, 1979, *34*(10), 932–937.

Anderson, C. M. *Society Pays the High Cost of M.B.D.* New York: Walker, 1972.

Anderson, L. "A Research Project for Twenty Out-of-School Young Adults with 'Mild' Neurological Dysfunction." In L. Anderson (Ed.), *C.A.N.H.C. Vocational Kit*. Los Angeles: California Association for Neurologically Handicapped Children, 1976.

Argyle, M. *The Psychology of Interpersonal Behavior*. New York: Penguin Books, 1967.

Argyle, M. *Bodily Communication*. London: Methuen, 1975.

Ausubel, D. P. *Educational Psychology: A Cognitive View*. New York: Holt, Rinehart and Winston, 1968.

Ausubel, D. P., and Sullivan, E. V. *Theory and Problems of Child Development*. (2nd ed.) New York: Grune & Stratton, 1970. (Originally published 1957.)

Bachara, G. H. "Empathy in Learning Disabled Children." *Perceptual and Motor Skills*, 1976, *43*, 541–542.

Bader, B. *Social Perception and Learning Disabilities.* Des Moines: Moon Lithographing & Engraving, 1975.

Baker, B., Brightman, A., Heifetz, L., and Murphy, D. *Steps to Independence: A Skills Training Series for Children with Special Needs.* Champaign, Ill.: Research Press, 1976.

Barsch, R. *The Parent of the Handicapped Child.* Springfield, Ill.: Thomas, 1976.

Bates, E. *Language and Context: The Acquisition of Pragmatics.* New York: Academic Press, 1976.

Bates, H., and Katz, M. "Development of Verbal Regulation of Behavior." *Proceedings of the 78th Annual American Psychological Association Convention,* 1970, *70*(5) (Pt. 1), 299–300.

Becker, E. *The Birth and Death of Meaning: An Interdisciplinary Perspective on the Problem of Man.* New York: Free Press, 1962.

Becker, E. *Angel in Armor.* New York: Free Press, 1969.

Becker, E. *The Denial of Death.* New York: Free Press, 1973.

Beckman, L. "Effect of Student's Performance on Teacher's and Observer's Attributions of Causality." *Journal of Educational Psychology,* 1970, *61*, 76–82.

Blatt, B., Biklen, B., and Bogdan, R. *An Alternative Textbook in Special Education: People, Schools and Other Institutions.* Denver: Love, 1977.

Block, J. "The Pinks and the Blues." Television documentary, Nova, Box 1000, Boston, 1981.

Bluebond-Langner, M. *The Private Worlds of Dying Children.* Princeton, N.J.: Princeton University Press, 1978.

Boulding, K. *The Image.* Ann Arbor: University of Michigan Press, 1956.

Bowlby, J. "Self Reliance and Some Conditions That Promote It." Paper presented at scientific meeting, Tavistock Clinic Jubilee, London, September 1970.

Brazelton, B., Tronick, E., Adamson, L., Als, H., and Wise, S. *Early Mother-Infant Interaction.* New York: Associated Scientific Publishers, 1975.

Bruinincks, V. L. "Actual and Perceived Peer Status of Learning Disabled Students in Mainstream Programs." *Journal of Special Education,* 1978, *12*, 51–58.

Bruner, J. S. "Personality Dynamics and the Process of Receiving." In R. R. Blake and G. V. Ramsey (Eds.), *Perception: An Approach to Personality,* New York: Ronald Press, 1951.

Bryan, J. H., and Perlmutter, B. "Immediate Impressions of Learning Disabled Children by Female Adults." *Learning Disability Quarterly,* 1979, *2,* 80–88.

Bryan, J. H., and Sherman, R. "Audiences' Immediate Impressions of Nonverbal Ingratiation Attempts by Boys Labelled Learning Disabled." Unpublished manuscript, Department of Psychology, Northwestern University, 1980.

Bryan, J. H., Sherman, R., and Fisher, A. "Learning Disabled Boys' Nonverbal Behavior Within a Dyadic Interview." *Learning Disability Quarterly,* 1980, *3,* 65–72.

Bryan, J. H., Sonnenfeld, L. J., and Greenberg, F. Z. "Ingratiation Preferences of Learning Disabled Children." Unpublished manuscript, Chicago Institute for Learning Disabilities, University of Illinois, 1980.

Bryan, T. H. "Peer Popularity of Learning Disabled Children." *Journal of Learning Disabilities,* 1974a, 7(10), 621–625.

Bryan, T. H. "An Observational Analysis of Classroom Behaviors of Children with Learning Disabilities." *Journal of Learning Disabilities,* 1974b, 7(10), 26–34.

Bryan, T. H. "Strangers' Judgments of Children's Social and Academic Adequacy: Instant Diagnosis." Unpublished manuscript, Chicago Institute for Learning Disabilities, University of Illinois, 1975.

Bryan, T. H. "Peer Popularity of Learning Disabled Children: A Replication." *Journal of Learning Disabilities,* 1976, *9*(5), 307–311.

Bryan, T. H. "Learning Disabled Children's Comprehension of Nonverbal Communication." *Journal of Learning Disabilities,* 1977, *10*(8), 501–506.

Bryan, T. H. "Social Relations and Verbal Interaction of Learning Disabled Children." *Journal of Learning Disabilities,* 1978, *11*(2), 107–115.

Bryan, T. H. *Social Skills and Social Relationships of Learning Disabled Children.* Chicago: Chicago Institute for Learning Disabilities, University of Illinois, 1979.

Bryan, T. H. "Children's Attributions and Others' Attributions About Them." Unpublished manuscript, Chicago Institute for Learning Disabilities, University of Illinois, 1980.

Bryan, T. H., Donahue, M., and Pearl, R. "Learning Disabled Children's Peer Interactions During a Small Group Problem Solving Task." Unpublished manuscript, Chicago Institute for Learning Disabilities, University of Illinois, 1980.

Bryan, T. H., and Pflaum, S. "Linguistic, Social, and Cognitive Analyses of Learning Disabled Children's Social Interactions." Paper presented at conference of International Association for Children with Learning Disabilities, Kansas City, March 1978.

Bryan, T. H., and Wheeler, R. "Teachers' Behaviors in Classes for Severely Retarded—Multiply Trainable Mentally Retarded and Learning Disabled and Normal Children." *Mental Retardation,* 1976, *14*(4), 41–45.

Bryan, T. H., Wheeler, R., Felcan, J., and Henek, T. "'Come on, Dummy': An Observational Study of Children's Communication." *Journal of Learning Disabilities,* 1976, *9,* 661–669.

Buber, M. "Distance and Relation." *Psychiatry,* 1957, *20,* 92–101.

Busse, T. V. "Child-Rearing Antecedents of Flexible Thinking." *Developmental Psychology,* 1969, *1,* 585–591.

Chapman, J. W., and Boersma, F. L. *Affective Correlates of Learning Disabilities.* Lisse, The Netherlands: Swets Publishing, 1980.

Chapman, R. B., Larsen, S. C., and Parker, R. M. "Interactions of First Grade Classroom Teachers with Learning Disordered Students." Unpublished manuscript, 1976.

Church, J. *Language and the Discovery of Reality.* New York: Random House, 1961.

Cobb, H. V. "The Attitude of the Retarded Person Toward Himself." In *Stress on Families of the Mentally Handicapped.* Paris: International League of Societies for the Mentally Handicapped, 1966.

Cohen, J. *Adoption Breakdown with Older Children.* Toronto: University of Toronto Press, 1981.

Constantini, A., Corsini, D., and Davis, J. "Conceptual Tempo, Inhibition of Movement, and Acceleration of Movement in Four-, Seven-, and Nine-Year-Old Children." *Perceptual and Motor Skills,* 1973, *37,* 779–784.

Crandall, V. C., Katkovsky, W. and Crandall, V. J. "Children's Beliefs in Their Own Control of Reinforcements in Intellectual-Academic Achievement Situations." *Child Development,* 1965, *36,* 91–109.

Cruickshank, W. "The Psychoeducational Match." In W. Cruickshank and D. P. Hallahan (Eds.), *Perceptual and Learning Disabilities in Children.* Vol. 1. Syracuse, N.Y.: Syracuse University Press, 1975.

Cruickshank, W. *The Learning Disabled Child in Home, School and Community.* Syracuse, N.Y.: Syracuse University Press, 1977.

Cummings, S. T. "The Impact of the Child's Deficiency on the Father." *American Journal of Orthopsychiatry,* 1976, *46*(2), 254.

Daly, M. *Beyond God the Father: Toward a Philosophy of Women's Liberation.* Boston: Beacon Press, 1973.

Davis, M. *Intimate Relations.* New York: Free Press, 1973.

DeMause, L. (Ed.). *The History of Childhood.* New York: Harper & Row, 1974.

Deshler, D., Shumaker, J. B., Warner, M. M., Alley, G., and Clark, F. L. *An Epidemiological Study of Learning Disabled Adolescents in Secondary Schools: Social Status, Peer Relationships, Activities in and Out of School, and Time Use.* Lawrence: Institute for Research in Learning Disabilities, University of Kansas, 1980.

Donahue, M. L., Bryan, T. H., and Pearl, R. A. "Pragmatic Competence of Learning Disabled Children." Unpublished manuscript, Chicago Institute for Learning Disabilities, University of Illinois, 1980.

Donahue, M. L., Pearl, R. A., and Bryan, T. H. "Learning Disabled Children's Conversational Competence: Response to Inadequate Messages." Unpublished manuscript, Chicago Institute for Learning Disabilities, University of Illinois, 1980.

Dore, J. "Children's Illicutionary Acts." In R. Freedle (Ed.), *Discourse: Comprehension and Production.* Norwood, N.J.: Ablex, 1977.

Dore, J., Gearhart, M., and Newman, D. "The Structure of Nursery School Conversations." In K. Nelson (Ed.), *Children's Language.* Vol. 1. New York: Gardner Press, 1978.

Doyleys, D. M., Cartelli, L. M., and Doster, J. "Comparison of Patterns of Mother-Child Interaction." *Journal of Learning Disabilities,* 1976, *9*(6), 371–375.

Dweck, C. S., and Repucci, N. D. "Learned Helplessness and Reinforcement Responsibility in Children." *Journal of Personality and Social Psychology*, 1973, *25*, 109–116.

Eisenberg, L. "Dyslexic Child." In J. Money (Ed.), *The Disabled Reader*. Baltimore: Johns Hopkins University Press, 1966.

Eisenberg, L. "Psychiatric Aspects of Reading Disabilities." Paper presented at the Orton Society annual conference, Minneapolis, 1975.

Elkind, D. *Children and Adolescents: Interpretive Essays on Jean Piaget*. New York: Oxford University Press, 1974.

Emery, E. J. "Social Perception Processes in Normal and Learning Disabled Children." Unpublished doctoral dissertation, New York University, 1975.

Epstein, J., Berg-Cross, G., and Berg-Cross, L. "Maternal Expectations and Birth Order in Families with Learning Disabled and Normal Children." *Journal of Learning Disabilities*, 1980, *3*(5), 273–280.

Erikson, E. *Childhood and Society*. New York: Norton, 1963.

Erwin-Tripp, S., and Mitchell-Kernan, C. (Eds.). *Child Discourse*. New York: Academic Press, 1977.

Exline, R. V., and Winters, L. C. "Affective Relations and Mutual Glances in Dyads." In S. Tomkins and C. Izard (Eds.), *Affect, Cognition, and Personality*. New York: Springer, 1965.

Farb, P. *Word Play: What Happens When People Talk*. New York: Knopf, 1973.

Farber, B. "Organizational Dynamics." In H. J. Prehm, L. A. Hammerlynck, and J. E. Crosson (Eds.), *Behavioral Research in Mental Retardation*. Eugene: University of Oregon Press, 1968.

Feingold, B. *Introduction to Clinical Allergy*. Springfield, Ill.: Thomas, 1973.

Fincham, F., and Barling, J. "Locus of Control and Generosity in Learning Disabled, Normal Achieving and Gifted Children." *Child Development*, 1978, *49*, 530–533.

Flavell, J. H. "The Development of Inferences About Others." In T. Mischel (Ed.), *Understanding Other Persons*. Totowa, N.J.: Rowman & Littlefield, 1974.

Forness, S. R., and Estveldt, K. C. "Classroom Observations of Children with Learning and Behavior Problems." *Journal of Learning Disabilities*, 1975, *8*, 382–385.

Freed, A. *T. A. for Tots.* Sacramento: Jalmar Press, 1973.

Freund, J. H., and Elardo, R. "Maternal Behavior and Family Constellation as Predictors of Social Competence Among Learning Disabled Children." Paper presented at conference of International Association for Children with Learning Disabilities, Kansas City, 1978.

Gardner, R. A. *Therapeutic Communication with Children: The Mutual Story-Telling Technique.* New York: Science House, 1971.

Garvey, C. "The Contingent Query: A Dependent Action in Conversation." In I. M. Lewis and L. Rosenblum (Eds.), *Interaction, Conversation, and the Development of Language.* New York: Wiley, 1977.

Garvey, C., and Hogan, R. "Social Speech and Social Interaction: Egocentrism Revisited." *Child Development,* 1973, *44,* 562–568.

Gergen, K. *The Concept of Self.* New York: Holt, Rinehart and Winston, 1971.

Giffen, M. "The Role of Child Psychiatry in Learning Disabilities." In H. R. Myklebust (Ed.), *Progress in Learning Disabilities.* New York: Grune & Stratton, 1968.

Goffman, E. "The Moral Career of a Mental Patient." *Psychiatry,* 1959, *22,* 123–142.

Goffman, E. *Behavior in Public Places.* New York: Free Press, 1963.

Goffman, E. *Stigma: Notes on the Management of Spoiled Identity.* Englewood Cliffs, N.J.: Prentice-Hall, 1964.

Goffman, E. *Ritual Essays on Face-to-Face Behavior.* New York: Doubleday, 1967.

Goffman, E. *Relations in Public.* New York: Harper & Row, 1972.

Goffman, E. *Frame Analysis: An Essay on the Organization of Experience.* Cambridge, Mass.: Harvard University Press, 1974.

Golick, M. *Learning Disabilities and the School Age Child.* Montreal: Quebec Association for Children with Learning Disabilities, 1977.

Gordon, S. "Psychological Problems of Adolescents with Minimal Brain Dysfunction." In D. Kronick (Ed.), *Learning Disabilities: Its Implications to a Responsible Society.* Chicago: Developmental Learning Materials, 1969.

Greenberg, E. S. "Brain Damage in Adolescence." *American Journal of Orthopsychiatry,* 1970, *40,* 333–337.

Griffiths, A. N. "Self-Concept in Remedial Work with Dyslexic Children." *Academic Therapy,* 1970–71, *6*(2), 125–133.

Guthery, G. H. "Difference in Attitudes of Educationally Handicapped, Mentally Retarded, and Normal Students: A Study of Attitudes Toward School, Teachers, and Academics." *Journal of Learning Disabilities,* 1971, *4*(6), 330–332.

Hallahan, D. P., Gajar, A. H., Cohen, S. B., and Tarver, S. G. "Selective Attention and Locus of Control in Learning Disabled and Normal Children." *Journal of Learning Disabilities,* 1978, *4,* 47–52.

Hallahan, D. P., and Reeve, R. E. "Selective Attention and Distractibility." In B. K. Keogh (Ed.), *Advances in Special Education.* Vol. 1. Greenwich, Conn.: JAI Press, 1980.

Harrison, A., and Nadelman, L. "Conceptual Tempo and Inhibition of Movement in Black Preschool Children." *Child Development,* 1972, *43,* 657–668.

Hartcollis, P. "The Syndrome of Minimal Brain Dysfunction in Young Adult Patients." *Bulletin of the Menninger Clinic,* 1968, *32*(2), 102–114.

Hartup, W. W. "The Social Worlds of Childhood." *American Psychologist,* 1979, *34*(10), 944–950.

Hayes, M. *The Tuned-In, Turned-On Book About Learning Problems.* San Rafael, Calif.: Academic Therapy Publications, 1974.

Hemming, J. "Some Aspects of Moral Development in a Changing Society." *British Journal of Educational Psychology,* 1957, *27*(2), 77–88.

Henry, J. *On Sham, Vulnerability and Other Forms of Self-Destruction.* New York: Random House, 1973. (Originally published 1957.)

Hirsch, J. G. "Individual Characteristics and Academic Achievement." In J. M. Beck and R. W. Saxe (Eds.), *Teaching the Culturally Disadvantaged Pupil.* Springfield, Ill.: Thomas, 1965.

Humphries, T. W., and Bauman, E. "Maternal Child Rearing Attitudes Associated with Learning Disabilities." *Journal of Learning Disabilities,* 1980, *13*(8), 459–462.

Hunt, J. V., and Hardt, R. H. "Developmental Stage, Delinquency and Differential Treatment." *Journal of Research on Crime and Delinquency,* 1965, *2,* 20–31.

Inkeles, A. "Society, Social Structure, and Childhood Socialization." In J. Clausen (Ed.), *Socialization and Society.* Boston: Little, Brown, 1968.

Izard, C. E. (Ed.). *Human Emotions.* New York: Plenum, 1977.

Jackson, P. *Life in the Classroom.* New York: Holt, Rinehart and Winston, 1968.

Johnson, D., and Myklebust, H. R. *Learning Disabilities, Educational Principles, and Practices.* New York: Grune & Stratton, 1967.

Jones, E. E., and Wortman, C. "Ingratiation: An Attributional Approach." Morristown, N.J.: General Learning Press, 1973.

Kagan, J., Kearsley, R. B., and Zelato, P. R. *Infancy: Its Place in Human Development.* Cambridge, Mass.: Harvard University Press, 1978.

Kantor, D., and Lehr, W. *Inside the Family: Toward a Theory of Family Process.* San Francisco: Jossey-Bass, 1975.

Kaslow, F,, and Cooper, B. "Family Therapy with the Learning Disabled Child and His/Her Family." *Journal of Marriage and Family Counseling,* Jan. 1978, pp. 41–48.

Katovsky, W., Preston, A., and Crandall, V. J. "Parents' Achievement Attitudes and Their Behavior with Their Children in Achievement Situations." *Journal of Genetic Psychology,* 1964, *104,* 105–121.

Keenan, E. "Conversational Competence in Children." *Journal of Child Language,* 1974, *1,* 163–183.

Kendon, A. "Some Relationships Between Body Motion and Speech." In A. Siegman and B. Pope (Eds.), *Studies in Dyadic Communication.* Elmsford, N.Y.: Pergamon Press, 1972.

Keogh, B. K., Tchir, C., and Windeguth-Behn, A. "Teachers' Perception of Educationally High Risk Children." *Journal of Learning Disabilities,* 1974, *7,* 367–374.

Kephart, N. C. *The Slow Learner in the Classroom.* Columbus, Ohio: Merrill, 1971.

Kirk, S. "Definition of Learning Disabilities." Paper presented to the Illinois Association for Perceptually Handicapped Children, Chicago, 1963.

Kohlberg, L. "Development of Moral Character and Moral Ideology." In M. L. Hoffman and L. W. Hoffman (Eds.), *Review of Child Development Research.* New York: Russell Sage Foundation, 1964.

Koppitz, E. M. *Children with Learning Disabilities: A Five Year Follow-Up Study.* New York: Grune & Stratton, 1971.

Kronick, D. *A Word or Two About Learning Disabilities.* Novato, Calif.: Academic Therapy Publications, 1974.

Kronick, D. *Three Families*. Novato, Calif.: Academic Therapy Publications, 1976.

Kübler-Ross, E. *On Death and Dying*. New York: Macmillan, 1969.

LaGreca, A. M., and Mesibov, G. B. "Social Skills Intervention with Learning Disabled Children." Paper presented at annual meeting of the Midwestern Psychological Association, Chicago, May 1979.

Lamb, M. E. *The Role of the Father in Child Development*. Monterey, Calif.: Brooks/Cole, 1974.

Langer, S. *Philosophy in a New Key*. New York: New American Library, 1951.

Larsen, S. C., Parker, R., and Jorjorian, S. "Differences in Self-Concept of Normal and Learning Disabled Children." *Perceptual and Motor Skills*, 1973, *37*(2), 510.

Lasch, C. *The Culture of Narcissism*. New York: Norton, 1978.

Lemert, E. "Paranoia and the Dynamics of Exclusion." *Sociometry*, 1962, *25*, 2–20.

Lenkowsky, L. K., and Saposnek, D. T. "Family Consequences of Parental Dyslexia." *Journal of Learning Disabilities*, 1978, *11*(1), 47–52.

Lerner, J. W. *Children with Learning Disabilities*. (2nd ed.) Boston: Houghton Mifflin, 1976.

Lesser, S., and Easser, R. "The Perceptual Aspects of Personality." *Journal of the American Academy of Psychiatry*, 1972, *11*(3), 458–466.

Lieberman, A. F. "Preschoolers' Competence with a Peer-Relations Attachment and Peer Experience." *Child Development*, 1977, *48*, 1277–1287.

Lieberman, L. "Territoriality—Who Does What to Whom?" *Journal of Learning Disabilities*, 1980, *13*(3), 124–128.

Lifton, R. J. *The Broken Connection*. New York: Simon & Schuster, 1979.

Light, P. *The Development of Social Sensitivity*. Cambridge, England: Cambridge University Press, 1979.

Lund, A., Hall, J., Humphreys, M. S., and Wilson, K. "Learning Disabilities and Sensitivity to Event Frequency." Unpublished manuscript, Chicago Institute for Learning Disabilities, University of Illinois, 1980.

Luria, A. "The Directive Function of Speech in Development." *Word*, 1959, *18*, 341–352.

McDermott, W. V. "Differential Interaction Patterns Within the Families of Reading Problem Boys." Unpublished doctoral dissertation, University of Western Ontario, 1977.

Mackworth, J. F. "Development of Attention." In V. Hamilton and M. D. Vernon (Eds.), *Development of Cognitive Processes.* New York: Academic Press, 1976.

Mahler, M., Pine, F., and Bergman, A. *The Psychological Birth of the Human Infant.* New York: Basic Books, 1975.

Marris, P. *Loss and Change.* New York: Random House, 1974.

Matas, L., Arend, R. A., and Sroufe, L. A. "Continuity of Adaptation in the Second Year: The Relationship Between Quality of Attachment and Later Competence." *Child Development,* 1978, *49,* 547–556.

Mehrabian, A. *Tactics in Social Influence.* Englewood Cliffs, N.J.: Prentice-Hall, 1969.

Meichenbaum, D. *Cognitive Behavior Modification: An Integrative Approach.* New York: Plenum, 1977.

Meichenbaum, D., and Goodman, J. "Training Impulsive Children to Talk to Themselves: A Means of Developing Self-Control." *Journal of Abnormal Psychology,* 1971, *77,* 115–126.

Mercer, C. D., Cullinan, D., Hallahan, D. P., and La Fleur, N. K. "Modeling and Attention-Retention in Learning Disabled Children." *Journal of Learning Disabilities,* 1975, *8,* 444–450.

Miller, D. R., and Westman, J. C. "Reading Disability as a Condition of Family Stability." *Family Process,* 1964, *3*(1), 66–76.

Miller, M., and Rohr, M. E. "Verbal Mediation for Perceptual Deficits in Learning Disabilities." *Journal of Learning Disabilities,* 1980, *13*(6), 319–321.

Minskoff, E. H. "Teaching Approach for Developing Nonverbal Communication Skills in Students with Social Perception Deficits. Part I: The Basic Approach and Body Language Clues." *Journal of Learning Disabilities,* 1980a, *13*(3), 118–124.

Minskoff, E. H. "Teaching Approach for Developing Nonverbal Communication Skills in Students with Social Perception Deficits. Part II: Proxemic, Vocalic, and Artifactual Cues." *Journal of Learning Disabilities,* 1980b, *13*(4), 203–208.

Morse, W. C. "Worksheet on Life Space Interviewing for Teachers." In N. J. Long, W. C. Morse, and R. G. Newman (Eds.), *Conflict in the Classroom.* Belmont, Calif.: Wadsworth, 1971.

Murray, H. A., and Kluckhohn, C. "Outline of a Conception of Personality." In C. Kluckhohn, H. A. Murray, and D. M. Schneider (Eds.), *Personality in Nature, Society and Culture.* (2nd ed.) New York: Knopf, 1953.

Muus, R. E. "Mental Health Implications of a Preventative Psychiatry Program in the Light of Research Findings." *Marriage and Family Living,* 1960, *22,* 150–156.

Neugarten, B. "Time, Age, and the Life Cycle." *American Journal of Psychiatry,* 1979, *136*(7), 887–893.

Nichols, J. "Quality and Equality in Intellectual Development." *American Psychologist,* 1979, *34,* 1071–1084.

Novak, M. "Affluence Paralyses Society—Philosopher." *Toronto Star,* May 11, 1977, p. 12.

Ojemann, R. H. "Incorporating Psychological Concepts in the School Curriculum." *Journal of School Psychology,* 1967, *5,* 195–204.

Opie, J., and Opie, P. *The Lore and Language of Schoolchildren.* London: Oxford University Press, 1976. (Originally published 1959.)

Opie, J., and Opie, P. *Children's Games in Street and Playground.* Oxford: Clarendon Press, 1969.

Orton, S. T. *Reading, Writing, and Speech Problems in Children.* New York: Norton, 1937.

Palomares, U., Ball, G. E., and Bessell, H. *Magic Circle Materials.* La Mesa, Calif.: Human Development Training Institute, n.d.

Parrill-Burnstein, M., and Baker-Ward, L. "Learning Disabilities: A Social Cognitive Difference." *Learning Disabilities: An Audio Journal for Continuing Education,* 1979, *3*(10).

Parrill-Burnstein, M., and Hazan-Ginsburg, E. "Cognitive Mapping and Social Cognition: Understanding the Impact of the Learning Disability." *Audio Journal for Continuing Education,* Summer, 1980.

Pearl, R. A., Bryan, T. H., and Donahue, M. L. "Children's Attributions for Success and Failure." *Learning Disability Quarterly,* in press.

Pearl, R. A., Donahue, M. L., and Bryan, T. H. "Learning Disabled and Normal Children's Responses to Requests for Clarification Which Vary in Explicitness." Unpublished manuscript, Chicago Institute for Learning Disabilities, University of Illinois, 1980.

Peck, B. B., and Stackhouse, T. W. "Reading Problems and Family Dynamics." *Journal of Learning Disabilities,* 1973, *6*(7), 506–510.

Perlmutter, B. F. "Rating Children with Learning Disabilities: Beauty Is in the Eye of the Subceiver." Unpublished manuscript, Department of Psychology, Northwestern University, 1980.

Piaget, J. *The Language and Thought of the Child.* New York: Harcourt Brace Jovanovich, 1926.

Piaget, J. *Psychology of Intelligence.* New York: Harcourt Brace Jovanovich, 1950.

Rabinovitch, M. S., Caplan, H., and Bibace, R. "Paranatal Stress, Cognitive Organization, and Ego Function: A Controlled Follow-Up Study of Children Born Prematurely." In E. N. Rexford, L. W. Sander, and T. Shapiro (Eds.), *Infant Psychiatry: A New Synthesis.* New Haven, Conn.: Yale University Press, 1976.

Radin, N. "Father-Child Interaction and the Intellectual Functioning of Four-Year-Old Boys." *Developmental Psychology,* 1972, *6,* 353–361.

Redl, F. *When We Deal with Children.* New York: Free Press, 1966.

Robbins, R. L., and Harway, N. I. "Reactions to Success and Failure in Children with Learning Disabilities." *Journal of Learning Disabilities,* 1977, *10,* 356–362.

Rosenberg, M. *Conceiving the Self.* New York: Basic Books, 1979.

Rosenthal, J. H. "Self-Esteem in Dyslexic Children." *Academic Therapy,* 1973, *9*(1), 27–39.

Roskies, E. *Abnormality and Normality: The Mothering of Thalidomide Children.* Ithaca, N.Y.: Cornell University Press, 1972.

Rothenberg, G. S., Franzblau, S. H., and Geer, J. H. "Educating the Learning Disabled Adolescent About Sexuality." *Journal of Learning Disabilities,* 1979, *12*(9), 576–580.

Rubin, Z. *Liking and Loving.* New York: Holt, Rinehart and Winston, 1973.

Sameroff, A. J. "Empirical Issues in the Operationalization of Transactional Research." Paper presented at biennial meeting of the Society for Research in Child Development, San Francisco, March 1979.

Sameroff, A. J., and Chandler, M. G. "Reproductive Risk and the Continuum of Caretaker Causality." In F. D. Horowitz, M. Hetherington, S. Scarr-Salapatek, and G. Siegel (Eds.), *Review of*

Child Development Research. Vol. 4. Chicago: University of Chicago Press, 1975.

Sarason, I. "A Modeling and Informational Approach to Delinquency." In E. E. Ribes-Inesta and A. Bandura (Eds.), *Analysis of Delinquency and Aggression.* Hillsdale, N.J.: Erlbaum, 1976.

Schumaker, J. B., Sheldon-Wildgen, J., and Sherman, J. A. *Observational Study of the Academic and Social Behaviors of Learning Disabled Adolescents in the Regular Classroom.* Lawrence: Institute for Research and Learning Disabilities, University of Kansas, 1980.

Selman, R. L., Jaquette, M., and Lavin, D. R. "Interpersonal Awareness in Children: Toward an Integration of Developmental and Clinical Psychology." *American Journal of Orthopsychiatry,* 1977, *47*(2), 264–274.

Shantz, C. U. "The Development of Social Cognition." In E. M. Hetherington (Ed.), *Review of Child Development Research.* Vol. 5. Chicago: University of Chicago Press, 1975.

Shur, E. M. *Labeling Deviant Behavior: Its Sociological Implications.* New York: Harper & Row, 1971.

Shuy, R., and Giffen, P. (Eds.). *Children's Functional Language and Education in the Early Years.* Arlington, Va.: Center for Applied Linguistics, in press.

Siegel, E. *The Exceptional Child Grows Up.* New York: Dutton, 1974.

Sigman, M. "Cognitive Aspects of Bonding and Attachment with Special Reference to Mentally Retarded and Autistic Children." Paper presented at meeting of the American Orthopsychiatric Association, Toronto, March 1980.

Simon, S., Howe, L., and Kirschenbaum, H. *Values Clarification: A Handbook of Practical Strategies for Teachers and Students.* New York: Hart, 1972.

Siperstein, G. N., Bop, M. J., and Bak, J. J. *Social Status of Learning Disabled Children.* Cambridge, Mass.: Research Institute for Educational Problems, 1977.

Spivack, G. "Childrearing Attitudes of Emotionally Disturbed Adolescents." *Journal of Consulting Psychology,* 1957, *21*(2).

Spivack, G., Platt, J. J., and Shure, M. B. *The Problem-Solving Approach to Adjustment: A Guide to Research and Intervention.* San Francisco: Jossey-Bass, 1976.

Stone, G. L., Hinds, W. C., and Schmidt, G. W. "Teaching Mental Health Behaviors to Elementary School Children." *Professional Psychology*, 1975, *6*, 34–40.

Strag, G. A. "Comparative Behavioral Ratings of Parents with Severely Mentally Retarded, Special Learning Disabled, and Normal Children." *Journal of Learning Disabilities*, 1972, *5*, 631–635.

Strauss, A. A., and Lehtinen, L. E. *Psychopathology and Education of the Brain Injured Child.* New York: Grune & Stratton, 1947.

Sutherland, D. *The English Gentleman's Child.* Middlesex, England: Penguin Books, 1980.

Thomas, A., and Chess, S. *Temperament and Development.* New York: Brunner/Mazel, 1977.

Thomasen, C. J. "Comparison of Three Parent Counselling Programs for Parents of Emotionally Disturbed Children." Unpublished manuscript, University of New Mexico, 1976.

Trower, P., Bryant, B., and Argyle, M. *Social Skills and Mental Health.* London: Methuen, 1978.

United States Office of Education. *Definition of Learning Disabilities.* Washington, D.C.: U.S. Office of Education, 1979.

Wacker, J. "The Dyslogic Syndrome." *Texas Key*, September 1975, pp. 2–7.

Warner, M. M., Alley, G. R., Schumaker, J. B., Deshler, D. D., and Clark, F. L. *An Epidemiological Study of Learning Disabled Adolescents in Secondary Schools: Achievement and Ability, Socioeconomic Status and School Experiences.* Lawrence: Institute for Research in Learning Disabilities, University of Kansas, 1980.

Warr, P. B., and Knapper, C. *The Perception of People and Events.* New York: Wiley, 1968.

Waters, E., Whippman, J., and Sroufe, L. A. "Attachment, Positive Affect, and Competence in the Peer Group: Two Studies in Construct Validation." *Child Development*, 1979, *50*, 821–829.

Watzlawick, P., Beavin, J., and Jackson, D. *Pragmatics of Human Communication.* New York: Norton, 1967.

Wechsler, D. *Wechsler Intelligence Scale for Children–Revised.* New York: Psychological Corporation, 1974.

Weitman, C. U. "Egocentrism, Perspectivism and the Child with Identified Learning Disabilities." Unpublished doctoral dissertation, Case Western Reserve University, 1974.

238   **References**

Wender, P. *Minimal Brain Dysfunction in Children.* New York: Wiley-Interscience, 1971.

Whalen, C. K., and Henker, B. "Psychostimulants and Children: A Review and Analysis." *Psychological Review,* 1976, *83* (6), 1113–1130.

White, W. J., Schumaker, J. B., Warner, M. M., Alley, G., and Deshler, D. *The Current Status of Young Adults Identified as Learning Disabled During Their School Career.* Lawrence: Institute for Research in Learning Disabilities, University of Kansas, 1980.

Wiener, J. R. "A Theoretical Model of the Affective and Social Development of Learning Disabled Children." Unpublished doctoral dissertation, University of Michigan, 1978.

Wiig, E. H., and Harris, S. P. "Perception and Interpretation of Nonverbally Expressed Emotions by Adolescents with Learning Disabilities." *Perceptual and Motor Skills,* 1974, *38*(1), 239–245.

Wilchesky, M. "A Comparison of Learning Disabled and Normal Children's Choice of Friends." Unpublished preliminary research study, York University, Downsview, Ontario, 1978.

Wilchesky, M. "Recognition of Peer Facial Expressions by Learning Disabled and Normal Children." Unpublished doctoral dissertation, York University, Downsview, Ontario, 1980a.

Wilchesky, M. "The Relative Effects of Treatment Programs on the Development of Interpersonal Competence in Children." Unpublished paper, York University, Downsview, Ontario, 1980b.

Winner, E., and Gardner, H. *The Comprehension of Metaphor in Brain Damaged Patients.* Boston: Psychology Service, Aphasia Research Center, Veterans Administration Hospital, 1977.

Witkin, H. A., Dyk, R. B., Faterson, H. F., Goodenough, D. R., and Karp, S. A. *Psychological Differentiation.* New York: Wiley, 1962.

Wolfensberger, W. *Normalization: The Principle of Normalization in Human Services.* Downsview, Ontario: National Institute for Mental Retardation, 1972.

Wolfenstein, M. "Fun Morality. An Analysis of Recent Child Training Literature." In N. Mead and M. Wolfenstein (Eds.), *Childhood in Contemporary Culture.* Chicago: University of Chicago Press, 1955.

Wright, B. A. "Processes and Tasks in Hoping." *Rehabilitation Literature,* 1968, *29*(11), 322–333.

Zaleznick, A. *Human Dilemmas of Leadership.* New York: Harper & Row, 1966.

Zimmerman, J., Rich, W., Keilitz, I., and Broder, P. *Some Observations on the Link Between Learning Disabilities and Juvenile Delinquency.* Omaha: National Center for State Courts, Creighton University, 1978.

Index

�֍ �֍ �֍ ✷ ✷